# CITY ON FIRE

## A BOYHOOD IN ALIGARH

# ZEYAD MASROOR KHAN

HarperCollins *Publishers* India

First published in India by HarperCollins *Publishers* 2023
4th Floor, Tower A, Building No. 10, DLF Cyber City,
DLF Phase II, Gurugram, Haryana – 122002
www.harpercollins.co.in

2 4 6 8 10 9 7 5 3 1

P-ISBN: 978-93-5699-824-7
E-ISBN: 978-93-5699-825-4

Typeset in 11/15.2 Scala at
Manipal Technologies Limited, Manipal

Printed and bound at
Replika Press Pvt. Ltd.

This book is produced from independently certified FSC® paper to ensure
responsible forest management.

*In the memory of my late father*
*and*
*to all those who have ever lost a loved one to religious violence*

The detailed notes pertaining to this book are available on the HarperCollins *Publishers* India website. Scan this QR code to access the same.

# CONTENTS

# PROLOGUE

'Perhaps home is not a place but simply an irrevocable condition.'
—James Arthur Baldwin, 1924–1987

THE SLOPE WAS red with bricks and blood. More bricks dropped from the sky like missiles. Once in a while, a bottle of acid or a petrol bomb made its presence felt among the variety of objects being hurled. Amid the clash of religious slogans and verbal abuses, gunshots were heard. The riot was at its zenith – and my home lay exactly in the middle of it.

Anger rose in the hearts of men flooding the streets. '*Har har Mahadev!*' they shouted from the bottom of the slope. '*Allahu Akbar!*,' shouted other angry men from the top of the slope. The body of a twenty-year-old boy lay somewhere between this mass of angry men, his intestines ripped out, his blood spreading across the tarmac.

But the memory that haunts me the most is the sound of women's screams coming from all directions at once. As if all the women in my mohalla were screaming in unison. '*Ya Allah!*' cried an old woman standing in a balcony in front of the foyer of my house, wiping tears with her dupatta. Her daughter called out to her brother urgently, repeatedly. 'Faisal! Faisal! Come back!' This was the first time I had noticed these particular neighbours. The woman started breaking away loose bricks from her balcony wall and dropping them out to Faisal. 'Don't give them an inch or they'll enter our homes!' she cried. Almost everyone picks a side when it comes to staying alive.

There was no shortage of bricks on our side of the fight. An unlucky neighbour had ordered a truckful a few days ago. Nobody asked his permission before taking a whole slab away to be used as weapons. Some men went inside an old house and demolished a broken wall for more arsenal to attack the marauding enemy. Apart from this advantage, we were also at a height. So, when the Hindu mob tried to push up the slope, they were easily turned back. 'I will return and fuck your mother in front of you,' cried one of them as a part of a brick hit his head and blood gushed down his face.

A few minutes later, they returned with more guns, and all our advantages turned to dust.

Inside our home, my mother was trying to decide whether it was time to run. She was reading *Ayatul Kursi*, the verse Muslims read when they are afraid. My father was at his office at the university on the other side of the town. Mother told my elder brother, Saad, to keep a watch and gauge the danger outside.

He came back in a rush. 'Ammi, bullets are being fired from everywhere. One missed my ear by a few inches,' he said, sounding more excited than afraid.

'Did it really go past your ear? Don't lie,' I asked circumspectly.

Before he could answer, Sayema, our sister, began to cry. She had been calling my father's office landline from her Nokia 1100 phone non-stop. Her husband had given her this brand-new phone with an orange keypad before she left Saudi Arabia to come home to deliver their first baby.

Of course, the eight-month-old baby in Sayema's belly was our primary concern. Running away involved the risk that she – or anyone else among us – could be shot. Or Hindus could enter our house through the garage door and set it on fire (like they once had when Sayema was one[1]). As my mother weighed her options, four strange men rushed into our home. 'Baaji, we need to go to the terrace to attack enemies from a height. Unlock your staircase,' said the shortest among them, his eyes wet with tears of anger.

'Forgive us, for Allah's sake! We don't want our home used for rioting,' said my mother as she pushed them out of the house.

'We are fighting to save you. If not for us, they'd have entered your homes by now,' he said before going away to knock on other doors.

As we latched our door, I heard the sound of stones hitting the ground. It was coming from across the foyer in Palle Ghar, the portion of our ancestral home inhabited by the twenty-one members of my paternal aunt's family. The attack had arrived there. I saw bricks raining down her porch, bypassing the giant peepal tree separating her home from Hindu neighbours. 'I have spent my whole life here but *never* seen such bad times,' said Mehro, my Phuppo, blankness reigning in her green eyes. Her sons had moved their children to safe places, far away from bricks and bullets. Two of the sons and their families would leave this home in a month.

The attack on Palle Ghar had also opened up another grim possibility: people firing bullets at our house. 'The Hindus are standing with guns on their terrace. I saw somebody firing from the roof of Punjab Bank,' said Nadim Bhai, Phuppo's youngest son. Anyone standing on their terrace now scared us.

'Ammi, should I close the window? They can see us moving inside our house,' I said.

'Don't act too smart. Stay away from the windows,' she said, reciting another set of *dua* with the women of Palle Ghar. I shut the window. I wanted to prevent them from seeing us moving around our living room. My brother promptly switched off the lights.

Suddenly, Tariq Bhai, my paternal cousin, came rushing into our living room. 'They are trying to climb up. You should run across the lane,' he said.

'What about Sayema?' Ammi asked, pointing to my sister's eight-month-old stomach bulge.

'Let's walk slowly,' said Saad.

Amid all the panic, Ammi took her time to lock the doors and hide anything that had a remote chance of being stolen. Finally, we left our home.

Outside, the screams of women mingled with gunshots, profanity and religious slogans to create a strange cacophony of chaos. We walked holding each other's hands before running into a narrow lane that led towards Jama Masjid. 'This way! This way!' said neighbourhood women we had never met, showing us the way to run away from our home while they were firmly planted in theirs.

After we left, the four strangers who wanted to enter our terrace returned to our home. They broke the rusty lock on the staircase. One of them later died of a bullet wound in a clinic nearby.

It was only later that I found out that Shadab had also died.

# PART 1

# Childhood

# 1

# THE U.K.

IF YOU ARE a starry-eyed thief riding a motorcycle on a dusty Aligarh road after snatching somebody's gold chain and know the intricate warren of lanes by heart, you can easily reach your hideout in less than fifteen minutes. Aligarh is *that* small.

But motorcycles with 200cc engines hadn't still arrived in the glassy showrooms of the Centre Point Market, so yesteryear robbers had to find rather complicated ways to outwit the law officers of their time. In this regard, the Dwarf Dacoit or 'Bona Daku' of Aligarh could be considered much ahead of his time.

The folklore says Bona Daku roamed on the potholed streets of Aligarh in the early twentieth century, the richest thief in Aligarh's illustrious crime history. He was so wealthy that he built his personal fortress on the outskirts of the city, a palace with an expertly designed array of little caves beneath it, where only the clever dwarf could enter. Nobody dared enter these caves to catch him.

The reason, according to an over-smart boy at a dhaba holding court outside the Aligarh Muslim University (AMU), was simple. 'Only Bona Daku could enter this place. If an enemy tried to attack

him, he would make his way through the little caves and attack
his adversary from behind,' the boy said over his tenth cup of tea.

But such things never came to pass. According to urban legend,
the robber lived a long life without fearing taller townsmen and
inefficient cops. Nobody knows the truth of this story, but many
who sit at Aligarh's dhabas believe it to be true – as if they had
personally visited the legendary dacoit in his fortress and drank a
cup of dhaba tea with him. Trapped in a web of illusions, they will
disregard the historians who say this fort was built by a governor
under the reign of Ibrahim Lodhi.[1] What on Earth do *they* know?

This story brings us to an inextricable part of Aligarh's culture,
the phenomenon of *slight exaggeration*. Everyone I know here
tends to *slightly* exaggerate whatever they say. Sometimes, it takes
the shape of half-cooked stories or outright lies, all of them more
intriguing than the truth. The moral of the story? If somebody
from Aligarh tells you a story, best take it with a grain of salt.

So, when you hear my Hindu neighbours say how Aligarh was
originally called Harigarh, be careful.

'It was named after the avatar of Lord Vishnu that takes away
everyone's pain,' somebody from the Hindu area Kanwari Ganj
would say. Another would say, 'It was named after a benevolent
Hindu king who was mercilessly butchered by the cruel armies
of Muslim invaders.'

When you hear these stories, remember what I told you about
the Dwarf Dacoit.

Never fall into this trap.

The Harigarh myth has long been told among the town's
Hindus, with occasional clamouring by fundamentalist groups
to have the name restored. They claim it is Aligarh's oldest and
*real* name – the perfect reason for renaming the city and all its
hospitals, schools and offices. Some would write this name in
addresses on postcards, others would have it printed on shop

banners. A Harigarh temple was later constructed, but I have never heard of anyone going to pray there.

Of course, Aligarh was not always known as Aligarh. The original name, in fact, came from Hindu mythology, but it didn't come from a God. It came from a demon – a fact that should explain a lot of things.

As per historical records, the city's older name was Kol – said to be named after the demon Kolasur who lived here and terrorized the folks until he met Balram, Lord Krishna's elder brother. After he found out about the situation, Lord Balram sought the help of some dairy farmers, came to the city, attacked Kolasur with his plough and killed him instantly. Afterwards, he went to wash his plough or *hal* at a pond in a village on the outskirts of Aligarh. The place came to be known as Haldua or Harduaganj, a village that still has a temple dedicated to Lord Balram.[2]

The name Kol was used to refer to the city till the eighteenth century. But the town existed before that. Historians say it was a seat of Buddhist learning in ancient times as the engravings and relics found in the city point out. Ibn Batuta, the famous Moroccan traveller, came here in the fourteenth century. He referred to Kol in his records as 'a fine town surrounded by mango groves' (slight exaggeration, folks!). In the nineteenth century, a Shia commander called Najaf Ali Khan captured the town from the Jats and named it Aligarh after the last caliph of Islam.[3]

Aligarh today is a city of a million people in western Uttar Pradesh. It lies in the fertile land between the two holiest rivers of north India, the Ganga and the Yamuna, but most know it for its university, lock industry and for being the place where the idea of Pakistan is said to be born. It is also where Chandrachur Singh comes from – the guy who got to woo Aishwarya Rai *and* outwit Shahrukh Khan's gang in the 2000 Bollywood film *Josh*.

And far from pageant-winning women and superstars with wax statues at Madame Tussauds, I was born and brought up in the Upar Kot area of Aligarh's old town. Upar means 'Upper' and 'Kot' means Fort, so it is named after an old fort which now exists only in the tales of elders. It is a place where small houses pack into each other to a point of annoyance amid grand mosques that dot its dense neighbourhoods.

The proponents of Harigarh lovingly call my locality 'mini-Pakistan', the name reserved for most large Muslim ghettos in India – a derogatory allusion to it being a place hostile to Hindu and Indian interests.[4]

My Muslim ghetto, Upar Kot, is situated on a higher ground than the rest of the city. According to my neighbour Tutu Bhai's son, when (god forbid) Aligarh is flooded and the people in the rest of Aligarh die a painful, watery death, the residents of Upar Kot will be lounging in their chairs, enjoying a hot *kullad* of tea. The mohalla is spread over five square kilometres with Jama Masjid, the city's largest mosque, in the middle of it.

Aligarh has two Jama Masjids: one is the famous one at the AMU where its founder Sir Syed Ahmed Khan is buried, and the older one in Upar Kot, where a thief is said to be buried – if I were to believe my neighbour Tutu Bhai's son.

Built in 1728 AD by a Mughal governor Saabit Khan, the white mosque is decorated with 600 kilograms of gold, the most of any Indian mosque.[5] 'When the flood comes, only one stair of Jama Masjid will be drowned,' Tutu Bhai's son once told me. However, I was more intrigued by the mosque's celebrity graves. Most were of Ulemas, religious leaders, who died fighting British imperialists during India's first war of independence. As a child, I had been curious about an unknown grave in a corner of the white marble-floored praying area. This was where Tutu Bhai's know-it-all son's conspiracy theory derived from.

'This grave belongs to a thief who once climbed the dome of the Jama Masjid to steal its golden *gumbad*. Abba tells me it is worth hundreds of crores,' he told a wide-eyed, gaping me. 'When the thief tried to climb the slippery dome in the dark of the night, he fell to his death. Before he hit the ground, on Allah's command, it parted, and this grave sprung up for the thief.'

Like almost all the children in Upar Kot, I also bought the story.

Less knowledgeable people than Tutu Bhai's son said this story was planted by maulvis to protect the Jama Masjid's substantial gold. However, nobody was sure who the occupant of this unknown grave was. But the tale of the thief's punishment continues to be told in Upar Kot alongside those of djinns roaming the rooftops at dusk, sadhus stealing children on summer days, and witches possessing Quran-reciting women on Shab-e-Barat.

Upar Kot's roads and lanes are full of magic and old tales. The lifeline of the neighbourhood consists of two roads that connect every place to every place. The first is Mohammad Ali Road, named after a leader of the Khilafat Movement. The second is Chandan Shaheed Road, named after a spiritual baba from Bareilly. Most locals just call the latter Penth, a famous market where burqa and sari-clad women jostle to buy fancy clothes at throwaway prices.

These two roads somehow hold together an intricate web of hundreds of narrow lanes crisscrossing through the unlikeliest corners. It is in these lanes Upar Kot lives and dies. This labyrinth is so dense that few will ever know it in its entirety. Lanes become narrow as you move inside them – sometimes, they further divide into narrower lanes or end in a lane or a road that seems geometrically improbable. Some lanes end up in dead ends, others in ruins or garbage pits. Few lanes are fortunate enough to sustain themselves till the mohallas of baniyas.

When posh kids come here, they are surprised. 'How can a lane be *this* narrow?' they'll say. A local will interject, 'These aren't *that* narrow. The ones that lie deep inside are as narrow as Pul-e-Sirat,' waiting to be asked what the Pul-e-Sirat was. 'It is the bridge through which everybody's soul will pass on the Day of Judgement. It is thinner than a strand of hair and sharper than a knife.' On cue, he'll take a well-earned pause, savouring the shock in the posh kids' eyes. 'Only the pious will cross it and reach the gates of Jannat. Sinners will fall into the raging hellfire below. Mostly, it is rich people who fall.'

If these rich kids ever reach the narrower lanes deep inside Upar Kot, they'll puke seeing the dirt. But never in their wildest dreams will they be able to imagine how beautiful, how full of splendour, these same lanes had been four centuries ago. The names of these mohallas, which now sound archaic, once represented the occupations of the finest workmen in the Ganga-Yamuna Doab.

Chirag Chiyaan, now just a chowk flanked by dirty stairs and crowded by banyan-clad men, was where workers made lamps to light up the homes of aristocrats and kings. Tantan Para made the finest bells, Atish Bazan made the best firecrackers, and Darziyan was where you'd find tailors who'd make the clothes of the wealthy. Ghosian was the mohalla of ghosis or cattle rearers, where Muslims raised cows and buffaloes. Rangrezan was where the dyers lived, and Parkatan was where people who skinned chickens lived.

In Turkman Gate lived the proud descendants of the Turks. Pathaan Mohalla housed the scions of the Afghanis. Sheikhan was the abode of those who claimed to be from royal Arab families. 'Never trust boys from Sheikhan. They make up tall stories and like bragging,' my father used to say. But he never said anything against the residents of Bani Israilan, the crown jewel of Upar Kot of yesteryear. 'Its habitants are the grandchildren of the Jews of Madina. They converted to Islam later,' he'd tell me proudly.

These riches survive only in the elders' stories. Now, their grandchildren sell towels and slippers from lovely homes. The present is ridden with poverty; the wealth remains with only a few, flowing away from the rest.

In the modern Upar Kot, every lane has three kinds of homes: poor homes, rich homes and the 'Manzils'. The poor homes belong to the workers. Their walls await the day when the owners can afford a fresh coat of paint. The curtains on the windows are old bedsheets or jute bags. The stairwells are narrow and dark. In rooms too small for their families, utensils, tools and clothes find company under worn-out beds.

On the contrary, the rich homes are too tall to be missed. They belong to a handful of lucky traders or factory owners. Sometimes reaching up to four or five storeys, they tell a tale of disposable money. Inside are decorated rooms with plastic paints and glossy showpieces, some never used. Uninterested in blending in, these homes were built to stand out from the surrounding poverty. Mostly, they come across as ugly anomalies.

The Manzils are basically in-between homes, originally constructed by a resourceful ancestor whose sole purpose in life seemed to be building a home for future generations. Caught between a glorious past and a harsh present, their inhabitants can be rich or poor. Plants sprout from corners or slither from centuries-old walls. Domed minarets befriend TV antennas. On the inside are crafted motifs, beautifully crafted pillars and expertly cut arches.

The architecture of Manzils synchronizes the elements of nature with human experiences, unlike modern homes. With time, many have become a hybrid of past and modern; old sheesham doors find space between sad walls with glassy tiles. The modern times are slowly taking these Manzils away. Some fall by themselves, others are brought down by labourers. Most end up as rich homes and contribute to the ugliness around.

Trees scoff at the modernism. They have mastered the art of hiding themselves in plain sight. The trees of Upar Kot are different from the trees in posh areas, which showcase their flowers, coaxing you to notice them. The trees here live almost secret lives, blending into decrepit surroundings, growing inside houses, on walls, on intersections, in mosques and on the sides of the lanes. 'Don't hurt trees. They are inhabited by spirits,' Badi Ammi, my father's eldest sister, told me when I broke a neem branch to brush my teeth. I still believe her. I see these trees as wise elders standing amid a mass of human beings, looking at their troubles from afar.

Unlike the trees, animals want to be noticed. The dogs of Goshtwali Gali will leave no stone unturned to gain your attention. They'll run around you, wag their tails and emotionally blackmail you into feeding them. They'll sneak into your home and steal whatever food is left in the open. There have been times when dogs have hidden inside people's basements for days. On the other hand, cats mind their own business and only enter homes for food or to have sex with your pet cat.

Here, open drains are an intrinsic part of existence. There's even a mohalla named after the broad drain that runs around it – it's called Chauri Naali. They carry everything: factory waste, vegetables, empty packets of Dilbagh gutkha and the blood of slain goats on Eid-ul-Zuha. Some drains are shallow, while others are so deep that a three-year-old could drown in them – not a rare occurrence. The drains are a part of childhood in Upar Kot, almost a playmate in cricket matches. Only a few shots don't end up in these drains, no matter how hard a young batsman might try. An average of four balls in every over end up in drains, sometimes politely strolling, sometimes in a rush. After a tantrum or two, the youngest boy pushes his small hands inside and takes the ball out.

Between the hundreds of balls going into and coming out of the drains, life goes along in Upar Kot. It's as if along with childhood, everyone's sorrows and worries are also left to flow in the drains. Most children are too engrossed in their own lives to understand their elders' struggles. Most walk about, nonchalantly talking to themselves; others run screaming on the streets for no reason at all (except to probably scare the posh kids). As they grow up, they master the art of avoiding the garbage on the side of the road and sticking to lanes they know well. Some become too clever for their own good. 'Nooruddin was born all bent and *tedha* from his mother's womb, so he will never do any *seedha kaam*,' they'd say to bully a meek boy.

Some of them grow up to be lock workers – the perennial example in Upar Kot for educated kids of what not to become. In the eyes of the privileged, they were the losers, the ones who never had the talent, the resources or the will to become something remotely respectable. 'Kids who don't study end up as *karkhaane-wale*. Do you want to become one?' Ammi would ask when I shirked homework. I would promptly go off to study. When I verbally abused my elder brother, she'd say, 'Why are you behaving like a karkhaane-wala's kid?' I would resist using invectives for a couple of days.

It was probably because I saw lock workers always covered in black, the colour of the grease that covered their facial features and their bodies, making them indistinguishable from each other. Blackness would cover the walls of the workshop and their tools. These men would sit hours in front of their noisy machines and work continuously for long stretches. They'd flick the multiple metal parts with their sweaty palms, making music from their tools.

Their days were spent amid sounds of welding machines and clanging metal. Some would be novices who'd shine metal parts or rub belt buckles in the sand. Veterans would immerse hundreds of bunched keys in yellow acid, its cancerous smoke fumes filling their lungs – and those of their unfortunate neighbours.

Like superhumans, these karkhaane-wale would spend the summers in closed rooms without fans or coolers, their sweat fusing with the dirt on their clothes. Some would work without a shirt, at risk from the sparks lighting up their rooms and hearts. 'Men like us don't burn. We are made of steel,' said Aiyya Bhai, who occasionally helped my family with tasks. As a child, I believed he was indestructible.

The karkhaane-wale mostly looked happy, though. Every day, they'd take a break from lunch, sit together, share food and jokes. The older ones would bully the younger ones but would help them in a moment of need. In between, they'd hustle for money, avoid friends looking to borrow, take naps and dream of opening their own workshops someday. It was between these moments they lived before they died, most of their dreams unfulfilled. Aiyya Bhai, the *indestructible* one, died of a lung disease he caught at his workplace. His eldest son replaced him within a month – the cycle repeating for generations.

Even in a ghetto-like Upar Kot, not everyone is poor. There are posh areas and less posh areas. I lived in a 'well-off' area of the ghetto, an area where garbage got picked up once in a while, bikes moved on cemented roads and tall mosque minarets adorned the skylines.

'*Mashallah*, our area is still one of the most open in Upar Kot. There is less garbage and thievery than in Teela and Usman Para,' Badi Ammi would say. 'Even the Hindus here are nicer than those from Baniya Pada.' Everyone would sing similar paeans for Atish

Bazan, my neighbourhood in Upar Kot. They loved pretending that their area was not a poor Muslim ghetto.

Denial is like an old beggar sitting outside a mosque. You don't see him because you don't want to. Because he brings you closer to the harsh reality of human existence. Because if you looked him in the eye, he would force you to recognize the bitter truths of your life. So, most pious worshippers would rather walk away as if they never saw the old beggar sitting on the pavement. They might even construe stories about the character of the beggar to lessen the burden of guilt on their hearts.

The people of Upar Kot mostly lived in denial – making up stories that portrayed them as a happier lot than the *unfortunate rich* who lived in planned colonies. 'You know what happens in Civil Lines? Rich people get robbed, lead a boring life and are left alone by their children who move abroad. People here take care of each other,' they'd say. These were the people who referred to Upar Kot by its anglicized name, 'The Upper Fort'.

Saad went a step further. Born with a talent for zany abbreviations, he famously shortened Upar Kot to the U.K., and keeping up with his British sense of humour, I will refer to it as the U.K. whenever I wish to.

༄

The U.K. had its problems. Hindus and Muslims disliked and distrusted each other with a passion that reminded one of blazing forest fires. 'You, the descendant of Shah Jamal, why don't you offer namaz in Pakistan?' they'd call out from their shops as we went to Friday prayers. Even politicians in Aligarh have publicly asked Muslims to 'go to Pakistan'.[6] The two communities kind of tolerate each other because it is good for business; Hindus are seemingly better off. 'But you know, water accumulates in their areas in the monsoon. Also, they'll die when the flood happens,' my cousin would tell me. It always lifted my spirits!

The Hindu areas had affluent upper-caste businessmen, baniyas with busy grocery shops and lower-caste labourers who were as poor as the Muslims. Then there were the Dalits. 'You clean everyone's houses. Why is your area not clean?' I asked Sanobar Bhai, who had been picking up the garbage from our house since my grandfather's time. He just narrowed his cataract-ridden eyes and laughed.

Every now and then, the Hindus and Muslims found themselves locked in heated battles over inconsequential local issues, got tired of it after facing curfews and business losses, but did it again after another quarrel. Riots were an inseparable part of our lives. I was very happy whenever there were riots – it meant not going to school. One or two boys dying in fights didn't alarm anyone. The violence was just another neighbour.

The U.K. was surrounded on three sides by Hindu areas. If there was a riot, we were cut off from the rest of the city. The only roads to reach the U.K. were Railway Road, Goolar Road and Mahaveer Ganj, Hindu areas where mobs could assemble to hunt Muslims. We were always worried because Papa would come back home through these roads, that too late at night.

'Can't you come back early when there is tension in the area? What will happen to our three kids if something happens to you?' Ammi would say angrily. Papa, usually the dominant one, would sheepishly go to bed. The children, the silent judges, would agree with their Ammi.

Another thing that irked the children, especially me, was my father's friendship with the Hindus from Kanwari Ganj. They came to our house to watch India–Pakistan matches, clapping boisterously when Sachin Tendulkar was on song. I never trusted them, but Papa didn't take ideological differences with his five-year-old son *that* seriously.

There were bigger issues in our lives. We were technically not considered part of the U.K. since our house was situated right on the border, at the end of the Muslim slope.

Our home was on the unofficial Line of Control between two adjacent Hindu and Muslim ghettos, a transition point for religious identities and culture. The place where two universes intersected. It was one of the many peculiarities of my ancestral home, Farsh Manzil, as my grandfather proudly named it.

As a naive five-year-old, I had no idea that like Farsh Manzil, the lives of its residents would soon be caught in a crossfire of hatred.

# 2

# FARSH MANZIL

WHILE MAN WAS sent from *arsh* (heaven) to *farsh* (earth) as part of his penance, I was sent down to Farsh Manzil, my ancestral home in Upar Kot.

On this earthly abode, Farsh was meant to refer to two slopes, separated from each other by my home. The two slopes had distinct characteristics. The one towards my portion was slanted and populated by more Muslims than Hindus, the one towards *Palle Ghar* was staired and was home to more Hindus than Muslims. Most mohallas in the U.K have opulent names. For these two unremarkable slopes in the middle of a ghetto, 'Farsh' was the grandest reference possible.

In between the two Farsh stood my century-old home. It had twenty-five rooms, ten families consisting of forty-seven members, and nearly 400 doors and windows. Some believe the name 'Farsh' came from the name of our home. Papa feigned ignorance. 'I think it's the other way around,' he said, much to my heart's dismay.

'It is the only place you can send a postcard without mentioning the mohalla,' Saad, my elder brother, told me as we slept on the terrace like tired prisoners, after another nightly power cut. 'If you write only "Farsh Manzil, Aligarh" as the address, it will still be delivered,' he told me as I gazed at the stars forming a ship, gliding through an infinite dark river. As mosquitoes tried to infiltrate the collar of my kurta, I flushed with pride.

At the dawn of the twentieth century, Farsh Manzil was built in British India by my grandfather, Ashfaq Ahmed Khan, and his brother, Aashiq Ahmed Khan. They came from a nearby village and found a plot in the heart of Aligarh. Eventually, they made a home where love met architecture and the present met the past.

Love dripped from everywhere: the limestone walls, petal-shaped arches, artistic pillars, rounded corners, secret stairs, giant windows and narrow passages. Like a clairvoyant, I could visualize a craftsman instructing sculptors and telling my grandfather: 'I'll make you a house your future generations will thank you for.' He kept his promise. And so, Farsh Manzil was my grandfather's magnum opus.

The architecture was experimental but consistent and symmetrical. Any design would be replicated exactly on the other side of the house or diagonally opposite. Made for a time before electricity came to Aligarh, the sunlight and wind would reach every space. Like elements in a painting, every room had a purpose: the living room where my Daadi sat with a handheld fan to comfort her kids, the basement where my grandfather ran his Unani medicine clinic, the sitting area where guests savoured cups of tea. Everybody liked coming to Farsh Manzil.

From the terrace, one could see the whole town. First lay the houses of Kanwari Ganj, then a transformer and the flagpoles of two temples, followed by houses upon houses extending to the horizon. On the other side, one could gaze past the houses to see the dome of Jama Masjid. During Ramzan, a bulb would light its dome to signify that it was time to break the iftar. We'd wait for this light with the eagerness of passengers waiting for a late-running train.

The keeper of the tales of the 'greatness' of this house and my family was Badi Ammi, originally Shahzad Begum, Papa's eldest sister and my favourite relative. My grandparents had died long before I was born, and so Badi Ammi told me all the family stories. 'We are Yusufzai Pathans, a warrior tribe, originally from Kabul. Our noble ancestors would be surprised at how *nalaayak* their descendants are,' she would tell me. She often said things that might hurt others, but that didn't stop everyone from respecting her. 'This generation has squandered both the wealth and reputation earned by their forefathers,' she'd say.

I was unsure of her theory that we came from a warrior tribe, but she did know the whole family tree. None of my relatives, however, looked remotely related to any warrior clan. We were indistinguishable from others in the U.K., with short, non-athletic frames, burgeoning bellies, broad shoulders, receding hairlines and soft features.

Badi Ammi lived on the first floor of Farsh Manzil with her husband, the Urdu poet, Kebab Sahab. Kebab Sahab was his poetry pseudonym. 'But you should call him Phuppha,' Ammi said, and I ignored her. Like a pair of old birds in a forest, the couple lived in a pretty room above us, which was partly covered by a tin shed and had three doors opening into a courtyard.

When I was seven, Kebab Sahab passed away, his book of poems still incomplete. After his death, it was either Sayema or I who slept with Badi Ammi. Ammi had shamed us into going. 'She is old and needs our company,' she'd say. And Badi Ammi, still active at eighty, really liked talking. These nights were when she told me our entire family history.

According to her, my grandfather, Ashfaq Ahmed Khan, was a helpful, pious and multi-talented man. He worked as a kanungo, a government revenue officer, who had served in many towns in United Provinces under the British regime. An avid horse rider and hunter, he socialized with British officers, zamindars and nobles alike. When he came to Aligarh, he bought a piece of land. 'It was a strange plot – just a slope, surrounded by a *nullah* and a big neem tree. When the foundation was dug, workers discovered the remnants of a fort, an underground tunnel and coal-filled vessels. But it was the discovery of Sayyed Baba's tomb that complicated his plans the most,' said Badi Ammi.

Like a witness on a payroll, Badi Ammi narrated her stories like she had seen everything with her own eyes, and the hero in each one was my grandfather. The honourable person he was, she said, he decided to forgo the land where the tomb was found. 'And Sayyed Baba returned the favour one day,' she recounted, cleaning her thick glasses for the umpteenth time. Badi Ammi's face was marked by deep wrinkles and surrounded by hair as white as salt. She mostly wore light-coloured salwar suits at home but wore saris for weddings. Though she didn't have a formal education, she was the brightest in Farsh Manzil.

When I'd once asked her about Sayyed Baba, she'd got angry. 'Don't ask such things at the time of Maghrib. Why do you play on the terrace at this time? Spirits come and go through this route.' This made me afraid to go back to my part of the house. I needed to climb down a dark staircase, the perfect place for spirits to attack their prey. I recited *durud* (the only dua I knew) and ran quickly through the stairs and reached our portion to have dinner.

Farsh Manzil was unlike any other manzil. A heavy door with sharp metal thorns led into a compund-cum-parking area. Palle Ghar, Mehro Phuppo's portion, was on the right, while ours was on the right. Our and Bade Papa's families lived on the ground floor, while Badi Ammi and Noorjahan Apa lived on the second.

Noorjahan Apa had been our tenant for over forty years. I had no idea she wasn't my Phuppo until I grew up.

As one entered our portion, they would come into a huge brick-laid courtyard, the centre of the home and lives of its residents. A bathroom, two kitchens and a water tank were on the right. On the left was a mud platform from where plants merged into the neem and peepal trees growing outside. Nearby was a big room where my uncle Bade Papa's family of five lived.

Outside our portion was a tin shed standing on carved sheesham pillars, which led into our hall, the centrepiece and unarguably the most beautiful room in Farsh Manzil. It had eight doors and two giant windows, making it the most spacious and lit. In the middle of it were three giant arches supported by craftily designed pillars. In Farsh Manzil, doors and windows occupied more area than walls. 'To provide woodwork for the 400 doors and windows, my father purchased a sheesham tree orchard. People have lived and died, but these doors are still there,' Badi Ammi once said.

Another peculiarity of our portion was that a new person wouldn't be able to guess which floor they were on. The guests usually entered the house from an entrance on the ground floor, but once they were inside, they'd be surprised to find they were on the first floor without climbing any stairs. (I later used this trick on almost all my friends who came home). Like a half-wrecked ship on a beach, the house was constructed partly on a slope and partly on flat land, so the basement was actually the ground floor, open on two sides with a door. This basement was huge with three rooms, probably made for a future time when some descendent would try to start a business.

After retiring as a *kanungo*, my grandfather became a Unani Hakeem and made this basement his clinic. After his death, the basement doors were kept shut for decades. I found out about its existence only after it was briefly leased out. 'Djinns roam there, but won't come to the upper floors because of Sayyed Baba,' Saad recounted. I imagined djinns moving around the basement, looking at the floor above, looking at me looking at them!

In the final year of his life, my grandfather tried to adorn Farsh Manzil with an unusual thing for Upar Kot – a rooftop glasshouse. However, Allah Miyan had other plans. He had a cardiac arrest and his attempts to further beautify our abode died with him.

∽

When the decades-long construction of Farsh Manzil was reaching its conclusion, something else was taking birth: the idea of Pakistan. In 1906, the All-India Muslim League emerged from the Aligarh Movement, demanding separate electorates for Muslims. The idea simmered for decades until 1940, when the Muslim League resolved to carve a separate state for Muslims. Suddenly, millions had to decide whether to stay in a secular India or migrate to a dream-like Islamic state. Mahatma Gandhi and Jawaharlal Nehru envisioned a secular, democratic India, while Mohammed Ali Jinnah wanted a state where Muslims wielded political power. Riots were taking place, people were butchered on streets, trains were robbed, and houses set on fire.

'Many advised my father to migrate. But he believed in Gandhi and wanted to stay in Aligarh,' Badi Ammi told me one night. But not everyone agreed with him, the foremost being Kebab Sahab, his son-in-law. 'I was afraid when my father and husband discussed politics. It got pretty ugly. My father believed in Maulana Abul Kalam Azad's promise that Muslims would be safe in a Hindu-majority nation.'

After my grandfather's death three decades after India's independence, my Daadi shouldered the responsibility of their nine children. The saving grace was that all the daughters were married before my grandfather died. While Badi Ammi and Mehro Phuppo lived in Farsh Manzil, the two other daughters, Bibban and Chotti Ammi, lived in Civil Lines. Daadi still had to worry about her sons. But the new nation of Pakistan, 'the land of the pure', snatched them from her. Unlike my grandfather, three of my uncles didn't believe in Gandhi and Nehru's promises. Their wives wrote to relatives settled in Pakistan, who narrated stories of better opportunities for Muslims there. They successfully marketed their country as a haven safe from communal violence that plagued India.

In the 1960s, three of the elder sons left for Pakistan. 'It was the wives who convinced their husbands to migrate. As the days for them to leave came near, everybody kept crying. It was the saddest time of our lives,' said Badi Ammi. 'It was as if Partition had begun and ended in our home,' she'd often say.

This was a time when love was not restricted to partners and parents. It engulfed the nephews and nieces, brothers and sisters, their children, family friends and neighbours. My father had only respect towards his elder brothers combined with equal amounts of love. The leftover family cried for days remembering those who had migrated. Only two sons remained in the now very-empty Farsh Manzil: Masood Ahmed Khan, Bade Papa, and my father. They'd decided to stay in India, unconcerned by fears that India was no longer safe for Muslims.

The head of my less-conservative-than-our-neighbours-but-still-patriarchal Muslim family was my father, Masroor Ahmed Khan. Papa was my idol, my hero and my best friend. When he learnt the Quran by heart at the age of twelve, he was declared the son who would carry his father's legacy forward. 'Ammi was so proud of him,' Badi Ammi told me. To my grandmother's dismay, however, he outgrew that religious inclination as soon as he was out of his teens. Worse, he became friends with Hindus from Kanwari Ganj and the Shias he studied with.

As he grew up, his brothers tried to lure him to come to Pakistan, citing the repeated religious violence in India. On more than five occasions, the teenage Masroor had visited the land across the newly formed border. 'I would go alone without asking anyone, take a train and spend weeks in Karachi and Lahore. Ammi was very afraid that I might also leave,' he told me one evening as I slept with him on his small single bed.

He loved Lahore and Karachi but detested Rawalpindi. 'I would take my brother's cycle and roam the streets of Lahore,' he recalled. Eventually, he found that he didn't have it in him to leave his home, city and the nation. Badi Ammi told me the real reason. 'He didn't have it in him to leave his mother,' she said, recounting the story in exchange for my bringing her a bulb.

As the borders solidified with time, the visits from the brothers in Pakistan became less frequent. Family bonds were weakened by the pressures of studying and making a career. As time passed, our family talked less about them. When their eldest brother passed away in Pakistan, Papa and Badi Ammi would cry together remembering him. It seemed really funny to me. *Who cries remembering their brother?* I would think.

After completing a course in library science, my father went to work at AMU as an officer in the Students' Union. He was a rebellious, anti-establishment officer who was utterly disliked by the administration. He spent his days with students and was biased towards their rights, fighting for them against his bureaucratic bosses. And thus, he faced many suspensions, transfers, blocked promotions and a general lack of goodwill from the vice-chancellors and registrars. The administration despised him so much that his name was once given to the CID as an instigator of students' trouble.

This involvement with university politics brought him recognition and clout. He knew local and national politicians from all parties and was on a first-name basis with most AMU employees. He was respected by the most powerful people of those times – the student leaders. He read and socialized a lot. And when he turned thirty, Daadi went to Etah to find him the daughter of a wealthy zamindar and a marriage soon took place.

That is how my mother, Parveen Jahan, became a part of Farsh Manzil. She left her pampered life and became a housewife and, later, a mother to three children.

She was raised in a family with dozens of helpers at the ready. Also, by nature, she was creative, messy and too bright to be interested in housework. But like most women of her generation, she had to fit into the mould of the devoted wife. This meant spending long hours in the kitchen, day after day, night after night, washing dishes and clothes for thankless children and taking care of them when they fell ill.

Ammi brought with her a good sense of humour to disarm her city-dwelling in-laws, who considered themselves more sophisticated. But at every point, she would prove that she was smarter, more hard-working and funnier. She was so good at tailoring that everyone was spellbound. But that didn't mean she was good at everything. She wasn't good at household chores or cooking, not for want of talent, but a lack of motivation. It was clear she did it because she had to. That meant years of her kids fighting her and comparing her cooking with what 'other mothers cooked'. Unsurprisingly, she cooked well when she was in a good mood or when guests came over.

She was the head of the gossip-cum-therapy centre in Farsh Manzil. Everyone came to our home to talk about their life's deepest worries. She was more interested in what was happening in their homes than in the lives of her own children. She'd hear everyone out – widows trying to get their daughters married to boys settled in the Gulf, daughters trying to avoid being married to balding men and men who couldn't marry early because of familial poverty. They'd talk about their complaints against their non-obedient daughters-in-law, haughty mothers-in-law or careless husbands. I was always surprised by Ammi's ability to be sympathetic to both sides at the same time. She'd listen to them patiently, ask them to come to a middle ground and divert their sadness by telling jokes. Whoever had come home, she was their best friend.

She wasn't as sensitive towards her children, though. She'd beat us for our mistakes, especially Saad for his countless mischiefs. Papa never raised his hands at us, but Ammi didn't hesitate. And that wasn't her only trick to get her way. She'd blackmail us to make us work. 'Beta, do this for your mother. Aren't you a lovely boy?' If we refused, she'd remind us that the Quran says that heaven lies under your mother's feet. Often, she was distracted and lost in her thoughts – a trait that she'd pass on to me.

The bulk of my relationship with Ammi involved finding ways to not massage her legs. Her legs always ached, and she felt sick almost every day. It was only later we found out that she had been suffering from rheumatoid arthritis for years.

Being an overprotective mother, she wouldn't let us mingle with the boys of the mohalla. 'I don't want you to become like other children of Upar Kot.' But when relatives came over, she'd say, 'My boys like playing in the house.' I always wished I could scream, 'That's because *you* don't allow us to go out.'

I was closest to my father and my sister, Sayema, the princess of Farsh Manzil. She was the eldest and the most beloved offspring (and according to her, the most sophisticated). Being the first child has its perks, and she unapologetically exploited them. She was the apple of her father's eye and the darling of all our uncles, much to the chagrin of her younger brothers. I, on the other hand, was slightly detached from Ammi. I was the third child, and by the time I arrived in the family, my mother's life was too busy with her chores.

But the person who almost hated Sayema was Saad, my elder brother, a bully and the nightmare of every kid. He was the crazy one, a born arsonist. When he was born, he was named Haaris, but then he began starting fires in different places in our house. Ammi called a maulana, who told her people named Haaris like to play with fire and the solution was to change his name. He asked her to name him Junaid. That didn't help. They changed a few more names before they decided to call him Saad. Even after that, the second-born child of our family kept setting things on fire and breaking things – including people.

He'd beat up kids everywhere: at school, in the rickshaw that brought him home and in the mohalla. Every once in a while, his rickshaw-wala would come to our house with his complaints. 'Oh, Saad beat up that child', 'Saad pushed that girl from the rickshaw,' 'Saad was beating the juniors in recess,' the teachers would call to complain. Unlike Sayema who went to Our Lady of Fathima, 'the best school in Aligarh' according to her, Saad went to Aligarh Public School. To put it mildly, the crowd was not as sophisticated there.

Saad was the reason Sayema and I became friends. We needed each other for protection when the elders weren't around. Because everyone else hated or feared him, Ammi always took his side. He was big and strong, and he'd beat up Sayema and me – throwing us from our beds, into wardrobes and scaring us with fake lizards. He could only be controlled by Ammi. 'My other two children don't do any mischief, but this one won't stop without beatings,' she'd say.

Saad never shared his toys. He didn't even let me touch his books or his cricket ball. If I touched any of his stuff, the result would be a thrashing. Many of my cousins and family friends' kids suffered nights of anxiety before coming to our home. 'Don't take us there. Saad will beat us,' they pleaded with their parents. But they came and were beaten again. Their parents cared more for their social obligations than the violence faced by their children.

I should say though that Saad kind of loved me. Only *he* could beat me up, nobody else. He'd sometimes kiss me when he needed some errands done and save me when other kids bullied me. When he slept next to me, he used me as his cushion.

Then there was me. The youngest of a whole generation – the youngest child of the youngest of the nine children of my grandfather. Almost everyone liked me, but I was, after all, the third kid. My parents were kind of bored of doing the kid stuff. A pampered kid, I was raised very independently, mostly by my elder siblings. I was exploited by everyone into running errands. I was the boy who wouldn't say no to anyone. I was the people pleaser, the kind who loved to hear 'He is a good boy'. I was creative, intelligent, slightly eccentric, remained lost in my imaginations and had terrible motor skills.

At school, I was the quiet but attention-seeking boy who'd perform stunts and acrobatics in the playground. I was a jester, who'd learn magic tricks from Saad and perform them for my class. I'd get into arguments with teachers and enjoyed a cult leadership among geeky boys. I was also arrogant and argumentative. 'You don't know shit and can never measure up to me,' I'd tell kids who'd argue with me.

As I later found out in life, I was also kind of resilient, something that was passed on to me by my Ammi. I didn't know at the time that I would need this resilience to exist in the strange time and world I was bestowed with.

# 3

# THE BUTTON

MY FIRST EXPOSURE to Aligarh's communal polarization came with my introduction to the Button. I was around four years old when the Babri Masjid was brought down in Ayodhya. It led to violent riots in India, and like always, in Upar Kot too.

A small, white, electrical switch hung in my drawing room near a window overlooking Kanwari Ganj, the Hindu area. It seemed a bit out of place. The Button wasn't attached to a switchboard and just hung above the windowpane. Its intertwined black and red wires led to our balcony and then got lost in a crowd of electrical cables near a blue metal grill.

It was at a height I couldn't reach. Then one day, Saad brought a chair to the drawing room. Bingo! I could *finally* reach the Button. I climbed up the chair and pressed the button. But there was no 'click'. No lights lit up anywhere, no fans began to circle. The elaborate setting seemed to be for nothing.

A few minutes later, all hell broke loose. 'The Hindus are coming!' somebody shouted, as if the end of the world had arrived. More screaming voices came from all directions. Panic reigned, and most of the men of my mohalla ran out of their homes and into the streets. Some gathered under my balcony. Two boys came inside without permission and entered the drawing room. 'Who pressed the switch?' they asked authoritatively.

Ammi feigned ignorance, and Saad denied he had even entered the room. 'It must be Sayema. She was here!' I lied. But somehow, they knew it was me. They began to laugh. 'Keep away from this switch from now on, Bhaiya,' the boys told me and moved the switch even higher.

The Button was actually an alarm wherein a lightbulb lit up in our neighbourhood to inform the Muslims that Hindu rioters were trying to move upwards on our slope. It signalled an enemy attack on Upar Kot. When I pressed it, someone sitting at a community area noticed it and informed the others. Soon, the boys of the mohalla got ready to defend the mohalla with their stones, knives, swords, bricks, country-made guns and, of course, acid bottles.

When they found out that it was a false alarm, the boys got angry. To placate them, my mother gave them a bottle of homemade chilli pickle that my Nani Ammi had sent from Etah. And so, it was a happy ending for everybody, my little misadventure with the forbidden switch a laughing matter in the neighbourhood.

It would be a few years before I'd understand the significance of this incident, when Ammi narrated the story to my friends to shame an overconfident me. Similar alarms were also installed in other homes on the border with the Hindu area Kanwari Ganj – little white buttons on which our lives depended.

The Button was just the beginning of a strange childhood. Living in a house on the border of a Hindu and a Muslim ghetto in communally charged times came with its risks. Spent at the cusp of two cultural universes, my childhood had somehow intertwined with the communal violence gripping the country in the 1990s and early 2000s.

Our biggest grouse at Farsh Manzil was that it was not entirely in the Muslim part of the locality. Our electricity bill came from the office at Delhi Gate, a Hindu area, because the government, for entirely unknown reasons, regarded Farsh Manzil as being in the Hindu part. Muslims lived on the top of the slope and Hindus at the bottom. Only unfortunate people like us were caught in the middle. My home was at the cusp of two warring civilizations – the Muslims of Upar Kot and the Hindus of Kanwari Ganj.

On our left was Goshtwali Gali, or the butcher's lane, where I once vomited because of the smell, and home to the most ferocious dogs in Aligarh. It was also where the shop of the most famous butcher, a man named the Collector, stood. Of course, the Collector wasn't a magistrate, but he sure acted like one. 'Why'd I give you bone-laden meat? Do you doubt my integrity?' he'd say, a thorough professional proud of his trade. '*Subhanallah*,' he'd say as he minced your buffalo meat like it was the most precious thing in the world. A magistrate at heart, he'd always treat his customers with respect.

Anyone who liked to be treated with respect while buying meat flocked to the Collector's shop. He wasn't ashamed of this title – a sign on the door proudly proclaimed that the shop belonged to Abdul Collector. Once I grew up, I found that the Collector's meat was a tad more expensive than others, but I always went there. Though he lived in Usman Para, where most butchers lived, his shop was in Goshtwali Gali. Professionalism ran in his family. His brother was called Judge, because he acted like a judge, often mediating when some dispute happened between men in Usman Para.

On the other side of our home was Tantan Para, where the owners of many lock factories lived. It was where Badi Mummy lived before Bade Papa saw her and fell in love at first sight. But we were far from being the most interesting people in our mohalla.

Ishrat Bhai's shop was the most happening place in our mohalla. If ever there was a contest in the mohalla, he would easily win the prize for being the most helpful. Everyone needed Ishrat's help at some point or the other. He knew all kinds of people. 'Ishrat, please get our telephone fixed', 'Ishrat, please ask the electrician boy to visit our house', 'Ishrat, do you know someone in the municipality?' He'd always do his best to solve everyone's problems. Everybody, even the Hindus from whom he bought goods in wholesale, respected him for his honesty.

For some reason, he always kept smiling – almost constantly and seemingly effortlessly. As he grew older, the smile remained, but it grew more and more forced with every passing year.

The neighbourhood rumours said that beneath the smiles, Ishrat had been sad for a long time. The reason was unrequited love. When he had fallen in love, he had shown my mother a photograph of his beloved. The girl was almost too beautiful for him, but they loved each other.

Ammi reached out to her network to send word to the girl's family, to tell them what a good boy Ishrat is. But her family declined. Because you know, decent families don't want to have their daughter married to the mohalla shopkeeper, however wealthy he may be, however clean his moustache might be, or however generous his smiles might be.

The life of a neighbourhood shopkeeper in India is strange and far too public. Though people meet them almost every day, they treat them as 'just a shopkeeper'. Few in Aligarh greet shopkeepers – they skip the niceties and go directly to 'six eggs, one Brittania bread, a quarter Amul butter.' Nobody asks them whether they are in pain, whether they have recovered from their last heartbreak or why they didn't marry.

Ishrat's shop was the centre of many things. It was where the skins of sacrificed goats were assembled in heaps after Eid-ul-Zuha and where *chanda* to make haleem was collected in Muharram. It was also the *adda* for most of the middle-aged men in Atish Bazan. They sat there every day but never talked to Ishrat about his personal life. They gibbered about who had a problem with whom in the mohalla, forced compromises between quarrelling families, pondered the fate of India–Pakistan matches and prophesied that the end of the world was near. But like most male friends almost everywhere on Earth, they never asked Ishrat how he was doing.

Not getting married was probably the most unpopular decision you could make in Aligarh. People are fine with Muslims not praying, they'll pardon even the ones who secretly drink alcohol from the *theka* in the Hindu areas, but almost nobody is fine with a person not getting married. It's almost as if that person had decided never to be happy. Men and women who don't marry are often sidelined at family functions (because most people are remembered through their families) and suspect them of being characterless.

Women have it worse. Like my neighbour Rasool's eldest daughter. She couldn't get married because she was too thin or probably because all her eight brothers and sisters looked like each other. It became almost impossible to distinguish one from the other. And because they had too many children, it became problematic for them to arrange a dowry – like every family, Hindu or Muslim, was expected to.

But because she couldn't get married, almost everyone talked about her sadly. Like she had failed her exams or something. Barring that, they were the bravest among all the Muslims of Atish Bazan. They lived in the last house on the Farsh, and most of their neighbours were Hindus. During riots, their house was attacked first, even if they acted all friendly with their Hindu neighbours. But they didn't know the truth – being nice to your

Hindu neighbours doesn't really help when the eventual attack comes.

Even Pappu, the poori-wala who lived in a lane populated by Muslims, acted friendly with Muslims. He seemed like a nice man and the Muslims never attacked him. Neither Pappu nor Rasool knew about the case in Dahiwali Gali, the small lane near Subzi Mandi, where people go to buy underwear, vests and bras. It was a place where Hindus and Muslims had lived like two estranged brothers with each other for decades, until a *piyaaoon*, a local water tap, came up near the mohalla mosque. Hindus claimed that the mosque had been a temple at some point in some version of their history. So, a riot broke out, the story of which was narrated to me by my Badi Mummy.

The self-explanatory title of the story was 'Daant Kaati Roti', meaning a friendship so deep and old that you could share a half-masticated roti with the friend.

In that story, a Muslim family lived in Dahiwali Gali (selling undergarments of course) and were friendly with their Hindu neighbours. Their daughter had literally been brought up by these neighbours and considered them her extended family. After riots broke out on one occasion, the girl heard a scream that seemed like it was her father's. When she looked out of her window, she saw her father being beaten. Among the mob were the ones whom she considered her family, her *daant kaati roti* friends. When she began to scream, the mob came to her house, dragged her out, beat her up and left her to die in the very deep drains of Dahiwali Gali. She was saved by some neighbours and lived to tell the tale, but remained traumatized for the rest of her life.

Rasool hadn't even shared rotis with his Hindu neighbours but still hoped he'd save his large family during a riot. Even after repeated warnings from more sensible Muslims, he continued to live in the most dangerous location on Farsh. But the fear of their house being burnt down wasn't the only problem they were dealing with. It was a very, very small house for his burgeoning family: they had more people in two rooms than all of Farsh Manzil put together. The only place that wasn't suffocating was their terrace, which was where almost all the siblings spent almost all their evenings. They flew kites every day, lit candles on Diwali, played contests with their Hindu neighbours, even smiled at them. All in vain.

During the next riot, the Hindu mob burnt down their son's brand-new car. The new jeep was set aflame right under my house, and we were worried that it would explode and damage some part of our balcony. But it never did. It simply burnt quietly for hours and hours.

When I saw the burning jeep on news channels like *Aaj Tak* and *Sahara Samay*, my fifteen-year-old heart was filled with pride. One way or the other, my balcony was on the national news.

For some time, Rasool avoided his Hindu neighbours. But by the next year, they were exchanging smiles and partaking in kite contests again.

When I was growing up, a very popular programme that people assembled to watch every evening on Doordarshan was called *Alif* Laila. It was based on *One Thousand and One Nights*. In this serial, a cruel king would marry a new girl every night and then kill her in the morning. One day, it was the turn of a young girl named Shahrzad, who devised a unique way to save her life. Every night, Shahrzad told the king stories about djinns, sailors, princes and princesses and noble caliphs. These stories were so intriguing that the king would listen to her all night, each story carefully told to last till morning when the king would begin to be sleepy. This way, night after night, the king kept her alive just to hear the end of the story.

I have often wondered: do we do the same to safeguard ourselves? Do we make up stories and lie so we may survive the next day? Was that what Rasool was doing with his neighbours?

Like a portal that took us to other worlds, the Farsh was the point at which religious identities, perceptions and cultures changed. Apart from a few deadly riots, the slopes of the Farsh had been a relatively peaceful interchange, where Hindus and Muslims lived in relative harmony, as compared to other 'border' areas like Baniya Pada, Kanjarwala Pul, Dahiwali Gali or Usman Para, where the communities came face to face on the slightest provocations. The elders of the Farsh had good relations with Hindu neighbours from 'down there'.

But this illusion of safety was shattered during riots. I could never separate a rioter from a school bully. Rioters were like bullies coming together and destroying things and killing people simply because they knew they could get away with it. They enjoyed inflicting pain on their hapless victims, mostly poor people, because that made them feel powerful.

The people butchered by the mob were almost always poor men – people passing by on their cycles, getting cheap mustard oil to their homes or filling their water bottles from a public tap in the Hindu mohalla.

Like bullies, a mob will continue to exert influence only till the people are terrified. When the victims began to stand their ground, they'd retreat – unless they had bigger weapons to scare the other side once again.

Rumours were worse and sometimes scarier than the actual riots themselves. Rumours of an impending confrontation were a monthly ritual, causing my mother to be on her toes constantly, even as she dealt with raising, feeding and bringing up her kids.

'Stone pelting is taking place in Usman Para, and now the Hindus are coming here,' was a sentence I had heard scores of times in my childhood. Another favourite was, 'A Muslim guy from Shah Jamal has shot his Hindu neighbour over a girl. It's just a matter of time before the Hindus take revenge.' Stone pelting always started in Usman Para or Dahiwali Gali, while the Hindu guy being shot down always happened in Shah Jamal. This was some sort of default for rumour-mongers.

Ammi was a staunch believer in the adage 'better safe than sorry'. So, whenever she heard a rumour of violence, she would pack our valuables in her purse, ready to run to a family friend's home near Jama Masjid, where the braver and more resourceful Muslims lived. 'The Muslims of the Farsh are soft. They wouldn't even be able to save themselves,' people from other mohallas often said. It was a fact known to each sensible man and woman in the U.K.

Saad and I were usually put on the lookout from our balcony, to inform Ammi whenever we sensed trouble. Sensing trouble is not an easy thing, and for most, it comes with experience. I had developed my own unique way to find out whether the Hindus were going to attack or not. I kept looking at the shutters of the shops. When they started to come down, it was a sure sign that things were not normal.

There was also a catch. My reference points were two shopkeepers: Shabbir Bhai and Alauddin Bhai. Alauddin Bhai was a little extra panicky and used to bring down the shutters at every false alarm. Shabbir Bhai was braver and not ready to shut shop until the Hindus had assembled at the fag end of the Farsh. Brave as I was, I used to rely on the courageous Shabbir Bhai to take a call. For when he shut shop, it meant there was real trouble based on accurate information, not based on paan-chewing rumour-mongers, whom I suspect did this more for their sadistic pleasure than their concern for the lives of their Muslim brethren.

Like false storms before the monsoons, the tension used to fade away as soon as it rose. In a few days, my not-so-affectionate mother would send me to buy *moong daal* in the Hindu mohalla, even after I protested that she would be responsible for my death.

Not all our neighbours were Hindus. One was Ravindra Jain, a blind musician, who often practised his singing in our basement in the morning – something that earned the ire of Muslims going for *Fajr* namaz, the first of five daily prayers. My grandfather was friends with his father Indramani Jain, the owner of the house adjacent to Farsh Manzil. He once had to talk to him to ask his son to change the *riyaz* timings to reduce the friction.

When Papa narrated this story, I realized that he was proud of Ravindra. 'He later went to Mumbai and became a Filmfare Award-winning music director. A star was born on our Farsh,' he told me. Whenever he heard the songs of Hindi films like *Saudagar*, *Ankhiyon Ke Jharokhon Se*, *Dulhan Wahi Jo Piya Man Bhaye* and *Nadiya Ke Paar*, he beamed. But I only warmed up to the legacy of Ravindra Jain, when I found out he also composed the music for *Alif Laila* – the serial on Doordarshan in which Shahrzad survives by making up stories.

But once in a while, somebody told us the truth without intending to.

A bearded man stood in a shop selling *shakkarpare* in Chowk Bundu Khan. He was talking about the rough times he was going through. It led one of the listeners, a man with a long flowing beard, to tell a story he had heard while growing up. It went like this: 'Once, enemies had attacked the Khana-e-Kaaba. Marauding armies surrounded the Muslims from all sides. During this, a *sahaba* (a companion of the Prophet) was busy taking care of his camels. Another man came to him and asked, "Enemies are going to attack the Kaaba and you are worried about your camel?" The sahaba replied, "Must I worry about the Khana-e-Kaaba? Hasn't Allah taken the responsibility of protecting it? I am only responsible for my camel, and I will save it. Don't worry about saving Islam – that's Allah's job. Save yourself if you can."

For some reason, at that moment, it sounded to me like a warning for times to come.

# 4

# LIFE IS BEAUTIFUL

THE YEAR 1994 is seared in my memory. It was the first year that I noticed. 1993 was kind of blurry, and 1995 too defined. Like a Bollywood movie at Seema Talkies, 1994 seesawed between magic and reality, while being endless at the same time.

It was a definitive year in other ways too. Both Miss World and Miss Universe were from India, a symbolic event in India's pop culture. The song '*Tu Cheez Badi Hai Mast Mast*' from *Mohra* became an earworm. The family entertainer *Hum Aapke Hain Koun...!* was released. Even though cinema was still considered a sinful indulgence among most in the U.K., almost every Muslim family flocked to see it in the Apsara theatre on Railway Road, where it was being screened. There were queues for tickets many days in a row.

It was the year I was in kindergarten at Carmel Academy school. 'Why does 1994 always remain on the class blackboard?' one day I dared to ask my teacher – the first among many stupid questions I would ask in life. 'Oh, that is called the year. It only changes once every year.' *Of course, you idiot!*

Carmel Academy wasn't my first school – that was a playschool named BabyLand. I would go there in a rickshaw along with Shazia, my neighbour's daughter. Her father, Anis Bhai, looked a lot like Anil Kapoor, everyone said. I didn't know that Anis had left his first wife and married a beautiful woman with hazel eyes from whom Shazia got her eyes. Anis's second marriage had been the talk of the entire mohalla. 'He shouldn't have divorced his wife.' 'No, it was the woman's fault. She charmed him with her pretty eyes.' 'She should have thought about marrying a married man.'

Shazia was my first friend. In the years to come, Anis Bhai would also leave her mother and marry another younger woman. 'He looks like Anil Kapoor,' everyone kept saying. 'No, he looks more like Jackie Shroff,' others would say. I had seen both actors together in *Ram Lakhan* and thought he resembled Jackie Shroff more. Whatever the case was, he still kept leaving his wives one by one, like they were stops in a bus journey.

My father was different. He loved his family and fulfilled his responsibilities. He was also my best friend. When he was out, I'd wait for him to come back so we could talk about 'the world'. If he came home after I'd gone to sleep, half-asleep, I'd go to his bed to sleep next to him.

When my rickshaw-wala didn't come, he'd wake up, flustered and under-slept, and drop me to school on his scooter, a sky-blue Bajaj Cub. He was, however, often late to pick me up after school. I would wait for him in the corridors as the peons waited impatiently to shut the school gates for the day. '*Arre mera bachha*, I am sorry,' he'd say. He'd then take me to a restaurant in Barula Market owned by his friend and treat me to an ice cream. And so I never minded him being late. 'Don't tell your mother that I was late,' he'd tell me. I ate the ice cream and never snitched on him.

During the students' elections in AMU, he was busier. Often, he'd send his office staff to pick me up. Sometimes, they'd drop me home, but they'd mostly take me to the office, the vintage, red-bricked building of the Students Union Hall. There, I'd sit with men six times my age and listen to them talk about national and university politics and take sarcastic digs at each other.

Papa was mostly nice to his office staff, but I also saw him shouting at them a few times, something he never did at home. 'How many times have I told you to do it this way? You people don't do anything until you are shouted at!' he'd say and send them off to get the job done properly. This was a totally different side of the man who created a ruckus if Ammi ever raised a hand at us.

Papa, for me, was a larger-than-life figure. He followed a strict schedule. He would wake up at 10 a.m., bathe and have a breakfast of two rotis with ghee and a chutney of green chillies, the breakfast his mother gave him as a child. He'd mostly be late to office, but he was the boss and not answerable to anyone.

Papa wasn't perfect. He'd struggle to find time for us. It was only on Sundays that the family spent time together. On most days, he would return late, after spending time at the non-teaching staff club or meeting his best buddy, Asad Ali Khan, the Shia Nawab of Pandawal, a small town in Anoopshahr. Sometimes, he'd go to their friend Raju Bhaiya's, the son of Kalyan Singh, the Chief Minister of Uttar Pradesh under whose leadership the Babri Masjid had been demolished. 'Every friend of Asad is a friend of mine, whatever their political affiliations might be,' he'd say as an explanation, which Achhe Mammu – my maternal uncle and a founding member of the Babri Masjid Action Committee – didn't buy.

Every night I would wait for Papa so we could talk. It was during these conversations that he'd tell me about his visits to Pakistan and how his brothers tried their best to make him settle there. Before he'd go to Pakistan, he'd tell Lala, the owner of the grocery shop our family had been buying groceries from for generations, about his trips. 'Can you bring back some Lahori salt? I'd pay you twice the price,' he'd asked Papa before one of his trips. The Lahoris were very proud of their salt. They called Indian salt '*khujli wala namak*' or the salt that causes itching. Papa knew Lala would sell it for ten times that price. He politely declined. Forty years later, Lala's grandson would identify me as a Muslim in front of a mob of Hindu rioters.

'If you had lived there, you'd have married a Pakistani girl. Would I have been born there?' I once asked him along with a thousand other existential questions. But I probably dozed off before he could answer. My father slept on a small single bed and sleeping with him would have surely caused him discomfort, but he always made space for me. I often watched television at full volume while in bed, and instead of telling me not to disturb his sleep, he'd move his legs to the side to give me more space.

When he rode his scooter, I always stood in the front. The world looked amazing as we rode through town, seeing the world passing by as though we were a whirlwind. It was almost as if I was riding the scooter myself. The wind breezing past my face, I kept asking questions about the things I saw on the streets. It was exhilarating. While Papa played the part of the parent who takes us closer to 'the world', Ammi was bent on protecting us from it.

'If you are influenced by the kids here, you won't get anywhere in life,' she'd say. I mostly listened to her and stayed at home. But Saad would often go to play marbles with 'bad kids' in the Haatha, the dusty open spaces that kids in Upar Kot had in lieu of playgrounds. I once went there to watch a cricket match and Ammi was furious. 'Play with the kids who go to your school instead,' she'd say. But like the devil tempting the faithful, Haatha kept luring me once in a while.

'It is called the "Haatha" because it is the place where elephants would be stabled for the night,' Badi Ammi told me. 'At first, there were soldiers, when there was a fort here. Later came the nobles to get medicines from famous hakims and the traders to buy their merchandise here,' she said. The Haatha was where kids swore at each other as they played cricket or marbles. '*Teri maa ki...*' I once heard somebody say. I repeated that at home – and all hell broke loose.

Sayema came after me with a matchstick and put it near my tongue. 'I will burn your tongue,' she said angrily, which was rare for her. Terrified, I called out for Ammi.

'What did you do?' she asked.

'He was abusing like the kids of Upar Kot, so I am gonna burn his tongue,' said Sayema.

To my shock, Ammi didn't interfere. 'She is right. What kind of kid are you?' she said and went away to Palle Ghar. I was now at Sayema's mercy. I blew out the matchstick. She took out another matchstick and tried to force my mouth open. 'Will you swear again? Tell me!' she shouted.

I kept crying, worried that if I lost my tongue, I would never be able to speak again. The tears extinguished the flame. Sayema, now the T-Rex from Jurassic Park, lit another one, opened my mouth wider and took the matchstick far too close to my tongue. I could feel the burn. 'I will never do it again,' I gathered the courage to say. I never went to the Haatha after that.

When not threatening to burn my tongue, Sayema was kind of nice to me. Like Ammi, she was a fan favourite at Farsh Manzil. She would show me off to her school friends, iron my school clothes and make me red chutney, which I absolutely had to have with khichdi and biryani. When Saad would beat me, she'd intervene; she supported me when Ammi didn't believe my version of the story. She'd teach me how to write my alphabets and often help me with homework. Moreover, she studied in Aligarh's best convent school. When she was admitted to Our Lady of Fathima, a few conservative relatives made a fuss. 'So, will she now wear a skirt and show her legs to every boy around?' they said. Later, most of them also tried to get their daughters admitted to the same school and forgot all about the skirt issue.

Sayema was also all kinds of cool. At school, she befriended Hindu boys and girls, who, unlike our neighbours, were kind of decent and lived in areas where there weren't pigs and cows roaming around. She was everybody's favourite, much more than Saad and me.

But she did have one weakness: clothes. She was obsessed with wearing the best salwar suits, ably supported by Ammi's skill at choosing clothes and tailoring them expertly. Going with Sayema to Penth every week and then sewing her clothes was one of Ammi's life missions. All our maternal uncles absolutely had to buy her clothes whenever they came to our home. Even though she received more Eidi than us, she'd usurp our share as well. 'What will you and Saad do with money? You are too young for all this,' she told us. Ammi didn't step in this time either.

For these reasons, I wasn't 100 per cent sure if Ammi even loved me. It reminded me of the time when one day, Badi Ammi had told me that Ammi had many apprehensions before my birth. 'Will we be able to afford a third child?' she would ask her. 'I told her, don't worry, Allah will take care of everything. Mark my words, this third child will make you proud,' Badi Ammi had told me. Ammi's love seemed more mysterious after knowing this secret.

Ammi was a lovable but moody person. She'd love us at some point or absolutely detest us at others – there was nothing in between. She'd wake up early and finish her responsibilities, no matter how sleepy she was. In joy, she'd kiss us to express her love, no matter how old we were. 'My kids are the nicest in the world,' she'd say. She'd cook something that we liked or made a lot of curtains and sweets made of dry fruits. Somehow, she'd try to make our lives comfortable.

In anger, she'd taunt her children, reminding them of their failures towards her and the rest of the family. In these moments, we were the worst kids in the world who'd 'leave her to die alone in her old age'.

When she had the energy, Ammi was a jack of all trades. When the electricity was busted, she'd try to take out a plier and screwdriver to set the wires in their rightful place. She'd varnish our doors and pillars by herself and sometimes our cooler. Often, she'd overestimate her skills, try to do a little plumbing job herself, fail badly and then blame us for not helping her enough.

When she was sad, she'd overthink. She'd retreat and sleep on the terrace, like she slept as a child in her village. She'd keep worrying whether all the taps were turned off, if all the windows were shut or the lights were on needlessly. She'd keep giving us tasks and remind us of them constantly until we did them.

Ammi was also in charge of raising us to be good Muslims. Once I asked her, 'What does God look like?'

'God is everywhere. He is around you. He is in the wind.'

'But I can't see the wind. How should I imagine God to be?' I asked her. This was a very loaded question. Muslims imagine Allah to be formless and giving him a form is one of the biggest sins in Islam.

'Just imagine yourself to be surrounded by light,' she told me. From then on, I'd imagine God as a very big bulb. In some time though, I replaced the bulb with a floodlight.

After someone raised the matter that I didn't know how to read the Quran, Ammi sent me to the madrasa. The Quran teacher here was Majeeb Sahib, a respected maulvi in our mohalla. During the summer vacations, I had to wake up at Fajr and go to the first floor of the neighbourhood mosque. On my first day, half-asleep, I put on a nice T-shirt. As I entered, I carefully put my slippers on the topmost stair to protect it from other kids. In the large hall of the mosque were kids in green plastic caps swaying up and down. With their book-rests in front of them, they kept repeating Arabic verses in a loud voice as if their lives depended on it. The rest of the time, they sat on plastic prayer mats in long rows, laughing over their own secret jokes. Occasionally, one of them would slap another without provocation. 'Allahmudillah-e-rabbil-aalameen,' a boy kept repeating, like somebody was holding him at gunpoint. Another one kept rereading a paragraph from the first *sipara*, a Quranic chapter.

I would find out the reason for their diligence later. 'If you can't recite your lesson, Majeeb Sahib will make you a chair,' a boy told me. Hearing that sent a shiver down my spine like only Saad could. Becoming a chair meant literally standing like a chair for an hour even if your legs hurt. For Majeeb Sahib, it was a good exercise-cum-punishment, but boys were understandably terrified of it. As we read our lessons, I kept staring at the two boys who were 'chairs'. If they faltered for a second, other boys shouted and informed Majeeb Sahib.

Madrasa kids everywhere are notorious for their mischief. On cold winter nights, they'd switch on the fans as men stood in rows after doing their *wudhu*, sending a literal shiver down the spine of namazis. At another masjid, they'd be more methodical in their mischief – first switching off the heater near the maulvi, before turning on the fans. On the rare occasion they themselves were offering prayers, they'd stand in the praying row to push or slap the kids pretending to concentrate. They'd run up and down the stairs shouting and jostling as adults looked disapprovingly. In Islam, kids are forgiven for their acts, so they took full advantage of the provision.

For their acts, these kids often earned scorn, insults or even beatings. But how can one be punished if nobody knew who did it? There was that kind of unity. When the teachers came in, they'd be the most obedient, reading their verses like they were the most pious of Allah's followers. 'Is this Tala or is it Allah Tala?' they'd say, banging a huge lock on the door towards the terrace, repeating an oft-used joke in Aligarh.

In Aligarh, it is said if a boy memorizes the Quran, becoming a Hafiz, his parents will be given the highest pedestal in heaven and will be forgiven their sins. My father was a Hafiz at eight, the only one of his nine siblings to do so. 'Your father had secured heaven for his parents. You should also do so,' Sayema once told me, putting a huge responsibility on my shoulders.

But Badi Ammi was critical of Papa. 'What did he do after that? Forget reading the Quran daily, he doesn't even offer namaz now.' Then, she told me something startling. 'It's a big sin if someone forgets the Quran after remembering it.' I imagined my grandparents being removed from the highest place in heaven. Nobody knew whether my father still remembered the whole Quran or not. I once asked him, and he said he did remember it but didn't sound very confident.

Being the son of a Hafiz meant extra pressure. I kept going to the madrasa day after day, trying to memorize the verses without success. Nobody had bothered to check whether I knew the Arabic alphabet or not, a crucial fact lost in communication. So, I sat trying to read my chapter in a language I couldn't understand. After two days, Majeeb Sahib called me and asked me to read a paragraph. I couldn't recite a word. Because I was new, he didn't beat me and simply asked me to become a chair. I was lucky as five minutes later, the *azaan* was heard and it was time to go home. Those were the five longest minutes of my life. Once I was home,

I talked about the chair incident, exaggerating it. Ammi never sent me to the madrasa again.

⌒

Home is where you remove the mask you wear in the world and become yourself, where you don't have to be courteous or diplomatic but can be your needy and moody self. It's where you can be a child no matter what age you might be. Home is where you can be feverish and expect to be taken care of, despite your protestations of not needing it. Home is where you can sit in a corner, your corner, without being pushed by the world to 'do something'. For me, home was where I could be my pampered, stubborn self, far from the overtly pleasing boy I was to the outside world. The only person who didn't listen to my demands was Saad. I was more pampered than him because I was cuter and less mischievous.

When I and Sayema joined forces, Saad was a little sidelined. She also had another follower, our cousin Nikki, who, like her elder brothers, also studied in Sayema's school. The two of them played games together but didn't let Saad play. For me, there was no dearth of kids in *Palle Ghar* to play with, but Saad didn't have anyone of his age around. This made him angrier, so he devised numerous ways to torture the rest of us.

Every day, he'd bully me in one way or the other. He'd beat me up when I didn't listen to his orders – bringing him *chhole* from Kanwari Ganj or the Sweety Supari that he chewed twenty packets of every day. I had to refer to him as 'Saad the Great' and if I didn't, I would be slapped. He'd never let me touch his toys or things. 'I beat up three kids when they didn't listen to me,' he'd tell me proudly. He'd blackmail me over imaginary offences that I did not commit. But the worst was the day he made me a thief.

One day, Zafar Motorwale, a friend of my maternal grandfather living in the nearby Chowk Bundu Khan, gifted me a plank of wood shaped like a cricket bat. It was the happiest day of my life. I now had a bat. As soon as I took it home, Saad snatched it from me. 'I want a bat too. Go to Zafar Motorwale and ask him to give you another plank of wood,' he ordered.

I pleaded, 'Where will I get one more plank of wood?' But he wasn't moved by my tears.

I went to Zafar Motorwale's house again and asked him if I could have the last wooden plank in his workshop. 'Beta, we need this plank for our work. We can't give you this. Didn't we already give you one?' the short, bespectacled man with grey hair told me sternly.

I returned home, told Saad what had happened and begged him to give my bat back. Instead, he went to the storeroom and brought out a saw. Slowly, he began moving the saw over the bat. 'If you don't bring me another bat, I will cut yours in two. If I don't get one, you can't have one either,' he said.

With folded hands, I kept pleading with him, crying, to return my bat. 'Please don't break my bat. I will do anything you want,' I said.

'If I don't have my own bat in half an hour, I will cut it in half, I promise,' he replied.

My heart kept pounding and the tears kept flowing. I went back to Zafar Motorwale's house. A carpenter was working in a corner of his workshop. Near him was a tiny iron door, which opened towards the Chowk, through which only a child could pass. I crept up silently, picked up the wooden plank and ran like my life depended upon it. 'Hey, stop, stop! Where are you taking it?' the carpenter shouted and ran after me, getting stuck at the tiny door.

I had never run that fast in my life. I gave the plank to Saad, and he returned my bat like he'd promised. A few minutes later,

Zafar Motorwale came to our house to complain to Ammi. 'Your son ran away from my karkhaana with a plank of wood,' he told her. My parents asked me what had happened, and I told them everything. I don't remember it now, but I hope Saad was beaten for this. Nevertheless, he eventually took away the bat.

But this wasn't the only time Saad had scared me. Every night he'd tell me that a hand would emerge from the back of the bed and strangle me. He would also tell me stories about Aligarh's most haunted location: Lal Diggi. It was a deserted road near the University where a woman in a white sari would ask strange men for a ride, and disappear when they looked back. Some would hear the sound of anklets. Others would feel somebody riding with them on their bikes. Almost everybody in Aligarh had stories of Lal Diggi Road. I thought my father as very brave because he always came home via Lal Diggi Road late at night. One day when Saad, Papa and I were returning from my friend Amir's home on our scooter, Saad reminded me that we'd have to pass Lal Diggi. This scared the shit out of me. 'Papa, please don't go through Lal Diggi – the witch will follow us!' I whimpered.

'There is nothing like a witch, Beta. These are all lies,' Papa answered and kept riding.

As we came closer to Lal Diggi, I began to cry. I was fully expecting a woman in a white sari to run alongside the scooter and drag us into the bushes. When we finally reached the area, I began to scream. 'Beta, don't be afraid, these are silly stories made by people.' When we reached home, he told me another story to calm me down.

Every night on his way back on Lal Diggi Road, he'd hear the sound of an anklet. Some of his friends had also heard the same thing. One night when he heard the sound, instead of running away, he stopped his scooter and started looking around. He then noticed a tent on the footpath. It was a traditional doctor, a *baidya*, who had set up his camp there. His two daughters wore anklets and often walked around the tent at night. 'If I hadn't stopped, I would have forever believed a witch was following me. You must be brave.' But I wasn't.

The scary stories, though, weren't limited to Lal Diggi Road. According to our relatives, parts of our house were haunted. A few days later, trying to be brave, I went to Badi Ammi's home to listen to the story of Sayyed Baba that she had left unfinished. There were, of course, many stories of Sayyed Baba in Farsh Manzil, and he was as much part of the house as the bricks, mortar and neem tree adjacent to it. Like always, Badi Ammi's story involved her father.

On a cold winter night, my grandfather was returning home after offering Fajr prayers. He found a gentleman with a glowing, white beard standing in his path.

'Don't you know it's getting late?' he asked my grandfather. 'Thieves roam around here at this time. Avoid going for Fajr prayers in the winter – offer them at home,' he said.

Not one to be overwhelmed by an old fellow with a glowing beard, my grandfather replied: 'I would never forgo *Jamat namaz* for anything on Earth, Bade Miyan. I don't fear anyone but Allah.'

On hearing this, Bade Miyan offered to accompany and save him from any dangers lurking in the dark corners of Upar Kot. On the way, he also held forth about the essence of Islam. When the duo reached the entrance of Farsh Manzil, Bade Miyan simply disappeared into thin air. This was when my grandpa realized he had been granted the privilege of being accompanied by Sayyed Baba himself.

There were many other stories in which Sayyed Baba had protected our family. One was when the Hindus had attacked our mohalla one night after Partition. Their evil forces were trying to move up the Farsh to kill Muslims. Suddenly, a divine horse-riding, sword-wielding man with a glowing, white beard appeared in their way. He wore white clothes and rode a white horse. The Muslims were not able to see this divine saviour; only the attacking forces saw him.

After the conflict subsided a few days later, and the Hindus and Muslims became best friends again (not uncommon in Aligarh), they told their Muslim neighbours about the miracle. The Muslims realized it could have been none other than Sayyed Baba. Thus, many Hindus also came to know about the greatness of our neighbourly divine protector.

Though he was a noble spirit and particularly protective of the habitants of my home, Sayyed Baba acted a bit vengefully when, as a child, Saad urinated on his grave through a window adjacent to his tomb. He fell sick the same night. My grandmother then narrated to Ammi what had happened to her eldest daughter-in-law. 'Before they went to Pakistan, Aftab's wife lived in the room adjacent to the tomb. She once slept with her feet towards the tomb. When she woke up, she was sick for several days,' she told Ammi.

This was now my parents' room. Heeding his mother's advice, Papa called a carpenter to seal the window, so no mischievous child like Saad could urinate on the holy grave ever again.

Sayyed Baba was not the only supernatural being in the home. It was said many unknown entities also visited parts of our house, something Badi Ammi referred to as 'Guzraat' (the passing by). There were many stories associated with our terrace and the mosque terrace adjacent to ours. Ballu Bhai, our tenant, told me that once he was beaten up by Noorjahan Apa and denied food. As he sat hungry and crying on the terrace, a hand came out of nowhere and gave him a plate of *zarda*. A few years later, a kid fell into the mosque well and drowned. The well was closed up, but the madrasa kids claimed that the kid's ghost could be heard doing *tilawat*, the recitation of the Quran, late at night. They also reported Quran stands being folded and prayer mats being rolled and unrolled on their own. Nobody remained on the top floor of the mosque at night.

'Djinns don't live here, but they probably do pass by sometime around Maghrib, the time of the sunset prayer. They are not bad, but if they find someone wasting their time, they get angry,' Badi Ammi told me. More than our terrace, such things happened on the Palle Ghar terrace. It was said to be where djinns had parties at night. Some mornings, our cousins found round black marks on the terrace as if a *deg*, a big cooking pot, had been used there.

The supernatural stories in *Palle Ghar* had been taking place since it was constructed a century ago. The wife of Aashiq Ahmed Khan, my grandfather's brother, saw a snake woman, known to everyone as Maya in her dreams. 'Sacrifice one of your sons to me, and I will tell you the location of the treasure buried under your home,' the witch exhorted her. Unwilling to sacrifice her son for gold, she called a maulana and recited a dua, after which Maya didn't disturb her. But other unexplained things kept happening. The wall next to a peepal tree in Palle Ghar kept breaking even after being cemented multiple times.

Something weird also happened to Saad in Palle Ghar. Being a mischievous boy, Saad was playing on the Palle Ghar terrace during the time for Maghrib. Their house was locked as everyone had gone to a wedding. Saad's rubber ball, which he was bouncing on the mosque wall, lost its direction and rolled to the lower terrace on the first floor of Palle Ghar. Then he got busy looking at a kite contest nearby. Like a ghost appearing out of nowhere, a few minutes later, the ball came up to the terrace on its own. Saad's first thought was someone was hiding on the lower terrace and had hidden again after throwing the ball to him. He went down to check, but there was nobody there. He felt shivers after finding that the door was locked from the outside. He swiftly ran up the terrace and came to our side, never playing on that terrace during Maghrib. Being a born sceptic, I thought that somebody had played a prank on Saad. Why would an entity trouble an idiot like Saad?

One day, Saad brought home a comic book on rent from a shop in the Hindu mohalla, Kanwari Ganj. Though he took considerable risk to fulfil his passion, bringing comic books home was probably the best thing Saad ever did in his life. It was something that would go on to change my life.

# 5

# SUPER COMMANDO DHRUVA

LOVE IS WHAT keeps us human. It is the silent angel that speaks to us on a dark night and turns bad times into good. It can turn anger into determination, sadness into reflection and pain into struggle. Love has the power to drown our sorrows into oblivion and shield our hearts from hate and derision.

I fell in love for the first time when I was five – with comic books. Being obsessed with comics and being a Muslim is related, though I will admit that it is a bit of a stretch. Let me explain. Before India won its independence, it was a norm for Indians to have large families. In Islam, contraception is forbidden and my grandfather, as we all know, was a devout follower. My father was the youngest of nine siblings. It meant that I was the youngest member of three generations of the Khan family spread across countries and continents. Most people of my age had cousins aged six or seven, but some of mine were fifty-eight years old. Some of them had even died after living a whole life in Pakistan.

This 'generation-gap-within-the-same-generation' meant that both my grandparents were dead long before I was born. My only interaction with them was going to their graves during our yearly visits to the *qabristan* in the Aligarh Eidgah. One could say that it is a grandparents' God-given duty to tell their grandchildren stories. But there were no '*Dadi Maa ki kahanaian*' for me.

Badi Ammi tried her best, but most of her stories were limited to the family. My childhood was also a time when there were just a few modes of entertainment, the only other options being family shows on Doordarshan or spending afternoons flying kites. To quench my thirst for fantasies, I had no other avenue but Hindi comic books.

The colourful, sketched figures of muscular men and women and white speech boxes placed inside little square panels looked immensely beautiful to me. I gazed at those frames like a besotted lover, turning the pages again and again, trying to get a sense of the story by looking at the pictures. The four or six boxes on every page took me to a world of brave heroes with superpowers, monstrous villains with evil plans and a joyful world of fantasies.

This world was more interesting than the one I inhabited in Upar Kot. The characters were brighter than most of the people I knew. Together, we were the saviours of the world. When I'd grow up, I'd go to Delhi and meet these superheroes. Then they'd find how righteous and brave I was and take me to meet a holy man or a scientist who'd bless me with the powers to battle bad people. This relationship between comic books and me deepened with every passing day. But just like every love story, there were several obstacles in our way.

Comic books were considered the pinnacle of vice in Upar Kot. Drawing or seeing pictures is frowned upon in some interpretations of Islam and comic books were filled with only images. Because he read comic books, Saad had already earned a bad reputation. 'Those who read comics end up behind the cash register in their maternal uncles' shops,' said the elders. This was probably the reason most kids in the U.K. preferred playing marbles, *gilli danda* or simply running cycle tyres with sticks.

Another obstacle was I didn't know how to read. With all the *'chhoti ees'* and *'badi ees'* and umpteen types of *'shs'*, Hindi was especially difficult. It was also the language preferred by Hindus, unlike the more refined Urdu. To overcome this, I used my innocent charm on Sayema and Saad. They read the comic books to me and explained their plots. That is, until Niki Baji, my cousin who had an odd fascination with being photographed in her karate outfit, didn't take them away to play useless games like *'Elli-dolli'*, *'Aao milo shilo shalo'*, *'Chuppan chuppai'* and so on.

In such a scenario, I, most grudgingly, had to try and read comic books myself. In a collective, and mostly selfish effort to get the burden off them, my siblings agreed to teach me how to read. They taught me Hindi alphabet, its *matras* and the impossible-to-pronounce consonants. If I didn't understand a word, they'd tell me the meaning. I learnt to read Hindi while in kindergarten, while the other kids were still struggling with *'ka, kha, ga'*.

But however brilliant you may be, I soon found out that life was a vicious circle of never-ending struggle. Despite learning Hindi and surmounting all obstacles, Saad began to show his true colours. Since he brought home comic books and was my only connection to this world outside Farsh Manzil, Saad stopped sharing his comic books. In his sadism, he began to hide them under his mattress. As you already know, anybody who touched his things without permission was beaten up.

In his version, he'd tell you that I sometimes tore the pages and he had to pay for physical damage. In my version, I don't remember tearing up comic books, and he just wanted me to be his unpaid slave in return for being able to read comic books. I was expected to do chores like bringing him his Sweety Supari from the paan shop or bring him chhole whenever Ammi made things like *shalgam gosht, mooli gosht* and *aloo saag*. He was the greediest person I knew.

But greed invites opportunity. It whets our appetite for 'more', an unachievable and dynamic goal. *If I can get more, why shouldn't I? Why should I listen to the meek and the losers?* you begin to think. Greed is often accompanied by success. *If I can do it, why shouldn't I?* your thoughts tell you. Under this intoxication, every bad action sounds rational. It is often reason fuelled by greed that drives us to kill and plunder. Reason wants us to survive as far as we can in this chessboard of a world. Anger is sometimes pure, even noble, but greed has a sinister edge.

Greed also leads us to plot schemes. It motivates us to find our opponent's weaknesses and inflict pain where they'd hurt most. *I will defeat them so they never rise up again.* No human advice or self-reflection can stop the one afflicted by greed. It's only pain or fear of loss that can stop its growth. Until you risk losing something you love, greed keeps growing.

I didn't want Saad's greed for exploitation to grow, so I took a stand. I refused to bow to his demands to be his slave. So, he began to hide his comic books and then stopped bringing them home altogether to pursue his new passion: kite flying. He was *that* mean. I had no option but to get the comic books myself, but there were no shops in the U.K. To do this, I had to take the biggest risk of my life – venture into the dark alleys of the Hindu mohallas.

When I shared this decision with the people around me, I was inundated with a slew of unfriendly opinions. I kept getting told things like this: 'The Hindus will cut you into small pieces,' or 'Don't you know what happened to the Muslim family that used to live there?' or 'Have you seen the well in Katra? Many bodies of little Muslim kids are found in it. They lure you in with comic books and then kill you.'

Some warnings came from my relatives, but most were from concerned neighbours. Everyone just seemed to care a bit too much for me because I was so cute. But there was nothing else to do. There was no way I was giving up comic books, even if it meant risking my life.

I asked Saad to take me to the comic book shop he went to. This also meant that he could read 'my' comic books for free. He knew I would never be able to be as cold-hearted as him. The next day, he took me to the shop of my first comic book-wala, Deepak, a shy teenager with a permanent smile on his face. I sensed deception, but there were no good comic book shops in the U.K. This was my first direct interaction with the Hindus of Kanwari Ganj. His shop was the nearest.

I expected the Hindus to steal from me, hurt me or kidnap me at the first opportunity. But more concerned was Ammi. She immediately went to meet Deepak's mother to build relations with them, assuming they'd probably think twice before hurting me. She even found some link within her family in Etah with Deepak's mother. I was safe in their shop. 'Don't go any further than the shop,' she made me promise.

The first comic books I read with my own money were two special editions: *Fighter Toads* and *Pret Uncle*. *Fighter Toads*, inspired by the Teenage Mutant Ninja Turtles, was a gang of four super-funny, crime-fighting frogs. *Pret Uncle* was a ghost, who saved a little girl from criminals wanting to kill her. I read the books slowly and asked my siblings the meanings of many words. I managed to finish an entire comic book in a single day. But tragedy struck soon: Deepak was now planning to concentrate on his own studies. His zeal towards running his bookshop started to wane. At the end of the summer vacation, I had to venture deeper into the Hindu area. For this, I had to break the promise I made. I did it without thinking. Love, for my beloved comic books, won.

By this time, I was adept at sensing danger myself. I began renting comics from Narayan. He ran a library-cum-confectionary-cum-general-store-cum-chakki. His main business wasn't renting comic books, but selling beauty items, breakfast items, aloo patties, and grinding some smelly pulses for their customers.

Narayan ran the shop with his three sons. All four of them came to the shop at different times, and I had no time to use my charm on any one of them. He had a much larger customer base and wasn't as flexible as Deepak. He'd rent by the hour and fine you if you were late even by a few minutes. 'You are thirty minutes late – *double kiraya lagega*,' he'd often say. Business was booming, and there was sometimes a queue of kids lining outside his shop, whom he used to rip off with glib disdain. Like devout worshippers going to a mosque, I would often visit his shop three-four times a day to know when the book I was waiting for would arrive. But he could only keep about 100 comic books under his counter. Soon, I was running out of comic books to read.

After I finished kindergarten, I was admitted to St Fidelis School in the first standard. It was a newly built convent school in Aligarh, just next to Sayema's prestigious school, Our Lady of Fathima. I loved it as it was bigger than Carmel Academy and had a huge playground with a dozen swings. It mostly had Christian sisters and fathers who taught us. 'Why is it sisters and fathers, and not sisters and brothers?' 'Because no boy wants to be called a brother,' the students joked. Since they didn't have space in the morning shift, I was admitted to the afternoon shift. They even had a third evening shift, in which they taught poor kids free of cost. 'It will become as big as Our Lady of Fathima,' Ammi told our relatives.

Thanks to comic books, I was getting the highest marks in Hindi. My Hindi teacher was startled out of her wits when I uttered words like '*raatri*', '*prayas*' and '*sankat*'. She interrogated Ammi when she went to collect my report card. *'Aap log toh Muslim hai na? Itni achhi Hindi kaise jante hai?'* Ammi had no clue that the secret was my voracious reading of comic books.

But Ammi was in the dark about a lot of things. She didn't know that I was now contemplating wandering still deeper into Hindu territory, further breaking the promise I made to her. Since I was running out of comics to read at Narayan's shop, I found out about Hemant's shop in Gudiya Bagh, an area with dark, narrow lanes and no Muslims in sight.

Gudiya Bagh was not as clean as Kanwari Ganj; in fact, it was even dirtier than my neighbourhood in the U.K. Pigs and cows roamed around freely. Hindu men sat outside their shops with protruding bellies and red *tilaks* on their foreheads. Though I was fine with the narrow lanes in Upar Kot, I was terrified when I ventured into this area. Hemant's shop was adjacent to a Shiva temple, where the more religiously hardened Hindus came to pray. A peepal tree where witches were supposed to live grew nearby.

But once I reached Hemant's shop, every fear melted away. It was the stuff of my dreams. Hemant, a lanky, dark fellow with well-oiled black hair had been reading comic books since his teens. A courteous gentleman, he never objected to me spending hours looking for books in his endless library. He had six large almirahs, full of comic books sorted by editions, years and publishing house. Some of these almirahs hadn't been opened for years. A lot of space meant children could even finish their books sitting in a corner. The shop smelt of damp walls and vegetable oil, the merchandise he sold along with comic books. A chhole-wala parked his cart just outside his shop and the *agarbatti* smoke from there diluted the smell of the broad drains of Gudiya Bagh.

Hemant charged half the rent that Narayan did. The going rate was 50 paise per day for a thirty-two-page edition and one rupee for the ones with sixty pages, also known as a digest. The new editions cost more, but I seldom read those. I mostly rummaged through the almirahs that were mostly unopened, which held decades-old comic books. Unlike Narayan, Hemant didn't charge me if I was late in returning the books. Moreover, he protected his books from badly mannered kids by putting them in polythene covers.

Hemant also had two elder brothers who sat at the shop once in a while, but I don't remember their names – it was Hemant's name stamped on every book. Within a few months, I became his top customer. He'd duly inform me when a new set was supposed to arrive. 'You come at 11 a.m. tomorrow, when Bade Bhaiya will arrive with the set,' he'd say. More often than not, Bhaiya would take till lunch time to arrive, which was when he'd lock his shop and go home to eat. As I'd have been waiting for two hours by then, he'd take me home too. With nothing on my mind other than the books, I'd readily go with him.

A compound adjacent to the temple led to Hemant's home. He lived in an old home with blue paint peeling off it, with some steel containers placed in a corner and photographs of Hindu gods on the walls. I'd sit in the baithak, which opened into a huge *aangan*. Soon, his mother and sisters began to accept me as a temporary part of their household. 'You want water or *daal chawal?*' the sister would ask me. I'd say yes to the water, and no to the food.

Hemant and his family's demeanour towards me changed little about the reality of Hindu-Muslim turmoil we existed within. Whenever I ventured into their area, a certain fear and prejudice was in my mind. Though, with time, I became more and more confident about the gullies of Gudiya Bagh. I knew that it was at the top of the list of places young Muslim boys shouldn't visit in Aligarh. I began to go into the narrowest of alleys, but I always stuck to the ones that I knew. All the time I was aware that however nice everyone might come across, they'd change colours as soon as a clash broke out.

In summer vacation between the second and third standard, my maternal cousin Talib had come to live with us – another child who would learn to deal with Saad's cruel ways. But for me, he was a friend and playmate. And he became my companion for my Gudiya Bagh trips.

Whenever we went to Gudiya Bagh, we'd think of 'original-sounding' Hindu pseudonyms. 'We shouldn't be Ram or Manoj. That's the first name a Muslim would think of as a fake Hindu name. If anyone asks, I am Abhinav, you are Sanchit,' I'd tell Talib, the names of two of my classmates. Like two secret agents on a dangerous mission, we were always watchful about whether we needed to run in case a riot happened while we were there. Often, we'd walk behind each other, so as to alert the other, if someone dangerous-looking was following us.

But what I had been afraid of finally happened. Ammi found out that I was going to Gudiya Bagh (I think the jealous Saad told her). A storm raged in the house. 'Do you know how dangerous it is to go there?' Ammi screamed. She then told me something that shocked me.

Until now, I had always thought that she hailed from a village in the Etah district. I didn't know that before she was born, her parents, of all the places in the world, once had a big home in Gudiya Bagh. In fact, two of her eldest brothers were born in that home. 'Your Nana and Chhote Nana lived here. They left their property after a riot,' she told me. Gudiya Bagh was once like Farsh, an area where Hindus and Muslims used to live in close proximity.

Back then, my maternal grandfather and his brother owned over fifty shops in the Madaar Gate area of Aligarh, now one of its busiest markets. 'Those shops were set on fire during the riots. The roof was made of wood and burnt along with all the merchandise,' Ammi said. The two brothers also had a zamindari in the Garkha village of Etah district. The riots and the destruction of their property forced them to sell their Aligarh property at throwaway prices and shift to their Muslim-dominated village. 'They wanted to concentrate on farming. That is why I was born there and not in Aligarh,' she finished. It was a lot of new information for me to digest. I had always thought of Garkha as my maternal home.

The stories of my mother's family's travails, however, didn't deter me from going to Hemant's shop. No matter how dark the history of the area might have been, the comic books that he rented talked of bonhomie. Some of the most popular heroes were Manoj Comics' leading pair, secret agents Ram and Rahim, a detective duo that had saved the country from terrorists, mad scientists, powerful aliens and immortal vampires.

The story went like this: Ram was the son of India's intelligence chief and his loyal sidekick was Rahim, the son of a Pakistani colonel who had defected to India and accepted this country as his home. He was so dedicated to his partner that in one episode, he sacrificed his hand to save Ram from an extra-terrestrial invader (later, however, he got a robotic hand which could do things his natural hand couldn't). Rahim, an orphan, was considered a brother by Ram, and his parents looked upon him as their second son. Though Rahim was more of a kind of sacrificial sidekick to Ram, he was the only main hero in an Indian comic book who was Muslim.

Though I had come to them for fantasy, comic books also introduced me to the realities of human life. I was introduced to people who had the powers to do good but opted for a path of destruction, 'righteous ones' who shirked from the fight when the time came, and those who overcame childhood traumas to become saviours for others. I was immersed in imaginary happiness, sadness, conflict, losses and victories. Flipping the pages desperately to reach the end of every comic book, my reading speed and vocabulary improved. As soon as I woke up, I'd take a comic book from under my mattress and start reading. I would eat with books in front of me and read in the bathroom. If there was a power cut, I would read by candlelight. 'Why can't you read your school books with this devotion?' Ammi used to say.

When the exam results for the second standard came in, I had topped the class. Except for one subject, I had scored full marks in all the others. My mother distributed sweets to let the others in Farsh Manzil know. Success is when everyone tries to be close to you and pretend that they have liked you for a long time. They begin treating you nicely and offer you tea and biscuits when you go to their home. They send their children to 'learn from you'. Little did they know I was mostly immersed in the world of comic books.

I didn't read Diamond Comics (they were for kids) or Tulsi Comics (too Hinduized). I loved Raj Comics the most, followed by Manoj Comics – the DC and Marvel of India. In this world, thanks to Raj Comics, I had my favourite hero. His name was Super Commando Dhruva.

Dhruva was an unmasked teenage boy with no superpowers. As a child prodigy, he grew up learning from the world's best acrobats. So he could drive a bike on a rope and hold his breath underwater. Sporting a tight yellow-and-blue costume, brown boots, and a utility belt, he protected the imaginary city of Rajnagar. And though he was Hindu, I loved him more than anyone else.

Named after the brightest star in the galaxy, Dhruva was born to Shyam and Radha, both artists at Jupiter Circus. At fourteen, he lost his parents in a fire started by their business rivals. In his first comic book, *Pratishodh Ki Jwala*, he avenged their killing. He was then adopted by the commissioner of Rajnagar. His foster sister, Shweta, a brilliant scientist, made non-lethal, projectile weapons for him including starblades, ropes, bracelets and skate-shoes. In between saving the world, he was just a normal boy who fell in love and was graceful even to his enemies.

Dhruva's enemies were mostly more powerful than him – superhumans, aliens, yogis with ascetic powers and human-animal hybrids. They underestimated him but ended up being surprised by Dhruva's intellect and scientific knowledge. Even gods accepted defeat at the hands of this boy, a mortal. If Dhruva could defeat gods, I believed, any human could be whatever they wished, stick to their principles and fight the good fight.

He taught me more than most people in Farsh Manzil ever did. It was through Dhruva comics that I learnt about pasteurization, photosynthesis, nuclear energy and states of matter, years before I learnt them at school. I knew everything most six-year-olds didn't. Love, violence, family problems, crime and terrorism. There was no doubt in my mind that I was as intelligent as Dhruva, someone who'd find solutions and emerge victorious against the bad guys.

But there was a slight problem. There were no Muslims in Dhruva's world, except Karim, one of the cadets in his commando force. In fact, Muslims were never the central characters in any comic books – they were only the sidekicks and villains, a trend that continued in almost all the ones I read. In Raj Comics' Inspector Steel series, Inspector Amar had Professor Anees, the doctor who operated on him to save his life, turning him into a cyborg named Inspector Steel. Raman in Diamond Comics had his friend Khalifa, who was always the most helpful but insignificant in the overall narrative.

Among the most popular Muslim sidekicks belonged to Doga, the Raj Comics superhero with the most traumatic background story. As is the case with most superheroes, Doga also had his parents killed off in the first book. An orphan named Suraj, he was found in a garbage dump by the cruel dacoit Halkan Singh.

The dacoit used the boy as protection against the police, took him and raised him like a dog. Under Halkan, Suraj witnessed endless brutalities that would cause him to harden his heart and hate all criminals. He developed an affinity for dogs and started identifying with them.

And this is where the sacrificial, noble Muslims arrive in the story. After escaping Halkan, Suraj was adopted by Adrak Khan and his three brothers, who owned the best gym in Mumbai. The four brothers didn't have generic Muslim names, for they were named after spices. Adrak Khan trained Suraj in bodybuilding, Haldi Khan taught him martial arts, Dhania Khan boxing, and Kalimirchi Khan marksmanship.

However, these noble gestures by Adrak Khan, his brothers and other Muslim side characters didn't change the real world. The riots continue to take place across India and in Aligarh. My problem with riots was that I was cut off from my beloved comic books. While the city was burning around me, my only focus was when I could venture next for my comic book fix. Whenever riots took place, Hindus who were once nice to me began to look threatening. In times of tension like these, their smiles disappeared and their gaze became suspicious. It was as though their eyes were telling me: 'You are a nice kid. We like you. But don't come here at such a time.' It was a strange cocktail of love and hate, where people were suppressing their natural inclination to care for me under the influence of outside factors. Perhaps they were battling their inner demons.

If you weren't from Upar Kot, it is likely that you may perceive communal tension to exist in binaries: either there is communal tension right now or there isn't. But for us, communal tension was a spectrum, a part of our existence, around which the lives of everyone around me were moulded. It simmered in the air around us all the time. Ammi would even go out to shop when the tension was less. She'd say: 'How long can we not leave our home?' The only rule was: don't trust the Hindus, or you'd end up in the well in Gudiya Bagh. Growing up in Upar Kot honed our judgement and made us confident about making the call on how dangerous it was to go outside. By the age of seven, I was a veteran who could sense communal tension like a pro.

There are several indicators to understand how much communal tension is in the air. Are the Muslims just sticking to their areas or are they going to buy groceries in the Hindu areas? How many police officers have been stationed in various localities? Are the shops closed? It also depended on the area. You could go to Railway Road near the Sabzi Mandi Police Chowki at any time. However, to go to Gudiya Bagh or Manik Chowk or Madaar Gate, you need to be completely sure that nothing fishy was going on.

You also need to be connected to friendly Hindus, who'd tell you what the scene was like. To survive, you need to have some friends in the enemy camp. This reminded me of a Raj Comics character named Gamraj who always ended up making friends with his enemies. Gamraj, the king of sadness, was an overly empathetic guy. He'd fight crime by listening to the traumatic stories of the villains and eventually turning them to the good side in an emotionally cathartic event. This was the story of all his comic books.

I often thought: *Can I, like Gamraj, turn Hindus into my friends by listening to their trauma?* Was it just a story or was there a kernel of truth in it somewhere? The answer was very important: it could decide whether or not I end up in the well in Gudiya Bagh on a trip to the comic book shop.

It reminded me of my kindergarten school, when a classmate named Pawan used to make fun of Muslims and their supreme god. 'Allah Ballah,' he'd jeer as Muslim boys passed him in the corridor. This really irritated me. The son of the neighbourhood kachori-wala, I had seen Pawan helping his father at the shop. So, whenever he said 'Allah Ballah' I called him 'Kachori-wala'. He denied this, which made me wonder whether the boy in the shop merely resembled Pawan. I continued chiding him for his probable family business anyway.

But one day, things got out of hand. In his zeal, Pawan started to curse Allah in the classroom. I got very angry. *There is no way this boy was getting away with this,* I told myself. But instead of calling him 'Kachori-wala', I decided to teach him a lesson.

I waited for the lunch break. Pawan was loitering around in the garden. As snot from his runny nose splattered on to his shirt, I began running towards him. As other kids looked on in shock and awe, I launched myself into the air and hit Pawan in the solar plexus with a dazzling flying kick. He crumpled to the floor, too afraid to react or fight back, tears flowing down his cheeks. None of my classmates had seen such a flying kick before, at least not from a kid.

Nobody messed with me after that. Nobody made fun of Allah again. And the flying kick had made me a hero among the Muslim boys. I felt like I was Dhruva.

# 6

# ALLEYS OF BLOOD

WHENEVER SOMEBODY WOULD sagaciously say 'The world moves around in circles', I would imagine a daredevil biker on his motorcycle speeding around the Well of Death at the Aligarh Fair. Man must be a fool, refusing to learn from the mistakes of his predecessors and dooming himself to go through the same suffering, again and again, until the end of time. Sufi saints say 'Suffering makes you pure', which implies that not everybody is equally pure because not everyone suffers equally.

I was taught by Papa that there was some virtue in suffering. 'You can never know how hard life was for us. You wouldn't learn if you don't understand the harshness of life,' he would say.

Being privileged in a ghetto meant you only acknowledged the presence of others in death, otherwise it was a crowd of nameless, faceless people. Only when somebody living nearby died in the riots would the violence lurking here become real for us. Otherwise, it was just a blur of random boys dying in random streets. Because I didn't know these boys, it didn't mean that the alleys of Upar Kot didn't have their share of spilled blood in the streets.

There's always a cool breeze blowing through Bibi Ki Sarai, a rustic neighbourhood with broad, well-lit lanes and old homes that takes you back a couple of centuries. It was nearly a kilometre away from my home on the outer fringes of Upar Kot, but in my mind, it was in a galaxy far, far away. It's one of those lanes that are always so quiet that you wouldn't believe there was a noisy road only a few metres away. Walking through Bibi Ki Sarai, you can hear birds in the trees, the sound of televisions playing in rich peoples' homes and the clanking of utensils from the less fortunate ones.

A predominantly Muslim mohalla, Bibi Ki Sarai was surrounded by Hindu families on all sides. Around the time my nose was buried deep in comic books, Shakir, the son of a karkhane-wala and a few years older than me, had to leave his home with his family in the dead of the night. The riots in their neighbourhood forced them to move to Tantan Para, a kilometre from Bibi Ki Sarai, where his eight maternal uncles lived. The oldest of the lot, Shamsuddin, was the success story of their family. He had been a balloon seller doing several odd jobs on the side before going on to own the largest tobacco business in the area.

'All eight brothers stuck together, and they enjoyed considerable influence in Bibi Ki Sarai. People would say it always felt like Eid in their house,' recalls Shakir. However, Shamsuddin's success ruffled the feathers of his Hindu neighbours. And yet, all was peaceful until 6 December 1992.

Babur, the Uzbeki king-turned-Mughal emperor, who set his sights on India when he got edged out of Fergana Valley, may or may not have built the Babri Masjid over the ruins of a Hindu temple. But since 1984, the Hindu outfit Vishwa Hindu Parishad had been calling for its demolition.[1] There had been quite a few *rath yatras* before Lal Krishna Advani, the party president of Bharatiya Janata Party at that time, set out on another yatra with members of his party. This time he had a trump card. Advani led a campaign claiming that the mosque was built exactly on the spot where Lord Ram, the ideal Hindu man-turned-god, was born. Thus, the Hindus needed to reclaim that land from the Muslims at any cost.

The demolition of Babri Masjid on 6 December 1992, captured live by TV cameras and news channels, was not the usual communal inconvenience Muslims around the country were used to. This was the real deal with events that rippled across India, from the blasts that rocked Mumbai the next year to the murder of Shakir's uncles in cold blood at Bibi Ki Sarai in 1990, here in Aligarh.

The violence related to Babri Masjid had begun in Aligarh even before the demolition took place. Communal tensions were rising since 30 October 1990 when *kar sevaks* were shot dead by the police in Ayodhya.[2] On 7 December, large-scale violence happened in Aligarh. Official accounts put the death toll ninety-two, two-thirds of them Muslims – many by the bullets of PAC (Provincial Armed Constabulary).[3]

'Some men occupied a terrace in their locality, shooting down any Muslim who passed by. My uncle Shamsuddin, and his eldest son, my cousin Zainul, were shot dead. The bullets hit their chests.' When their younger uncle, Qayaam, someone who generally avoided trouble, tried to pull them inside an open doorway, a bullet grazed his arm. 'As he thanked Allah for being saved, he noticed blood pouring down from his right arm. He couldn't feel any pain; it had become numb,' Shakir said.

His arm would have to be amputated; the doctors pronounced when Qayaam got to the hospital. 'But the students from AMU would not allow it; they assembled outside the hospital and protested. The doctors were forced to find a way to save the arm,' recalled Shakir. For the next twenty years, Qayaam would constantly feel a searing pain shoot through his arm, now rendered unusable. Painkillers, and later intoxicants, shadowed the rest of his days.

While Qayaam was suffering in pain, the virus of fundamentalism was spreading fast in India. The conspiracy theories were getting more absurd by the day and their consequences more real. More and more Hindu saints began having political dreams – and nobody could deny them. They were, after all, saints.

There was no doubt in the minds of fundamentalists who brought down the Babri Masjid that it was built upon an ancient Ram temple. After this dream was realized began the demands to destroy other Indian mosques: the Gyanvapi Mosque in Varanasi, the Shahi Idgah Mosque in Mathura, the Quwwat-ul-Islam Mosque in Delhi. Later, a self-styled historian named P.N. Oak wrote an account that the Taj Mahal was not a mausoleum, but a Shiva temple.[4] It became the new truth.

In this new truth, India was a magical, spectacular country in ancient times and the only thing that was needed now was to restore our lost glory. In this truth, the crimes committed (or not committed) by someone became timeless and needed to be avenged in the present. People dead for centuries would now dictate our future. Time would come out of the boundaries and the past, real or imagined, would influence our present and future. For Qayaam and his dead brother and nephew, the past had eroded any hope for the future.

As most of Aligarh's rioters weren't brave enough to venture into rival territory, the riots almost always happened in 'border areas' like mine. The locals rarely fought where they lived. On both the Hindu and Muslim sides, they avoided the fray, afraid of being identified by their neighbours. And so, they resigned themselves to giving tips to the actual fighters. On the Hindu side, most of the fighters were from Hindutva organizations and far-flung areas or villages. On the Muslim side, most came from other mohallas such as Teela, Ladia, Junglegarhi and Usman Para.

Paul Brass, an American researcher who studied communal violence in Aligarh for over three decades, says that this difference was because Hindu mobs were more planned and organized than Muslim ones, because of the presence of Hindu militant nationalist organizations under the Sangh Parivar. 'The maintenance of communal tensions, accompanied from time to time by lethal rioting at specific sites, is essential for the maintenance of militant Hindu nationalism,' says Brass.[5] So riots that caused Qayaam's trauma were, after all, petty politics for the powerful.

The young boys who worked in karkhanas were usually the ones who died in riots. As a child, I wasn't perturbed by their deaths, but I did envy them when they were alive. They earned their own money, and they had their freedom. They could live the way they wanted, and perhaps, they even chose the way they died.

Usman Para is a mere half a kilometre from Bibi Ki Sarai. It lies at the bottom of the slope that leads from Jama Masjid and is the most densely populated area of Upar Kot. It is mostly dark as the Sun can't penetrate the canopy of tall buildings that line the narrow lanes. It is where most butchers live. The smell of meat from the shops diffuses with that of the filth that is rarely cleaned. It is one of those Muslim areas where cops are afraid of entering because of the close relationships between everyone who resides here.

In a corner of Usman Para lived Samiullah aka Nawab, a tall, fair, pious, handsome man who was a little out of place in comparison to his loud neighbours. 'He only spoke when he had to and never interfered in anyone's lives. He respected his children and let them be themselves. Never did he raise his hand on anyone,' said his son Wasiullah, when I met him at his crockery shop in Upar Kot in October 2021. After doing his B.Com from AMU, Samiullah used his skills to become Aligarh's top lock supplier to Delhi in the 1970s.

Apart from his silent and business-like nature, the things that defined Samiullah were his love for food and for his mother. 'Mother and son kept to themselves and just ate their hearts out. Abba was fond of bringing home various types of food, and Daadi was fond of cooking. Both were very religious, offered all five prayers and cried during the Tahajjud prayers every night.'

Samiullah's love for food didn't go to his waist because every day after offering morning prayers, he would go jogging. As there were no places to walk or jog in Upar Kot, he would go to the market area of Railway Road.

It was where he was shot dead while jogging on 1 March 2002.

The riots had been happening in the faraway state of Gujarat for the previous three days and stories of Muslims being killed were all you saw on TV. That day, Parveen Togadia, a far-right Hindu leader had said the violence had strengthened the resolve of Hindus,[6] but nowhere outside Gujarat had the fire spread. Nowhere, that is, except Aligarh.

'Abba usually took our youngest brother, then ten years old, to run with him. That day, he left him behind.' As Samiullah, sporting a long beard and skullcap jogged outside the Tonga Stand, some Hindus standing outside a lane tried to drag him. However, he was too strong for them. 'Unable to physically overpower him, one of them took out his gun and shot Abba dead,' said Wasiullah. Thus, the shy, quiet, food-loving Nawab of Usman Para was taken away from his family.

For days, nothing was cooked in the family of ten, nor did anyone laugh. They kept seeing the TV news coverage of the Gujarat riots and cursed their luck. 'The district administration gave us compensation of 50,000 rupees, but did it matter? The most priceless jewel of our family was gone.' Later, the police arrested four random people on suspicion, but they were let off after the family did their own investigation. The real culprits ran back into the lanes and were never identified. 'Even if they were found, would that have brought him back?' asked Wasiullah as he instructed workers to clean up the crockery shop that his father had set up.

Hate, at its strongest, has the power to overwhelm and defy logic. Samiullah's death was a random killing: the killers didn't know him, his family, or his heart. It wasn't even spontaneous but an act of planned revenge for events that had happened hundreds of kilometres away. The spatial distance didn't matter, nor did reason. Did his killers believe they were helping their community and safeguarding their religion? Or was religion just a plank to carry out a random act of violence and satisfy the animal inside?

This animal lurks inside each of us – some keep it on the surface, while others hide it deep inside. It begins to dominate our humanity when we fight, guard our territories, compete for partners, plan conspiracies for a few inches of land or kill to instil fear in the hearts of our enemies. The enemies, in this case, were Muslims – the ones with beards, burqas, long flowing kurtas and net skull caps decorated with stars and a crescent moon. It didn't matter whether or not they were innocent.

Samiullah's killers were standing at the edge of a lane simply to terrify their 'enemies' by killing someone who appeared to be Muslim. Wasiullah's shy, quiet father simply happened to be at the wrong place at the wrong time and in the wrong attire.

At different points in the day, Aligarh is painted in different hues. The sunset is when it changes from a tinge of yellow to a shade of red. As the Sun relinquishes its ego and disappears from the horizon by throwing a majestic tantrum, hundreds of kites fly against the fading wind and dot the cloudy sky.

On most evenings, the call for Maghrib, the dusk prayers, fills the ears of the faithful and the unfaithful. The world slows down a little; its sounds drowned by time. Birds stop chirping. Women sit in their homes in silence. Men sit in reflection in mosques. All the parts of Upar Kot are flooded with the sound of the azaan coming from its hundreds of mosques, at every corner, in every lane. Some go out to meet friends, others look for an evening snack.

It was around this time, the twenty-seven-year-old Azimullah and his newly wedded wife, Uzma, decided to watch a film in the theatre. Azim drove his moped to the Grand Surjit Cinema, his wife on the backseat. 'A man changes when his girl is sitting in the backseat,' men often said to jibe with their married friends.

Azim was a Bollywood-obsessed boy who never missed a hit film, while Uzma was a conservative, burqa-clad girl from Budaun, a small town a hundred kilometres away. 'Their wedding was fixed by their families, and they had married in a simple ceremony two months ago,' said Muheeb, Azim's cousin when I met him at his home in Junglegarhi in September 2021.

Before this, I had never been to or heard of Junglegarhi – the word means 'forest fort' in Hindi. Nobody knew if, and when, this forest had existed and when it burnt down to become what it was right now. Now Junglegarhi was a mohalla with dusty paths for roads, the abode of hungry dogs and the site of a powerful bad smell that emerged from a warehouse nearby where animal bones were crushed into gelatine. It is around two kilometres from Farsh Manzil in a direction I usually never went and hadn't intended to go either. It was where people who couldn't afford to live in Upar Kot lived.

From their home in Junglegarhi, Azim and Uzma went to watch *Fanaa*, a film in which Aamir Khan, unironically, plays a Muslim who woos a mute and blind girl, Kajol, to use her to camouflage his identity as a Pakistani terrorist. When the couple was watching the film, something sinister was happening at Hathiwala Pul, around three kilometres away. A few masked men arrived on a motorcycle and shot down an influential Hindu businessman in his home. 'The Muslims have killed him!' went out the word in the Hindu locality, spreading as fast as the forest fire that might have decimated Junglegarhi.

To slake their anger against the unidentified assailants everyone believed were Muslims, young and old men took out their clubs and swords. It was again time to kill Muslim passers-by at Railway Road.

Unaware of this, Azim and Uzma would have watched the climax, where the Muslim terrorist is killed by his beloved girl and takes his last breaths in her arms. They would have got up from their AC seats and discussed the ending. Then Azim would have driven his moped out of the parking lot towards Junglegarhi on an unusually deserted road. When they arrived at the crossing at Kutte Ki Qabar, some people on the street warned Azim, 'A Hindu man has been shot. We have heard that the Hindus are looking to kill Muslims on Railway Road.'

'I have to go home. I will be careful,' Azim told them and went on his way. The rumours of riots had been circulating every other day for the last two months. As he drove his moped, the road got more and more deserted, but he kept on. At Sabzi Mandi, a few metres away from the border of Upar Kot, Hindus had assembled with weapons in their hands. 'Look, burqa-wali on a bike,' they pointed at Uzma and ran towards them. Azim tried his best to turn around, but it was too late. The mob had dragged his wife off the moped and had begun to misbehave with her. Azim would have had a few seconds to run away and save his own life, but he didn't. He went back to the mob and pleaded, 'Please let my wife go. Take me instead.'

The mob now had one more prey to hunt. They caught Azeem, slapped his face, tore his clothes and threw him on the ground. 'Kill the bastard,' the mob screamed. Uzma tried to save her husband and saw among them an ice-cream seller from whom they had bought ice cream a few days ago. He was leading the mob. Before they could get to her again, Uzma ran to a police chowki a few metres away. 'Help! They will kill my husband,' she shouted at the cops. The police did come but took their time. By then, somebody had broken Azeem's head with a bat. He died that day, not in the arms of his beloved like Aamir Khan did in *Fanaa*, but amid a mob of hateful men.

'He was the most educated person in our family – the only one who was studious and spoke fluent English. Whenever he found me wasting time with the boys on the street, he would tell me to go home and study,' Muheeb told me, his legs folded near the shutter of a shop in Junglegarhi. 'After Azim Bhai's death, his father lost his mental balance and started talking like a six-year-old, at times. When he was in his senses, he only talked about his son.' Two years after Azim's death, his father died a heartbroken man – but not before fulfilling his responsibilities.

'He talked with his younger brother and arranged for Uzma to marry Azim's cousin. She had her whole life ahead of her and didn't deserve what had happened,' he told me. Azim's new bride, now a new widow, was married within their family. As is the way of the world, everyone got on with their lives, with Azim's tragic love story to be retold in Junglegarhi for years to come, as a reminder to always keep your guard up when you ride through roads. You never knew where death was lurking.

Earth didn't stop spinning on its axis. The culprits were never caught. Justice was never served. Uzma's trauma wasn't resolved. The killers went back to their wives and children, took doctor's appointments, bought groceries and milk in case a curfew was imposed, and probably bragged about their bravado to groups of men. They wouldn't have, under any circumstances, considered themselves evil.

For society, many of them would be good men: people who loved their families, did their work honestly, cared for their friends and helped friends in need; men who taught their children moral lessons and protected themselves from any hurt.

In a 1961 essay for the New Yorker, philosopher Hannah Arendt grappled with the banality of evil. She interviewed German officers who worked in concentration camps and presided over the killing of Jews. Among them, Arendt found 'terrifyingly normal' men who were neither perverted nor sadistic, who remained detached from the reality of their murderous acts.[7] They did it not because they wanted to do it from an ideological position; they did it without any consciousness of the consequences of their actions. They were monsters who killed without thinking.

What were they thinking when they were hitting Azim on his head? Was he a living person or just a Muslim who deserved only to be beaten to death in the middle of the streets on a hot summer day? We can never know.

⌒

I knew Yaseen Bhai as a good person. He lived in the last Muslim home in Gudiya Bagh after other Muslim families, like my mother's, had long left the area. He probably believed that his helpful nature would save him from violence. Or his family probably didn't have the money to buy a new home.

Mohammed Yaseen was a brown-haired man with hazel eyes. He ran a video game parlour a stone's throw away from Hemant's comic book shop in Gudiya Bagh, and I was one of his regular customers. I went there because he had something that other video game parlours didn't – a 16-bit Sega console with awesome graphics and expanded controls, unlike the regular 8-bit gaming consoles the other shops had.

Almost every day after school, I and Fahad, my friend and rickshaw-mate, came to Yaseen's parlour. For hours like addicts, we'd play games like WrestleMania, Mortal Kombat, Aladdin and Sonic. My favourite was WrestleMania where we could fight with popular figures like Yokozuna, Bret 'The Hitman' Hart, Bam Bam Bigelow, Shawn Michaels and Lex Luthor. I couldn't master the game: I was a slow learner and this game cost thrice as much as regular games to play. 'Your time is up. Do you want to play another?' I hated Yaseen Bhai every time he asked me that after losing another round to Fahad.

The ones who actually despised Yaseen down to his very bones were his Hindu neighbours. 'Most of them didn't like us living in their midst and kept trying to force us to sell our home for peanuts. We didn't take this seriously until they killed our uncle and cousin,' said Yousuf, Yaseen's younger brother when I talked to him in September 2021.

The uncle didn't live in their home but in a house in another lane close by along with a few Muslim homes. It was where Yaseen, Yousuf and the rest of their family ran to when there was any danger of riots. 'I think it was 1992 when riots were taking place everywhere. My uncle and his son were caught by their neighbours on the way home. They were taken to a lane in Gudiya Bagh. We only found their deformed bodies later,' said Yousuf. The postmortem report came a few days later. 'It said my uncle had been cut into hundreds of pieces by knives and swords. His son saw him dying before being stabbed seventy times on his body and shot three times.'

The uncle had lived in a 'safer' area than them, and this made the brothers try, for the first time, to look for another home. Of his brothers, Yaseen was the oldest, bravest and most practical: he knew the only way to move out was to earn money. 'More than once, he was beaten up by people who wanted us to sell the house at their price. Once, some men dragged him into a lane and beat him up with sticks for refusing to listen,' said Yousuf.

Paul Brass had observed the same thing in his study on Aligarh: 'The riots between Hindus and Muslims often occur where Hindu and Muslim areas are in close juxtaposition with each other, in nasty slums where landlords or businessmen of one of the other community seek to displace persons from the other community in order to acquire valuable real estate,' he wrote.[8] Was this the reason behind the torture meted out to Yaseen's family by their own neighbours?

Sometimes, I had found Yaseen to be a bit irritated and angry. 'Don't overextend your time,' he snapped. I didn't know that beneath his curly brown hair, his mind was an ocean of anger and betrayal. For years every day, Yaseen opened his parlour in the morning, switched on his Sega console and waited for the rich kids to come. However, many like me were easily bored. Long after I got tired of WrestleMania and Fahad moved to Lucknow, I would see Yaseen with his shop open, now just emptier. This kept going until 2006, the day Azim was killed by a mob on Railway Road.

The same day that Azim and Uzma were engulfed by the mob, a crowd of hundreds assembled outside Yaseen's Gudiya Bagh home and began setting it on fire. 'We ran away to safety in time, but for the next three days, they'd keep robbing our home: first the gaming console, then the television, then breaking the lock and taking away our cash and jewellery we had left in a hurry.' When Yaseen took the risk to come to his own home after three days to pick up the remaining stuff, something died inside him.

'His business and dreams had vanished. He became depressed and anxious. We tried to help him but couldn't,' Yousuf told me. Pain is a strange thing. While joy can't erase past pain and is fleeting, pain can corrupt your present joy through your memories and become a part of your existence. It can even turn you into a shadow of yourself.

Yaseen's mental and physical health declined, and one day, he became paralysed. 'It was in 2013 that he died of diabetes and other complications,' said Yousuf. The brothers eventually sold the home and bought another home in a Muslim ghetto, three kilometres away from Gudiya Bagh.

Gudiya Bagh is now free of Muslims. Yaseen Bhai's video game parlour and his home have been demolished. In their place stands a new building with a wholesale market.

# 7

# THE TYRANNY OF KNOWLEDGE

P RIVILEGE, AS I would come to learn, is a double-edged sword: it offers you power but also hardens your heart and blinds your conscience. You think something is not very much of a problem because it's not a problem that affects *you*.

One side of the story included Yaseen, Qayaam, Shamsuddin, Samiullah and Azim. When they faced misfortune, I was engrossed in comic books, video games and television. When Qayaam was pushing painkiller injections into his hand, it was likely the time I was heavily into the Cartoon Network, a 24-hour channel dedicated to shows like Dexter's Lab, X-Men and Powerpuff Girls.

More than the ones I liked, I remember the cartoons that I absolutely detested but watched anyway. On top of that list was Samurai Jack, a Japanese Samurai sent to a dystopian future ruled by the fascist, evil king Aku. Though Jack had a magic katana that could cut through everything, Aku would shift shapes whenever he was about to be killed. Episode after episode, Jack tried to kill him but failed, a very frustrating thing for someone who liked seeing superheroes saving the day. But even amid the boredom, I could always feel his pain – so close to happiness, yet so far.

Then there was Courage the Cowardly Dog. In it, the title
character is a pink dog named Courage who is, ironically, the most
cowardly dog in the world. He lives in a farmhouse 'in the middle
of nowhere', with an elderly couple called Muriel and Eustace. In
every episode, their home is attacked by demons, ghosts, spirits,
who can only be seen by the dog. Even with all his cowardice,
Courage would always be the enabler of circumstances leading
to the defeat of his owners' evil enemies. I didn't like cowards.
Muslims are taught never to be afraid and accept death like
Bravehearts. Courage the Cowardly Dog didn't know that he only
needed to be afraid of Allah. So, I disliked him.

But what disgusted me most were the characters named Ed,
Ed and Eddy. In every show, the trio did some sort of dirty thing,
like playing with their saliva, urine, blood or mucus. Why would
anyone like boys as yucky as them? Especially Muslims, who
performed ablutions five times a day. Somehow, I hadn't noticed
people living amid dirt in Upar Kot.

As I grew up, I got interested in the Discovery Channel. It
ruined everything I knew about the world. 'Ignorance is bliss,' my
English teacher had once told me. I agreed. Too much knowledge
can kill our feelings and might push us towards tyranny.

Discovery Channel went on to teach me many things I shouldn't
have ever known. It also altered my view of love. A show 'explained'
love as hormones guiding a male to choose the female most likely
to bear children. So if a boy thinks a girl is beautiful, he approves
her waist-hip ratio, and thus an increased likelihood of bearing
their future children. And if a girl considers you handsome, it is
her biological approval of the shape of your jawline and shoulders
as indicators of your virility. So much for a feeling that poets and
philosophers have been writing for centuries!

Discovery Channel would also manipulate my expectations
from the future. A show called 'Beyond 2000' predicted what

the world would look like after the year 2000. It painted such a rosy picture that I believed that the end of human suffering was imminent. In the present I inhabit, I have yet to see flying cars, robot workers in homes, superfood pills to end world hunger, or the cancer cures they promised. Neither have I seen people going on vacations to the Moon, colonies on Mars, super-cheap housing and human clones walking the roads.

I then turned towards animal shows and realized that folks on the Discovery Channel are obsessed with snakes. They try to pass this obsession on to everyone. Whenever I went out to anybody's lawns, I first checked for snakes. The sound of baby toys reminded me of rattlesnakes. Then, there were shows about surviving in a jungle if ever your flight crashes in it. It would be decades before I set foot on a plane, but I was prepared to eat insect shells, identify poisonous plants and remove leeches from my body – just in case my plane ever crashed over the Amazon rainforest.

My favourite programme on the Discovery Channel was 'The Haunting', which explored the vilest demons, witches and poltergeists living in American homes. It made me piss my pants. Because if it must be on Discovery, it must be true. These demons slowly tortured families that had just moved in, possessing their youngest child and flipping crosses from their walls. Usually, the story ended after an exorcism. But in one episode, the demon followed the family to the hospital even after the exorcism! I saw that demon in my dreams and told Saad about it. He was surprisingly comforting.

'The demon didn't go away because they had called a Christian priest. If they had called a maulvi, the demon would have run,' he told me. That made a lot of sense. 'But why aren't the Americans being haunted by djinns? Why do they only haunt Muslims?' I asked him. 'Oh, it's actually the djinns they call demons. It isn't that easy to tell the difference,' Saad said. For me, the easiest explanation was that the spirits are as communal after death as they were in life and would thus haunt only people of their religion.

Though Discovery Channel shows explained a lot, they never explained why it was so easy to hate Muslims. In Hindu imagination, we were dirty, illiterate, patriarchal creatures, who looked at women as baby-producing machines. Paradoxically, we were also lecherous and charming beings, which we used to seduce Hindu girls and convert them to Islam. That's because we've had sex with all of our relatives. 'But you do marry your cousins. So you can fuck everyone, *right?*' a Hindu boy once asked me.

When they didn't consider us sex-obsessed, they considered us radicals. 'Why are you people so overtly religious?' asked a Hindu boy wearing a *teeka* and Ganesha amulets to school, to ten-year-old me, who didn't know how to offer namaz. In their worldview, Muslim men and women could never be loving, kind, decent people, trying to get by in the world as they are.

Apart from demons, I was also afraid of lizards. I saw them in my dreams, falling down on me from imaginary walls. The worst thing about living in an old Indian house is that you share it with countless lizards. In my home, lizards were under windows and doors, next to bulbs and tubelights, under the curtains and near the washbasin. They were the most active in the mornings when I was getting ready for school. But the fear was mutual and lizards were as afraid of me as I was of them.

There was, however, one that was particularly brave. It lived behind the dressing table and came out when I was getting ready for school in the morning. We sort of played hide-and-seek, often startling each other, but with time we became strangely comfortable around each other. I didn't startle it and it didn't move suddenly. Playing mind games with a lizard was how I began my day.

Raja Bhaiya was my first rickshaw-wala at St Fidelis. Only a few rickshaw-walas dared to take kids from Upar Kot to Ramghat Road, over five kilometres away. After me, he'd go to pick up Yasir-Natiq, Fathima and Zeeshan, my rickshaw-mates. We'd then pass Katpula (the bridge where my Phuppa died of a heart attack) to reach Marris Road. Here, we'd pick up Harshal, the richest person in our rickshaw. He was the scion of the owner of Nandan and Surjeet Talkies, the only two air-conditioned cinema halls in Aligarh.

Nobody made a fuss when Harshal took his time to get ready. We'd quietly roam around his home and his luscious garden, playing with his expensive toys as he got ready. When he arrived, we'd give him the main seat of the rickshaw without fuss. It was mostly because of Harshal that we'd reach late and wait in the queue outside the school assembly. The students who lived nearby and came on time looked at us latecomers with judgemental eyes. 'Zeyad, you should come on time at least one day,' my class teacher would often say. She didn't know I was coming all the way from Upar Kot.

Everyone mocked me when I told them that I was from Upar Kot. 'Really? You don't really look like someone from there.' I didn't know what someone from Upar Kot looked like. I told them that my father was an AMU employee and we were convent-educated, reasonable, non-violent people. But it didn't matter. There was a marked difference in the way people treated me before and after they knew I was from the U.K. After some time, I stopped telling them. When someone asked, I said that I was from 'Sheher', the term by which Aligarh's old city is often referred to by the people who live in elite, newer areas.

We were believed to be troublemakers. 'Upar Kot is the Pakistan of Aligarh,' a friend once told me. According to him, we were a monolith, who fought and killed at the slightest provocations. Sometimes, I wished Papa had taken the government quarters he was given by the university. Then I'd have more friends and grassy playgrounds, unlike the dusty Haatha. But he was in love with Farsh Manzil, and that is how love works.

In actuality, Upar Kot boys were like all boys around the world. They wanted to be some sort of Superman. If they had a chance, they'd give their eyes to be able to fly, have enormous strength and gadgety suits that ran on nuclear energy and deflected bullets. If Spiderman had really existed, a lot of Upar Kot boys would be inspired to get bitten by all kinds of toxic spiders and die because of it. And if there was a serum to give superhuman strength like Captain America's, they'd probably find some *jugaadu* relative to get them a cheaper version.

By the second standard, I became the class topper. I only studied just before the exams, never took tuition but remembered everything anyway. Everybody thought I studied secretly. Little did they know I was just brighter! My class teacher Suman Ma'am treated me like the king of the class and said things like: 'Zeyad also has only twenty-four hours in his day – you all should take tips from him.' But in the third standard, Neha, a tall girl with curly hair and kohled eyes, got the first position. I was relegated to the second position. It hurt.

This was my introduction to the competitive part of me who was obsessed with winning. I won poetry recitation competitions, quiz competitions, essay writing and creative writing. Though I always got a B or C in drawing, I once even won a Diwali card-making competition because of a unique idea!

I was also the boy who helped everyone. If there was someone who didn't have a pencil to write his exam, I'd break my pencil into two and give them the other half. Most other toppers would build a kind of wall around their answer sheet, but I would position it such that those sitting behind would be able to look easily. Sometimes,

I'd give them my answer sheet when the teacher wasn't looking. And so, those who sat near me always got high marks.

In our school, nobody wanted to befriend kids who failed their exams. 'They fail because they are lazy,' everyone would say. I felt bad for them. Some of them were nice and even read comic books. So I helped them cheat in exams. Perhaps there should have been a comic book where Dhruva fails to save the world from evil *Mahamanav*, and everyone is kind of okay with the world ending. Or better, stories where the evil men eventually win like they often do in life, where people die of police bullets without a reason, nobody vows revenge for them and are conveniently forgotten. Like the boys of Upar Kot who died of gunshots and intelligent, powerful people kept mum.

Nobody embodied this better for me than Bhediya, a popular Raj Comics character who defended the forests from greedy 'civilized' men. In one issue, he was captured by a villain and split into two beings: *Kobi* (the wolf) and *Bhediya* (the human). The human half was intelligent and calm, whereas the wolf half was hilarious, aggressive and powerful. Kobi possessed animal power and the ability to grow his tail extremely long. Despite his lack of powers, Bhediya tried his hardest to save innocents. But Kobi never used his superpowers unless something affected his interests or his half-girlfriend, Jane.

I never understood why the writers divided the original hero into two. Was it to remind us we are human only if we use our powers to fight injustice? And if we only thought of ourselves, were we any different from the villains?

⌒

In the third standard, like a king deserting his throne, Raja Bhaiya passed the responsibility of taking the U.K. kids to Lalu, his 'cousin from Bihar'. Lalu already had nine children in his rickshaw, and when we added four from ours; it took the tally to thirteen – all in one rickshaw. We'd call ourselves 'the unlucky thirteen'.

Lalu's rickshaw was as crowded as a hospital after a riot. After me, he'd pick up Fahad, who would later go on to be my video game companion. Then we picked up Yasir and Natiq from Hathiwala Pul. After that, we'd enter the Hindu area and pick up Neha from Goolar Road. As we waited outside her home, a shopkeeper made fun of us, '*Katua, katua, katua*,' he chanted. Natiq, the oldest among us, knew what he meant. 'He is abusing us. The next time he calls you katua, call him kaafir.' So, henceforth, whenever he called us katua, we'd call him kaafir. Before this, I hadn't heard either of the two terms, but they soon became a part of my lexicon.

Lalu's rickshaw took its time covering half of Aligarh at a snail's pace. Three children sat in the main seat, three sat on the back, and four sat on a customized wooden bench. Rest (including me) stood along the rickshaw's back frame. Someone was injured every now and then, but no one complained. Because Lalu was almost pulling an entire planet, we were always late for school but never made a fuss. The only thing that worried me was being seen by other kids in my class like this. What would they think?

'Our rickshaw moves so slow. Why don't we walk to school instead?' Natiq once suggested. He was especially good at turning everything into a game. Walking through Aligarh's roads and discovering shortcuts sounded fun. In fact, we reached school before Lalu did. He, of course, didn't mind the burden being taken off.

One day, Natiq suggested we tear our general knowledge aka GK books to mark the end of exams – a yearly milestone in student life. It was akin to getting out of prison. So on Natiq's advice, we tore apart our General Knowledge textbooks piece by piece, threw away the remnants on the tarmac of the road, and screamed '*Padhai murdabad!*' 'Look at these rowdy Muslim kids, they are tearing their books apart!' kids from other rickshaws would exclaim, not knowing that Hindu and Muslim kids stood together in this revolt against the education system. Anyway, it felt like a fitting end to the school session!

Hoisting remnants of textbooks in the air from the moving rickshaw felt utterly liberating. It was probably because, throughout the year, I struggled with keeping my textbooks intact. It seemed like a curse – while others' notebooks looked new even after the end of the term, mine would start looking ragged within a month or so. Every year, when Sayema and Saad put brown covers on my notebooks, they'd tell me, 'Keep them safe this year.' But within months, I would start losing pages even after trying my level best not to. I kept thinking: *Is there something wrong with me? Why couldn't I do simple things that others could?*

There were other things I couldn't do well. I couldn't fold my clothes nicely, ride a bicycle or run as fast as other boys. I would look down when I walked and dragged my feet. I couldn't properly hold a spoon or tie my shoelaces properly. Because I was forgetful, I lost all the umbrellas, pencils, erasers, sharpeners, sunglasses and water bottles my parents got for me. Others had pencil boxes in which they'd press buttons and a pencil would come out. I would search for a pencil in my bag and after failing, I would ask whoever was sitting next to me. It would be the beginning of a long life of bad motor skills, coupled with a short attention span, that made simple tasks look insurmountable.

I also wasn't good at sports. But nobody, including myself, knew this. So, when a new physical training teacher brought a games period along with him, Suman Ma'am chose me as the cricket captain of the class. I vehemently believed I could bat because I had played cricket in my courtyard with Badi Mummy's washing machine as a wicket. Moreover, there weren't any playgrounds in Upar Kot, except the Haatha, and I had nearly got my tongue burnt one time I went there. For at least four periods, I kept convincing my classmates that I was just trying to find my rhythm. But even the best lie can travel only a few miles. Pretty soon, they caught my bluff and elected another captain.

I was also terrible at handwriting. Worst in the class, it looked like ink-dipped ants had taken a walk on my notebook. I would have an A in almost every subject, but in handwriting, I got a D. 'We'd give him more marks if we could understand what he wrote,' 'He can't even hold a pen properly,' my teachers would tell parents on rare occasions when they met them. Ammi tried her best to correct this 'flaw' in her son. She brought every cursive writing book in the city, but her little son kept failing her. My friends would often try to cheer me up. 'Even Einstein had bad handwriting, but he went on to become the greatest scientist.' Though it was a lie and Einstein had a fine handwriting, I'd use this 'fact' whenever someone tried to make fun of my handwriting.

Despite being the topper, I set a really bad example for the class. I never listened to the teachers and ridiculed students who studied too much. When they scored less than me, I would ridicule them more. 'You know what, I am just brighter than you,' I'd tell them, unapologetically. I had a sharp memory, could remember my lessons easily and was good at reading – all thanks to my comic books.

I would make up for these insecurities by being the class clown. I would sing songs like '*Meri Marzi*' and was the star player in Antakshari. After school, I could mostly be found in playgrounds on the swings. 'I can get on the top of the slide just by running up. Can you do that?' I would say. I would also do different stunts on swings, which meant falling in the dirt and taking dirty clothes to Ammi every day, who mostly didn't scold me for that.

I was also too stubborn to listen to the others. 'You'll fall down because of your open shoelaces and break your leg,' other kids would tell me.

'I have walked with open shoelaces for years. I will live the rest of my life like that. Concentrate on your life,' I would tell. And I never fell.

'Why don't you look ahead while you're walking and not at the ground?' some kids would say. But I kept walking like that and never ran into anything.

I wouldn't follow a rule until it made sense to me. I would argue with teachers, call them out if they made an error and was often proved right. 'Expecting students to ask permission before going to the toilet is an idiotic rule,' I would tell other kids, who thought I was crazy. I also found excuses for not attending PT classes, even as other kids fell down like ripe guavas while exercising under the harsh summer Sun.

'You are too naive. The world will eat you up,' everyone would say. 'The world will not eat me. I will eat the world,' I would say.

This dream to eat the world was what probably made me a fan of the new show *Kaun Banega Crorepati*, which aired on Star Plus. Being a quizzer in my school, I dreamed of going to KBC. In my imagination, I calculated how much money I would win if I was in the 'hot seat'. On most days, I won Rs 6.5 lakhs, usually quitting the game at Rs 25 lakhs. Then I'd imagine how people would react after I won that much money. Would my school felicitate me? Would media persons throng my home in Upar Kot to interview me? None of that happened. I could never get through the phone lines constantly busy with thousands of other dreamers.

Aside from the crushed dreams of becoming a millionaire, there were other irritants in my life. A new show called *Kyunki Saas Bhi Kabhi Bahu Thi* had debuted on television. Ammi and Sayema weren't initially interested, but Rubina Bhabhi from Palle

Ghar persuaded them to watch it. Saad and I both detested the show. 'Aside from fights between sisters-in-law and mothers-in-law, what do they show?'. I'd say.

We watched it with them, pretending we didn't care about this 'womanly' serial, but soon we became more addicted than we realized. When Mihir, the central male protagonist, was killed, I went from being a passive, judgemental critic to becoming more engaged with the show. It brought us more grief than the death of our Chhote Nana in Garkha. It became such a big deal that it sparked national outrage, forcing the show to change its plot. After an episode of amnesia, the producers finally brought Mihir back.

Aside from the concept of amnesia, the show taught us something else that would have made my religious grandfather turn in his grave. We learnt the Gayatri Mantra, Hinduism's first mantra, similar to what *kalimas* are to Muslims. Tulsi, the show's heroine, would recite it whenever she needed to summon the courage to deal with evil mothers-in-law and Mihir's mistresses. '*Om Bhur Bhuva Swa, Tat-savitur Vareniya, Bhargo Devasya Dheemahi, Dhiyo Yonah Prachodayat*'. I recited it to shocked friends and appreciative Hindi teachers.

'Who taught you the Gayatri Mantra?' they'd ask. On this attention, I reacted like a street boy brandishing his new suit. 'Oh, I am interested in all religions. I hope to finish memorizing the Quran and reading the Gita and Bible by the eighth standard. I don't watch cartoons now,' I would lie and they'd all believe it.

More than just being a boast, I was sure that Gayatri Mantra would someday save my life. If I was ever caught by a Hindu mob, I'd recite it to prove my Hinduness. I didn't know that the mob would simply check my penis for circumcision and not rely on my knowledge of the mantra. But this illusion did provide a sense of safety during my sojourns to Hindu areas.

Most of us are trapped in a cage of delusions. Only in extreme pain do we notice things our minds are attempting to avoid. Palaces in other people's minds appear strange to us, but palaces in our own minds appear as real as the stench from drains in Upar Kot. When these illusions are shattered, it feels as if an army has destroyed a palace you built with your own hands. 'Only fools are ever happy,' wisemen say. But it is human to hope.

Even these wise men and women wait for something to happen, some sort of revolution that will take ours and everyone's pain away. All these revolutions are always 'around the corner', but they never arrive. Though suffering has always been present, few hope it'd *always* be there in the world. Perhaps because it stops us from despair – a sin in some interpretations of Islam.

That's probably why, despite the death and suffering in Upar Kot, life continued. The world continued to spin, as it always did.

∽

A year later, like an enemy trying to enter into a peace treaty, Saad told me of a place in Upar Kot where you could play video games. It was a small house in Chowk Bundu Khan, in the same lane as Zafar Motorwale. There were three TV screens and a very excited homemaker delighted to see an obsessed customer. For many months, I would ask Ammi for money on some pretext and simply go missing for hours. All my free time was spent at the parlour. As is its nature, the truth came out. One day, Ammi found out.

Burning with anger like shops did during riots, she arrived at the parlour and dragged me home. Rather than being worried about my studies, she was concerned that I was now going out in Upar Kot. *Now she can't brag that her sons don't go outside*, I thought but didn't say out loud. I cursed her and kept crying. After this, my trips to the game parlour became rarer and secretive. The owner was not as excited to see me as before.

Nevertheless, I kept fighting with Ammi to go to the game parlour more. She was like a banyan tree holding on to the soil and didn't want to budge. It became an issue at home. A few months later, Papa went to Lucknow and brought home a video game.

The world of video games was as beautiful as the one of comic books. Here, *you* were actually the hero, someone who protects cities, saves princesses in distress, becomes the karate champ, fights extraterrestrial terrorists or just proves himself the best clown in the circus. Soon, the lure of comic books began to wane. My game cassette had sixty-four games, and I would play all of them, one by one, every day. The first game I'd play was *Islander*, then *Mario*, *Road Fighter*, *Contra*, *Lode Runner*, *Bomberman*. Sayema mostly played *Bomberman*, while Saad was really into *Lode Runner*. The villain in *Bomberman* was Lode Runner, and the villain in *Lode Runner* was Bomberman; it kind of suited the animosity between Saad and Sayema.

Initially, there was a competition between Saad and me, but he soon got bored and went back to kite flying. After that, I would game on our BPL colour TV for sixteen hours at a stretch. Ammi and Sayema struggled to watch TV. Papa, who had brought it home, suffered the most, because the TV was in his room. Every morning at 6, I would go to his single bed, find a little space near his legs, turn on the TV and connect the game. I kept the volume up and moved a lot. Papa would simply glance up from under his blanket and move his legs to give me space.

I would get better at gaming, sometimes playing it even when I was not deriving any pleasure from it, like an addiction. At school, I would borrow game cassettes from others and give them back after completing all the games. 'So, you crossed that level?' they'd ask. 'Oh, it was too much of a breeze until the seventh level,' I'd say proudly. But I'd soon discover every joy has its price.

The more I sat for hours in front of the TV, the redder my eyes became. Then the redness became darker and more permanent. I looked like an eight-year-old drug addict. Ammi was concerned and took me to the medical college at AMU. 'This is not redness, ma'am. These are actual wounds in his eyes. They happen to those who sit in front of a colour TV for hours,' the doctor said. Oh, so that was why it hurt when I blinked! My mother now had the unenviable task of putting eye drops and stopping me from playing video games.

Like a lion in captivity, I kept restless and fought with her a lot. Papa came up with a solution. He bought a new black-and-white Onida TV, attached an additional glare-reducing screen and moved it into the room next to his. It was no fun playing games on a black-and-white TV. It was like a chess game without its pawns. I began to lose interest in video games and began to play chess with Saad and Papa. Pretty soon, I was defeating them. But I now had a void in my life. This was when I fell in love again – but this time with a human being.

She was a classmate in the fifth standard, a shy, elegant girl with a beautiful smile. She smelt nice, wore clean clothes, spoke very little and laughed at all my bad jokes. This made me want to impress her with my attention-seeking antics: sliding down the staircase side grill, saying smart things in class and balancing my pencil box on my fingers during 'hands up' punishment for the class. Sometimes, her shy smile turned into shy laughter, and I liked her even more. I was mean to all the other girls, but I was helpful and kind to her. I kept finding new ways to talk to her. Once, I gave her a Tazo, the toy which came in a packet of Lays chips. She took it and smiled, but didn't understand that I loved her more than anyone else.

At St Fidelis, there was a specific area near the stage where all good-looking girls hung out during recess. We mostly stayed away from that area, lest the girls suspected us of being boys who stalked places where beautiful girls hung out. So, my friends and I would roam around in the area where ugly boys and girls went. But one day, I gathered the courage to go into the space of beautiful people. I went up to her, held out a packet of Britannia Little Hearts biscuits towards her and said really throatily, 'Would you like a little heart?' She smiled her shy smile and took one. It was probably a sign that she liked me too. But I didn't know what to do next.

Love is where rationality goes to the dogs. You worry about the eventual separation from your beloved and cry along with sad songs. Love is also scary. It is like entering into a war without any guns.

I was never brave or old enough to tell her what I felt and so, I began offering namaz. 'If you ask Allah for something with a pure heart, he will give it to you,' Sayema had told me once. So I prayed for the health of Ammi and Papa, to become a pilot, and to marry my beloved – all in that order. But my prayers didn't work. The next year, her section changed, and now I would only see her in the school corridors. Sometimes, I'd go by her class to catch a glimpse of her sitting in the back row.

Apart from love, something else was happening in our lives. A machine called a computer had arrived in Aligarh. 'In some time, the world will move on computers, and anyone who doesn't learn how to use them will be left behind,' our teachers would say. We now had a computer period, where we learnt how to use MS Paint and languages like LOGO and HTML.

As the year 2000 drew closer, the world was changing fast. A song from an Aamir Khan film called *Mela* was becoming popular. '*Dekho, 2000 Zamana Aa Gaya*' it went. In the song, Aamir Khan danced with skimpily dressed girls amid rain, fire and studio lights celebrating the new millennium. Even in the real world, the year 2000 was something to look forward to.

In school, the other kids were talking about conspiracy theories. 'All the computers will stop working after the clocks move to the year 2000 because of the Y2K bug. The world will collapse,' Shamlan told us. I didn't give a shit as I didn't have a computer. No computers meant no computer period and no learning the silly LOGO and HTML languages. It also meant we didn't have to bother taking our shoes off when we went inside the computer lab. It anyway stank because of the dozens of smelly socks inside. Unfortunately, Shamlan was wrong. 2000 arrived with gusto and no computer stopped working.

I asked my class teacher what was so special about 2000. 'The millennium is changing. It happens only once in a thousand years. You are lucky to witness this.' This made me happy. We were the millennials, those who'd usher in the twenty-first century and shape it. We'd soon have flying cars, medicines to cure cancer and take rocket trips to Mars as the Discovery Channel had predicted. Everyone was celebrating the beginning of the new millennium, the grand twenty-first century the human civilization was waiting for.

Little did we know what was really in the offing.

# PART 2

# Boyhood

# 8

# OSAMA BIN LADEN

WHEN I WAS in the sixth standard, my father bought us a subscription to *The Hindu*, a newspaper considered informative and educational, one that didn't rely on titillating pictures to tempt their audience. By this time, my father's interest in politics had begun to rub off on me. I was too old for comic books and video games – newspapers were my new obsession.

After scanning the headlines on the front page, I would go to the editorial and op-ed sections. Then, I would read the letters to the editor. Like a dying man going through his will thoroughly, I read almost every news item from beginning to end. Except for business news, I read everything: the classifieds where the grooms demanded tall, fair and young brides from their caste and religion, the TV guide, and the complete scorecard for all cricket matches. I knew which horse had won the equestrian championships in Chennai and what happened at a nondescript volleyball game in Goa.

Then, I would read the supplements: especially the *Hindu Young World* and the *Sunday Magazine*. After that, I'd go to Bade Papa's home to get their copy of the *Times of India*. It had salacious pictures on page two, a daily cartoon, sudoku and horoscope section on the end pages. This was when many new news channels like Aaj Tak, Zee News and Sahara Samay were making their mark. They were more sensational and less informative, but I still preferred them over the entertainment channels.

I had turned twelve that year. The evening of 11 September 2001 was slow and sunny like most autumn evenings in Aligarh. I was studying while watching Cartoon Network (my parents didn't interfere with how I studied). The most precious instrument in our home, our landline phone, rang in the lobby at around 6.30 p.m. Aamir Hasan, the only other boy in my class as interested in politics and world affairs as me, was on the other end.

'Turn on the news. Something big has happened!' he said.

'What is it?'

'Two planes have crashed into the Twin Towers at the World Trade Centre one after the other.' I had heard about those buildings – in a fourth standard General Knowledge exam, there had been a question about the world's second-tallest building and at the height of 1,368 feet, the North Tower was the correct answer.

'Damn, was it an accident? Were the planes flying too low?'

'I heard that it might be a terrorist attack.'

I knew what a 'terrorist' was, but I didn't know they existed in the real world. They were nameless, bad people whose evil plans were regularly defeated by superheroes like Dhruva or Doga.

I turned on Aaj Tak, the new Hindi news channel everyone was watching. My first reaction was shock and then sympathy for the families of the victims. But deep down, I felt the first stirring of a strange excitement. It was like a Hollywood movie coming to life. *Well, supervillains have arrived. Superheroes might arrive soon,* I thought. But that didn't happen. The news later revealed that two planes had been hijacked by terrorists and deliberately crashed into the buildings. Everyone was now glued to the news channels. All the flights over American airspace were immediately grounded, and all tall skyscrapers were evacuated.[1]

As the details of the attack emerged, I began to respect these supervillains. *Whoever they are, they've planned it well,* I thought. All the kids I knew were also in awe. The loss of human life was an afterthought, somewhat like what would happen after violence in Upar Kot. I was more interested in the details of how it had been carried out. If someone could do this in the US, the world's most powerful and secure nation, anything could happen anywhere. I had watched enough TV shows and movies to know America was the land of Arnold Schwarzenegger, the very zenith of wealth, scientific advancement and military prowess. A land where the roads didn't have potholes, there were no power cuts and no garbage was strewn in public spaces. Who had the audacity to carry out *such* an attack there?

Of course, it was planned by the Israelis, that cunning, barbaric nation with a mad leader. 'When Ariel Sharon dies, even maggots won't eat his body for the sin of killing children,' Badi Ammi had once told Papa during their regular morning discussions as he ate his staple breakfast of ghee–roti and green chilli chutney. Even though she was in her eighties, she was acutely aware of politics.

A few days later, I found who the supervillains were. It was us, the Muslims.

'Muslims couldn't have done this!' we cried in shock.

When Osama Bin Laden, a gaunt-looking Arab man with a long beard, the leader of Al-Qaeda, a terrorist organization not many had heard of before, was held responsible for the attacks, he became the most talked-about person in the world. Editorials in *The Hindu* raised questions about how he went from being a 'prime suspect' to the 'mastermind' in no time. Letters to the editor talked about America as a state that initiated wars for their benefits.

New York is thousands and thousands of kilometres away from Aligarh but 9/11 led me to wonder if I, a Muslim, was somehow responsible for all this death. Were Muslims a danger to others for the crime of existing?

Every time I heard of a terror attack, I'd pray for the attackers to not be Muslim. If they weren't, it was a great relief. If they were, it was a burden on my soul. Now it wasn't just the people of Kanwari Ganj who hated us – the entire world had joined them.

'Why are all Muslims terrorists?' a few Hindu classmates asked me after 9/11. And even though some Muslims agreed with this new labelling of their people, most were ashamed of it.

Like insecure lovers trying to hold on to a failing relationship, my fellow Muslim classmates began to act extra patriotic so that the others would not be afraid of them. 'Islam has always been a religion of peace,' they'd tell everyone, but that didn't help. I, on the other hand, spent my days reading more deeply about international affairs and responding by talking of atrocities committed on Muslims in Afghanistan, Iraq and Palestine. But it didn't cut any ice. Muslim lives were, seemingly, not as important as American lives – sort of like the lives of young men of Upar Kot.

Along with terrorism, another word became a part of our lexicon – jihad. It was the subject of every TV debate and column. Hindu boys asked us when we were going for jihad. Some Muslim boys, mostly those who had no idea what it meant, thought it was a cool thing to do. 'Only the noblest and bravest have the courage to go for jihad,' they'd say with pride.

It's interesting how people choose sides in a political conflict. Instead of going with a side that appeals to their morals, they were likely to go with the one that claimed to fight for them. Herd mentality, which came into existence when humans began to form tribes, grew when they migrated in groups, and solidified when they began to farm, became the driving force again. In the old days, at least, people didn't have much of a choice. Modern life brought with it the burden of choosing our identity, a complex permutation of our upbringing, nation, ideology, gender, caste and religion.

When George W. Bush threatened the Taliban and demanded they hand over Bin Laden, most Muslims made fun of him. Compared to Laden who looked like a strong man in a beard, with dark intense eyes on a mission, Bush looked like a chimp in a suit. When Bush threatened to attack Afghanistan, they said, 'They'd never dare attack.' And when they did, some Muslims said, 'They can never win. Nobody has managed to conquer the rough Afghan terrain.' When the Taliban began losing to the rebel Afghan alliance supported by America, they prophesied, 'It won't last.'

On the day America attacked Afghanistan, a Hindu classmate celebrated like she had won a lottery. 'It's about time,' she said, amid cheers from the others. I was disgusted. How could anyone support the beginning of a war?

As American bombs rained down on Afghanistan, I kept track of civilian casualties. I didn't understand how America, the doyen of democracy, could kill civilians and call it collateral damage. Thousands of questions raided my mind like planes dropping bombs in Kandahar. 'Don't they have high-tech satellites that target people precisely? Don't they have the CIA which knows everything about everyone? Are they killing Muslims just because they *can*?' But I didn't get any answers – except from my cousin Danish who was incredibly sure that 9/11 was an inside job by the US military because they wanted to start a war for global domination.

What was unbelievable, though, was his prediction of the future of the world order. 'Osama Bin Laden will defeat the Americans in Afghanistan, and this will precipitate the fall of American power.

After that, the Taliban will become stronger, take over Pakistan and get their hands on their nuclear weapons,' he said as I listened attentively. 'Indian right-wing politicians like Advani and Vajpayee are on Pakistan's payroll and are trying to weaken India from the inside by their communal rhetoric. They will help Pakistan take over India. After that, Osama will take control of the whole of the Middle East,' he pronounced as I tried to memorize everything. 'Then will come the Islamic domination of the world. Forty years after that, of course, will be Judgement Day,' he declared with absolute conviction. I later claimed this as my own prophecy and narrated my first conspiracy theory to my classmates.

The mainstream media's larger-than-life depiction of Osama Bin Laden only deepened my interest in him. While my Hindu classmates were also intrigued by him, there were some like me who increasingly began to view him as a messiah taking on the enemies of the community, righting the wrongs inflicted on Muslims around the world. The fact that he had humiliated America in their own backyard – something no country could even imagine – was incredible. The more I read about him, the more obsessed I became with him. He was an engineer, an Arsenal fan and a man who had a multi-million-dollar business inheritance, but he'd left it all behind to fight the world's most powerful nation. You could love or hate him, but nobody, absolutely nobody, could ignore him. I didn't foresee how badly this stance would age in time, but back then, it sounded like the right thing to believe in.

Two months after 9/11, on 13 December 2001, the Indian parliament was attacked by terrorists from Lashkar-e Taiba and Jaish-e-Mohammed, and nine security men and other personnel lost their lives.[2] This felt personal. 'It is our parliament that the Pakistanis have attacked,' I said to my followers in school. The Hindu classmates looked at me approvingly.

Soon, the winter break arrived like a diligent clerk, and I went to my mother's village in the Etah district. They subscribed to a local Hindi newspaper there, which was very different from *The Hindu*. It talked about 'the plague of Islamic fundamentalism' and how Muslims weren't doing enough to stop it. They were overly fond of using pictures of bearded men and burqa-clad women in these articles. The message was clear: all Muslims supported the terrorists.

Meanwhile, the Indian Prime Minister, Atal Bihari Vajpayee, held Pakistan responsible for the attack and warned them of retaliatory military aggression. The Hindi newspapers claimed that a war was imminent, almost as if they wanted the war! Eventually, my month in the village passed amid fears of a possible nuclear war. *If Delhi is attacked, the radiation might reach Aligarh but not Etah*, I thought while imagining my friends and the Farsh Manzil burning to the ground in a Hiroshima-like blast or like the Twin Towers.

By the time I returned to Aligarh, it was clear that the threat of war was not entirely a hoax. The Indian government began acting against its 'internal enemies'. Some students, associated with the Students' Islamic Movement of India, aka SIMI, which was founded in Aligarh, put up posters mocking Vajpayee's decision to support America in parts of Delhi. The organization was linked to Al-Qaeda and banned a few weeks after 9/11.[3] Among those arrested were students from AMU – the war on terror was coming closer to home.

The new year only brought fresh terrors. On 27 February 2002, a train was torched near the town of Godhra in Gujarat, killing fifty-nine Hindu pilgrims returning from Ayodhya. The Gujarat police said a Muslim mob was responsible, while other enquiries called it a fire accident.[4] The following week, communal riots erupted across the state. The official death toll was 1,044 people, the majority of which were Muslims.[5] The toll from unofficial sources was more than 2,000 people.[6] More than 2,500 people were injured and over 50,000 people were displaced.

The newspapers I read carried witness testimonies of how Hindu mobs ran amok in the streets to avenge the death of the pilgrims, not unlike the anti-Sikh riots in Delhi after the assassination of Prime Minister Indira Gandhi in 1984. In Gulbarg Society in Ahmedabad, sixty-nine people were killed after Hindu mobs ransacked the Muslim neighbourhood.[7] In the Naroda Patiya area of the same city, ninety-seven Muslims were killed by a mob of thousands.[8] In Vadodara, fourteen people were killed when the Muslim-owned Best Bakery was burnt down by a mob.[9] Three of the bakery's employees were Hindus, who didn't have the chance to prove that they were, after all, Hindus.

But what really remained etched in my memory were the horrific rapes, especially that of Bilkis Bano, one of the few women who made it out alive. After the riots broke out, her family tried to flee in a truck but were intercepted by a Hindu mob. On the outskirts of Ahmedabad, fourteen members of her family were killed in front of Bilkis Bano's eyes.[10] Somebody smashed the head of her two-year-old-daughter Saleha on the ground, killing her. Though Bilkis was pregnant with another child, she was gang-raped and brutalized, left behind only because the mob mistook her for dead.

Muslims in these areas alleged that police either stood by as mute witnesses, or worse, helped the rioters. In the years to come, most of the people charged with these crimes would be acquitted for want of evidence.[11] Sitting in Farsh Manzil, I dreaded reading the newspaper. All anyone in Aligarh could talk about were attacks in retaliation. We lived in fear and hoped that the fire wouldn't reach our town.

A few days later, a bearded, Muslim man woke up in Aligarh, offered his morning prayers like a faithful and went for his daily morning walk. He was shot dead at Railway Road, a five-minute walk from my home. A day before the shooting, I was practising a song from the classic Bollywood film *Anari* for a school event.

*Kisi ki muskuraahaton pe ho nisaar,*
*Kisi ka dard mil sake to le udhaar,*
*Kisi ke waaste ho tere dil mein pyaar,*
*Jeena isi ka naam hai*

On the day of the shooting, I had an important rehearsal. But, of course, my parents forbade me to go to school. 'Why don't you understand? The teacher will throw me out of the choir,' I told an unrelenting Ammi. 'You people are fools. All the other kids will show up, and I will be kicked out.'

'They don't live in Upar Kot; it's not safe out there,' said Ammi. And as always, she prevailed and was eventually proven right. Cases of fighting followed, and the situation remained tense for days. When I returned to school a week later, the music teacher understood why I'd been absent and allowed me to perform.

As I sang that timeless song on stage, something was changing inside me. More than ever before, I was aware of my identity as a Muslim. I was angry about the atrocities against Muslims around the world, with no courts or laws protecting them. This soon translated into a growing belief in the religion, and at the age of thirteen, I finally became a practising Muslim. I regularly went to the mosque, asked Allah for forgiveness and prayed to keep my family safe from harm. The mosque, adjacent to my home, became my sanctuary.

I would offer namaz four times out of five. I didn't know the verses, but I thought standing with other worshippers would save me from Allah's punishment. If I missed any prayers, I would offer *Kaza namaz,* the prayers you offer in place of the ones you have missed. In the holy month of Ramzan, I would wake up at 5.30 a.m., perform my ablutions with cold water and offer Fajr prayers. Badi Ammi and Shamlan, my best friends, were delighted, and suddenly, my neighbours and elders began treating me with more respect.

But only I knew why I had become religious. It was because I was afraid. Even though hell scared me, I somehow could imagine enduring the eternal fires, being cut down by swords and feeling intense pain, dying and then being brought to life again to be punished again till the end of time. The thing that actually scared the wits out of me was 'the torment of the grave', referred to by our maulvi as '*qabr ka azaab*'.

'After a person dies, once their relatives and friends start walking away from their grave, two angels called Munkar and Nakir arrive to interrogate the deceased. They're terrifying, with solid black eyes, shoulders that stretch for miles, and a hammer that can't be moved even if the entire human race joins to lift them. They'd ask us three questions: Who is your lord? Who is your Prophet? What's your religion? The correct answers are Allah, Prophet Muhammad and Islam. But there is a million-dollar catch – you will only be able to answer correctly if you have lived by Allah's way. You can't lie,' he said.

If your answers satisfy the two terrifying angels, the grave would expand and be filled with beautiful light and smells. 'They'd spend their time in comfort until Judgement Day,' said the maulvi as the old man next to me at the mosque began to weep. Then the maulvi told us what would happen to the sinners. It was the most frightening thing I had heard. 'Their graves contract, and their ribs are crushed into each other. They are held and punished in a place called *Barzakh* at the lowest levels of the earth, a precursor to hell.' I had heard about Barzakh, a place where the fire of one's sins would burn them until the end of time. It was said on Judgement

Day, Allah converts time into a little goat, sacrifices it and takes stock of everyone's deeds.

But the maulvi kept going on about sinners. 'Hundreds of lizards and snakes will cover them in their graves and bite them, causing them immense pain.' The thought of lizards crawling over my body in a small, dark grave horrified me. I came home and asked Ammi to teach me the verses to read during namaz. I didn't know Urdu or Arabic, and she gave me a book that had all the verses in Hindi. I memorized the whole book in a day.

I prayed every day, but my worldly fears persisted. Whenever I passed Railway Road, I thought about the man who had been gunned down on his morning walk. *Will my father be shot at while returning from university? Does he look too Muslim?* I thought. As the coverage of the Gujarat riots subsided, things returned to normal in Aligarh. Ammi began sending me to get groceries from Hindu mohallas again.

Soon, I began to assert my Muslim identity at school. I began arguing with anyone who said anything derogatory about Muslims. At lunchtime, Natiq would arrange for me to debate senior Hindu boys, who said that Islam was the root of all evil. 'Muslims are responsible for their own plight. The Hindus have been the real victims for centuries,' they'd say. We'd always end recess telling each other that 'debate was critical to learning' while thinking of our opponents as idiots. Soon I earned a reputation for being a radical Muslim from Upar Kot, a closet jihadi and troublemaker.

Apart from debates, I was also into proving how fearless I was of authorities. I'd also do anything to win bets. I'd walk on the railing of staircases and jump down five stairs in a single bound. I would attack the class monitor's nose with a Tazo. I'd bunk classes, take a stroll around the staffroom, and if a teacher caught me, I'd lie my way out of punishment. If a boy wanted a girl's landline number, I'd go into her class during recess, take her diary from her bag, copy her number from the personal information page and give it to the boy. I would raise students' demands with teachers, even asking a very strict sports teacher to let us play cricket and not football.

One day, however, my bravado backfired. That unfortunate bet was placed by Natiq. It came up when we were questioning the school rule of wishing our teachers a good morning and afternoon. 'This is the way of the Christians. If we are true Muslims, we should wish teachers *As-Salam-Alaikum* instead of good morning.' I was blown away by Natiq's wisdom. 'Somebody should have the guts to say that to D'Souza,' he said.

Father Dennis D'Souza was the school principal, known for beating the shit out of boys and girls alike. We called him Dennis the Menace, and even the bravest shivered at the mere mention of his name. 'If you can greet him with As-Salam-Alaikum, you're the bravest boy in school.' Pride mixed with righteousness – what a heady cocktail. I was sold!

Same day near the end of recess, I waited on the porch outside the principal's office. This was usually when he came out to address the short assembly that happened after the lunch break. As soon as the peon rang the recess assembly bell, the short, bald and fair-skinned menace came out in trademark white cassock and black-rimmed spectacles. 'As-Salam-Alaikum, Father,' I said and began to run away.

'What? *What* did you say?'

I turned back for a second and said, 'As-Salam-Alaikum, Father. I mean, good morning, Father.' Before he could react, I ran away and got lost in the sea of kids in the playground. Natiq later told me that Dennis the Menace stood still in shock for a few seconds.

A few minutes later, in the assembly, like everyone else, I repeated our prayer thrice, 'O God, bless me and my food.' Once the assembly was done, I began moving towards my class in a queue. But like a lizard waiting for a bug near a lightbulb, Father D'Souza was waiting for me at the bottom of the staircase leading to my class. With incredible speed, one hand shot out and grabbed me by the collar and holding my long brown hair with his other hand, he dragged me out of the queue. If I hadn't been so terrified, I would have complimented him on his phenomenal strength. For the next five minutes, he kept slapping me as hard as he could until my face was red with the imprint of his fingers.

The other kids gawked at this scene in complete silence; one of my classmates looked at me with tears in her eyes. Even after this public humiliation, I summoned all my courage to ask, 'Father, why?' He continued to slap me.

'You were laughing in the assembly like a ruffian, weren't you?' I was not but both of us *knew* what I was being punished for. He could at least have been truthful! When somebody was beaten by Dennis the Menace, the news travelled through the school like wildfire. The respect that I had earned over the years dissipated in seconds, and I was now a notorious kid.

This incident didn't stop me from being the face of Muslim assertiveness at St Fidelis. A few months later, a cartoon strip in *The Hindu*'s *Young World* supplement featured Prophet Mohammed, though in a respectful way. However, many Indian Muslims objected as depicting the Prophet Mohammed is believed to be against Islamic traditions. 'It is banned because it might promote idol worship among Muslims, and there is no bigger sin,' Sayema had told me. *The Hindu* later issued an apology. But the cartoon strip was still pinned on to the school noticeboard, continuously and aggressively hurting my religious sentiments.

I didn't dare take this issue up with Father D'Souza and invite another beating. So, I went to the office of the much gentler Father Joseph, the school's vice-principal. I had expected him to refuse my demand, and I looked forward to proving to other kids how

Muslims were systematically oppressed under Father D'Souza's dispensation. But to my surprise, Father Joseph promptly ordered the peon to remove the strip. It was a win, and I was a Muslim hero.

The next year, my battles with the school administration were less successful. The school choir that I was a part of had to perform a series of songs at our annual function. We were singing a patriotic song, a *bhajan* and a rendition of the truly terrible Vengaboys song '*Shalala Lala*'. As a fan of Enrique Iglesias and the Backstreet Boys, I hated the Vengaboys and anyone who listened to Vengaboys. But here we were, rehearsing to perform this vulgar song in the holy month of Ramzan. For this performance, we were also being asked to buy our own costumes. *The nail in the coffin?* We were to dance as we sang. The prospect of dancing to this ridiculous song in ridiculous costumes gave me sleepless nights.

The other Muslim boys in my group didn't seem that worried. Some of them (God forbid) even liked the Vengaboys. Some were concerned about performing but none of them had the guts to take it up with our music teacher. I had never fasted in my life, but to save myself the shame of dancing, I decided to play the religion card. As the leader of the Muslim singers, I took 'our' case to the teacher.

'Ma'am, we won't be able to sing and dance during Ramzan.'

'Hmm. Is this because you must spend on the costumes?' she asked.

'No, ma'am. It's about our faith. We can't dance while fasting,' I said confidently.

She looked worried. We were upsetting her plans at the last moment. 'Okay, will you wait here?' she said and left the room.

After some time, she returned. 'Father D'Souza wants to meet you in his room.'

I nearly shat my pants. I had never imagined that Dennis the Menace would get involved. Shivering with fear, I walked along with the music teacher to the principal's office. I wanted the earth to swallow me, and I began reciting the *durud*. 'You are in the right and you shouldn't back down,' I muttered to myself. It had been a year since the As-Salam-Alaikum incident, and perhaps there was a chance he might have forgotten my face.

He hadn't. When I entered the room, his eyes glowed with recognition. I turned my gaze to the files on his desk. 'What is your problem with the song?' he asked me in a surprisingly calm and friendly tone.

Trembling like an old railway bridge on the passing of a train underneath, I explained to him how dancing during Ramzan was prohibited. After I was finished, the friendliness was gone; I could see him trying to control his anger and curling his fists. Then he asked me, again, in a calm voice, 'You say it is against your religion. Do you follow each and everything that is written in your religion?'

'Yes, Father, I do,' I answered without thinking.

'Oh, you little ruffian! I will teach you how religious you are!' he shouted and tried to grab me, but the desk between us was too wide. I stepped back and stared at the music teacher with pleading eyes. Dennis looked so angry that I thought he'd slam my head on the desk. He was now screaming at the top of his voice while trying to grab my hair.

The music teacher was shocked by Father's sudden outburst. She stepped between us and said, 'Father, let him go! I will make him understand!'

'No! I want to talk to his parents! Tell them that if he doesn't perform, they can pick up his transfer certificate and get out of our school. If not, I will rusticate him.'

I had never imagined my little rebellion would put me in danger of being kicked out of school. Before I could say anything else, the teacher dragged me out of the office. By now, though I was ready to dance to every Vengaboys song there was, I persisted.

'Ma'am, it's just "*Shalala Lala*" I want to avoid. I am not good at dancing,' I said softly.

'So, you and the other boys will sing another song if you don't have to dance to it?'

I nodded. I later told the other boys in the choir about how I faced Dennis the Menace and got us out of dancing. For months, these boys would narrate my story to others who didn't believe that anyone could stand up to Dennis. By now, I was addicted to fame. For the next two years, I kept arguing with teachers and fighting with them over Islam. I was obsessed with flirting with danger.

A year later, when I was in the seventh standard, there was a discussion in my classroom. During our English class, we had to speak about our role models. While other kids spoke about Mother Teresa and Mahatma Gandhi, I spoke about Shah Rukh Khan.

'Why do you like him?' the teacher asked me.

'I like his acting, films and sense of humour,' I said.

'That is fine, but why do you really like him?' she probed again, and I gave her another answer that I don't remember. 'Now tell me the real reason you like him?' she asked me again.

I could tell that she was baiting me; I was going to give her what she wanted. 'I like him because he is Muslim,' I answered. The class went silent.

'So, you would support anyone if they were Muslim?'

'Yes, I would,' I answered.

'The attackers on 9/11 were Muslim. Do you support them too?'

I hadn't anticipated this question, but I replied without hesitation. 'I would support everyone in the world if they were Muslim.' There was pin-drop silence in the class.

'Then you are a supporter of terrorism. It is people like you who bring a bad name to your community,' she screamed.

'America also kills people across the world,' I replied. In less than a minute, the discussion had moved from a Bollywood heartthrob to the investigation of the 11 September attacks.

'Do you know how many Indians were killed in the attack? If you support terrorism, I will take it up with Father D'Souza,' she said.

I nearly had a heart attack. I softened my stance and said, 'Ma'am, you asked me why I liked Shah Rukh Khan, and I answered truthfully. If it is wrong to like him because he is Muslim, I am sorry.'

This trick worked. 'Meet me after the class,' she said and the tension in the classroom subsided. After the class, she gave me a long, moral lecture on how religious fundamentalism is bad. And it was now clear to many of my Hindu classmates that I was a radical Muslim.

∽

By 2002, America had invaded Afghanistan, but Osama Bin Laden had escaped. He had become a mythical figure, much like someone who would fake his death and return decades later to fulfil his destiny.

At the end of the academic year, I was busy preparing for the Moral Science exam. One of the easiest subjects to score in, it taught us ways to live in a society, to be just and humane towards others. The questions in a Moral Science test would present hypothetical situations and test our moral beliefs in essay-like answers. Having won many creative writing competitions, it was easy for me to write impromptu essays and score well.

This time, however, the exam was on a day I was angry about an incident that had taken place during America's war against Iraq, the second instalment of Bush's war against terror. One of the questions was the one which had got me into trouble with my English teacher: 'Who is your idol and why?' By now, I knew better than to write Shah Rukh Khan and was confused between the two other contenders for the winning answer.

The first option was Mother Teresa. I had visited the Aligarh branch of her organization, the Missionaries of Charity and was mighty impressed by what she had done for the poor and the disabled. But everybody else had gone there too and were likely to write about her. So I went with the other option – Osama Bin Laden.

I remember feeling a tinge of uneasiness and a bit of fear when I wrote the sentence: 'My idol is Osama Bin Laden.' *But shouldn't I write what I really think? Isn't this what exams are for?* I thought and kept writing as the exam clock kept ticking. It was a very long essay praising the virtues of the world's most wanted man. I still remember the primary argument of my essay: I had compared Laden to the Buddha. It went something like this:

'Bad people are selfish and don't think about others. Good people sacrifice their pleasures for others' welfare, like Lord Buddha. He left his kingdom and went to live like a poor man to find himself. Similarly, Osama Bin Laden was born into one of the richest families in Saudi Arabia. He could have comfortably lived in air-conditioned rooms, driven BMWs and married beautiful women.

'But instead, he hid in a desert, his kidneys failing, in a place where he and his family faced enormous, constant threats to their lives. When he could have had the best doctors for his ailment, he probably now sits in a cave where there are no toilets. Can he, who left all these to fight for the weak, be a bad person? Can't we celebrate his dedication and sacrificial spirit?'

After the exam, I told my friends about the subject of my essay.

'This time, I think you'll *finally* be thrown out of school,' said Shamlan.

A few days later, my class teacher, Sara Job, called me to her room. 'Zeyad, your essay had caused a storm in the staff room,' she said. 'Some teachers wanted to take it to the principal and have you rusticated. If I had not defended you, you would be in a lot of trouble right now.'

My mind began racing. *They* had asked *me* who my idol was! If my answer was so wrong, why had she given me good marks in the exam? Had they expected me to lie? However, I didn't say any of this to her – I knew she cared for me.

'Zeyad, I know you will go far, but you should learn to keep your opinions to yourself. It can get you into trouble someday,' she told me, looking into my eyes. 'Can you promise me that you won't do such a thing again – at least until you are a student at this school? Can you promise me that you will be a good boy from now on?'

I looked down at my shoes, I felt guilty for the trouble I had caused her. 'Yes, Ma'am. I promise,' I said. Unlike the ones I made to Ammi, I kept this one.

With time, my fascination for Osama Bin Laden started to fade. It was replaced by a Muslim religious organization named the Tablighi Jamaat – where I'd meet Shadab.

# 9

# ALLAH MIYAN KI POLICE

IN 1926, A religious scholar from the Nizamuddin area in Delhi, Maulana Muhammad Ilyas, went on his second pilgrimage to Mecca. On his way, Ilyas had an idea – to set up a religious movement in line with the Prophet Muhammad's teachings to reform society through personal spiritual renewal. Towards this purpose, he founded an organization that later came to be known as the Tablighi Jamaat.

Over the next seventy-five years, it would grow to become one of the world's largest religious movements – with a presence in over 150 countries, over 300 million followers, most of whom lived in South Asia. As it was my destiny, at the age of thirteen, I became one of them.

On a winter afternoon in 2002, as I tried to rush home after offering the Asr prayers, a boy stood near the shoe stand. 'Brother, can you please wait in the sanctum for a talk on Islam?' he asked so politely that I couldn't refuse. It's always difficult for a Muslim to say no to religious discussions. A few minutes later, I sat cross-legged in a congregation of young, idealist boys on a mission to lure the Muslims of Upar Kot towards Allah's path. Their leader,

Ghiyas, was a short, fair-skinned young man with a sincere smile that reminded one of Rishi Kapoor. 'Us, Muslims can't change the world unless we change ourselves,' he said, radiating a sense of comfort and peace. And thus, the desire to somehow change this terribly broken world began to form inside me.

The idea of God is a powerful one: it offers one a purpose in their lives, a succour for grief, someone unblemished to look up to, and an answer to the eternal question: what happens to us after we die? It also gives us something we desperately need to cope with the madness around us – hope. The hope for divine justice is often the ultimate relief for the weak and the destitute. Wouldn't the structures we hold in high regard crumble if someone told the weak there is no justice in this world or the afterlife?

In all the tales of survivors at sea, it's always the hopeful who swim across mercurial waters to reach an island. One film that used to play on Star Movies was *Titanic*, the only film with a sex scene I'd watched with my parents. Overwhelmed by the tragic love between Rose and Jack, they were strangely okay with me seeing their lovemaking endeavours in a pricey car that would soon be at the bottom of the ocean. But how would the film have unfolded if Jack had told Rose, 'Look, darling, the *Titanic* would sink, and we'll certainly die a painful death, so let's have sex anyway.' Would my parents have allowed me to watch it then?

We, the boys of the Tablighi Jamaat, were motivated by a higher calling than sex. Our purpose was *daawat*, the invitation to participate in preaching missions to promote Islam and its way of life. The Jamaatis divided themselves into groups of ten, men and boys, who ate, slept, washed, prayed, travelled and spread the word of Islam together. In many South Asian mosques, they would engage in 'patrolling' their neighbourhoods to entice other men to the mosques. In Aligarh, it earned them a humorous sobriquet – Allah Miyan ki Police.

Within no time, I became an active member of this virtuous force. Like army recruits driven by a hope of victory, we'd assemble every day after the night prayers, read interpretations from the Quran and Hadith and devise ways to bring 'wayward youth' into our fold. I began to avoid fighting with Saad and swearing at him (which he most likely deserved). The Jamaat gave me a sense of camaraderie, community and purpose. Pious and ethical when together, we were Allah's soldiers fighting to save whatever little good remained in the world.

'It doesn't matter if you are a king or a servant, we're recognized by how we treat others. Don't you see Muslims of all classes praying shoulder to shoulder?' Ghiyas Bhai said. I now thought of the neighbourhood kids, whom I once looked down upon, as my brothers. 'It is as tough for a rich person to enter heaven as it is for a camel to pass through the eye of a needle,' said Ghiyas. This brought me utter joy. Somewhere, the poor *actually* had a better chance!

Each of us who gathered at the mosque was an outsider in our respective circles – quiet, introverted boys driven by idealism and a distrust of the world. But one person didn't fall in this category: Shadab, the tallest, thinnest, politest and funniest among us.

Shadab lived in Naaiwali Gali, the lane of the barbers, but he wasn't a barber. Soon after reaching his teens, he worked as a shopkeeper in Kanwari Ganj selling *bura-batasha,* cheap sugar candies that Hindus and Muslims considered a devotional offering and distributed to the poor. Like a railway clerk on his way for his prayers, he'd always wear a light shirt and formal pants along with a woven skullcap. A hard-working boy who dropped out of school to support his family, he'd learn the ways of Aligarh fast. Every day, he'd hear comments from neighbouring Hindu shopkeepers calling him a *katua*, a jihadi or a *mullah*.

Everyone in the Jamaat loved Shadab because of his wry sense of humour. He would always have a mischievous smile on his face. Like a part-time clown finding his audience everywhere, he'd laugh and make others laugh. He'd crack jokes in the mosque and in the middle of religious discussions, much to the irritation of Ghiyas Bhai. 'Is it a sin to ask a girl for his number you like?' he'd ask. Once, Ghiyas was teaching us about the things which might end the validity of the wudhu, and Shadab asked a cheeky question about masturbation. 'Does the wudhu end even if one doesn't ejaculate?' he asked. 'Yes, impure thoughts can take away the sanctity of the ablution,' Ghiyas Bhai said sternly, not at all pleased.

Shadab would bring a human element into the working of a rigid Jamaat. He offered his namaz at right times, fasted for Ramzan, and was more considerate than others. If an elder boy tried to bully a younger one, Shadab would intervene. To newbies like me, he'd give effective insider tips. 'Tell them about the many thousand years they'll live in hell for skipping a namaz. Always works.'

Learning quickly from Ghiyas and Shadab, I became a reliable preacher. The schedule of the Jamaat became my schedule. On Thursdays, after Asr prayers, we'd go for our 'patrols' and take our learnings to others.

When we, the Jamaatis, walked on the street, people disappeared into thin air. When the young and older men saw the skull-capped boys standing outside their homes, they'd run out the backdoor or have their mothers lie and say they were out buying groceries. 'Oh, but I just saw him come home,' Shadab would reply. Like a reluctant child being taken to a dentist, a half-asleep middle-aged man would come out and listen to our sermon at the door. A true Muslim mostly doesn't interject when quoted a verse from the Quran. 'When somebody comes close, he comes beneath the shadow of Allah's benevolence. Their hearts turn softer,' Ghiyas Bhai taught us.

But once in a while, some men would respond in harsh words. 'Don't reply in their language. Just pass Allah's message on and pray for them,' said Ghiyas Bhai. He often talked of the 'hardness of the heart' and said, 'As people inundate their lives with greed, material desires, and sins, their heart turns hard. The people who live lightly and take everything in their stride are loved by Allah.'

But our strides wouldn't go everywhere. We wouldn't venture into the territories of other mosques, and the Shia Mosque in Tantan Para. Like every Shia mosque, this was said to be haunted by djinns. 'If somebody tries to cut it down, they will die,' children would say. If ever we had to go through neighbourhoods that had mixed populations of Hindus and Muslims, the Hindus would stare at us like we were made of dangerous combustible material.

On our patrols, we visited the homes of those who were somewhere in the middle: neither were they very religious, nor were they complete heathens. They were men who once offered prayers regularly but had now grown lazy; boys who were once a part of Tablighi Jamaat but had succumbed to the ways of the material world. 'If we change even one person from a family, we help the entire family,' Ghiyas Bhai declared.

Other times, we'd just aimlessly wander about, visit homes randomly, ring the doorbell and ask the men to join us outside for a discussion. Most times, it worked. After consistent visits to somebody's home and providing them with a stable spiritual support system, they'd start praying regularly. Some even joined the Jamaat.

Once a month, we'd attend an *isthma,* a congregation of all Tablighi Jamaats in Upar Kot. I'd observed that there were three levels of Jamaatis. The first were those who went for a three-day Jamaat at another mosque in their town or outside it. Above them were the ones who had done a *chilla*, a forty-day religious trip outside their town. At the top were the people who devoted four months of their lives to the Jamaat.

The way Jamaatis convinced people to devote this much time to Islam was an exercise par excellence. After the Asr prayer, a young boy would stand up in the mosque and say, 'We will now talk about Allah's message. Please stay back.' Many did, and then a speaker would give a speech filled with Quranic verses about a Muslim's purpose in life and how the material world keeps us away from it.

When the audience was fully engrossed, the speaker would emphasize 'the duty of taking the message of Islam to those who have been deprived of it'. Pre-empting a variety of excuses – work, study, family – that audience members might bring up, he would say, 'Work won't end until you die. Allah wants to test whether we can walk on his path while fulfilling our worldly duties. Can't you give three/forty/one hundred and twenty days to Allah's way?'

Absolutely nobody in the audience would say yes at first. Then a local Jamaati boy with a pen and paper would begin writing names. 'It's as tough for us as it is for you, but we still do it, don't we?' the speaker would say, trying a different tack. A local boy among us would give his name. 'Anyone else? You are allowed to cancel, but surely you have some willingness to find time for Allah's way?' The option to cancel would result in some more hands rising up. 'I can go for three days,' one person would say.

That was it, one fish had been hooked! Once you got one name, it was easier to reel in the person's friends. Pretty soon, the list would have ten names.

'Now who wants to go for a chilla?' the speaker would ask. One or two people would give their names, and their friends would admiringly pat them on the back. It was time for the last option. 'And who wants to go for four months?' Not really expecting a reply, he'd wait for 30 seconds and then ask the boy to close the register.

At this time, I would focus on the intricate patterns of prayer mats like I was staring into the abyss of my consciousness. If someone asked me, I would talk about a test or an exam. If I was asked to join them because it was a holiday, I would tell them that my father didn't want me to go. They'd look disappointed and let me go. But I was telling the truth. While Badi Ammi was extremely happy that I was part of the Jamaat, Papa wasn't. 'These Jamaatis will take my kid's mind off his studies by talking about the afterlife. I have seen it with many other boys,' he'd tell Ammi and Badi Ammi.

One evening, I returned home after a lecture where the speaker said that Prophet Muhammad had a beard and that every Muslim should do the same. I thought Papa would be happy about this, but he wasn't. 'Do you know what happens to Muslim boys with a beard? Not only will you not get a job, but the cops will also pick you up on the slightest suspicion.' After the cops had randomly arrested many SIMI boys, he was worried that I would pay the price for looking traditionally Muslim. 'You should stop hanging around these Jamaati boys,' he'd tell me. I listened to him but didn't agree. In hindsight, it was the beginning of the end of our friendship.

Apart from the friction between father and son, this was also an ideological difference between the two kinds of Muslims that inhabit India. I was the one escaping from the world, seeking sanctuary inside the mosque, a boy for whom nothing mattered except his religious identity. Anyone, including my own father, who disagreed, was a sinner and an obstacle to a larger goal. *He is a selfish person who cares only for himself and not for the community. These are the Muslims who make us weak*, I thought.

Papa, on the other hand, was the older man who had seen many hardships while growing up and knew what it meant to be an Indian Muslim in the real world. He knew that ideals don't survive long in the face of necessity – a concerned father who wanted his son to be a normal college-going kid, and not a religious preacher. Seeing TV news and hearing things from people in the university, he was afraid for his younger son, his friend. 'Do you know what's happening to boys who were picked up? Everybody says things, but nobody comes to help them once they are in jail,' he told me.

I was the fundamentalist and he the pragmatist, both struggling with their ideas of what it takes for a Muslim to survive in a fast-changing world. But instead of coming to a middle ground, we began growing apart. My idea of Papa was the man who would side with the 'right thing' against all odds. When that idea collapsed in my mind, I began to lose respect for him. The love, or admiration, that had raised him to an idol, came crashing down. He was just a mortal who couldn't understand that the world meant nothing and that the afterlife meant everything. 'There are prices to be paid while following the right path,' I heard them say at the mosque every day.

As I read more deeply about Islam, I became more sensitive towards the misery of the poor of Aligarh. I noticed the beggars at Kathpula, Aligarh's oldest bridge, once made of wood but now a mere heartless concrete structure. It was the bridge over which Papa had cycled to the university as a student and where my Phuppa had died of a heart attack. Kathpula also marked the border between the old town and Civil Lines, the alien place where most rich people lived.

On Kathpula, there would be a crippled man, a woman holding an infant under a green dupatta, a boy trying to sell you agarbattis – all asking for your alms. A three-year-old kid would wrap himself

around your leg until you paid him. A man would nearly block
your path and show you his festering wounds.

I got only Rs 20 every day as pocket money, which I used to pay
for my daily rickshaw rides. I sometimes gave the beggars a few
coins, but I knew that was nothing. However much I, as a young
Jamaati, wanted to save the poor, I'd still fail. 'If we can't help the
poor with our money, we should pray for their afterlife. They will
have it better than us there,' Ghiyas Bhai would say. But it still
sounded unfair to me.

Much to my father's chagrin, I kept attending the discussions
at the mosque and the patrols. In fact, I got better at it. Using
Shadab's tips, I found out what really worked – polite requests to
join us in for prayers. I would, of course, scare my audience too, by
emphasizing the 'torment of the grave' and the duration of hellfire
for skipping namaz. It almost always ended any resistance I faced.

Soon, Ghiyas Bhai began to depend on me. Like a teacher's
pet trying to score points with his schoolmaster, I began leading
patrols when the older boys had gone for a religious trip; on
occasion, I even led the religious discussions after the Asr prayers.

The first time I stood up on the podium at the mosque, it gave
me a feeling of power like never before. I could see people listening
to me with respect in their eyes. In school, I was seen as a ruffian
who was alienated for who he was, but here at the mosque, I was
seen as a role model to be emulated. Before this group of religious
preachers and friends, I had never felt so sure and content about
myself. After I'd given speeches from the dais of the mosque, boys
would congratulate me. 'It's more important to try and fail, than
being afraid of failure,' Ghiyas Bhai once told me. I kept trying
and got better at preaching with every passing day.

I became so enamoured by this role that I hated going home.
Wasn't the mosque also my home? On the days when there were
no religious discussions, I'd feel purposeless and sinful. If I miss

a prayer, the guilt of missing it would keep playing in my head like an irritating tune that got stuck in the mind. Slowly but surely, religion had become the centre of my universe. Everything else, the material world, was just background noise.

∽

But if Allah was working his miracles over time on me, so was Shaitan.

In Islam, Shaitan is a djinn named Azazel/Iblis, who was once Allah's most obedient follower. He was so pious he was promoted to the rank of angel. When Allah created Adam from clay,[1] he asked everyone to bow before his new creation. Everyone prostrated, except Shaitan.[2] He had a disdain for humanity, he thought man was corrupt and flawed.[3] Allah then breathed life into the clay, and thus Adam and Eve came into being.[4]

Azazel scorned in his pride, then tempted Adam and Eve to eat the apple, the forbidden fruit. 'Your Lord has forbidden this tree to you only to prevent you from becoming angels or immortals,' he kept whispering to them, luring Adam and Eve to eat the fruit.[5] Allah was angry. 'Did I not forbid you from that tree and did I not tell you that Satan is your sworn enemy?' he called out.[6] Everyone knows how that story ended for both Adam and Eve.[7]

After that, Shaitan turned into a rebel, walking the earth in many forms. Even now, he lies in wait for us, takes advantage of human selfishness and tempts people to take the wrong path to finally prove his point to Allah.

Therefore, it was most likely Shaitan, who at the height of my religiousness, whispered into my ear and pointed me towards FashionTV, a channel which broadcasted shows of models walking the ramp in revealing outfits 24x7. And then a friend at school (bless him) told me about 'Midnight Hot', a programme where one could see (God forbid) a woman's bare breasts. I knew it was a sin, but I would still stay awake till midnight to watch the show every night. This was also when Papa came home and so, like a vigilant traffic cop, I'd always keep one finger on the remote control.

But that was not the only sin I was committing. I also listened to music, which is forbidden by some interpretations of Islam, and very strictly by the Tablighi Jamaat. 'Those who listen to music will have lead poured into their ears in the afterlife,' was a very common saying.

I was lured to this sin when Sayema outgrew listening to music on her tape recorder. Earlier, we'd listen to songs from Hindi movies, such as *Phir Teri Kahani Yaad Aayi*, *Tamanna*, *Fareb*, and *Barsaat*, and Urdu ghazals together. But as her interest faded, music became my next big obsession. The first music cassette I bought was *Aks* by Lucky Ali, a singer Shamlan worshipped. Soon, I clutched the tape recorder with my not-so-tiny hands. That was the year when *Kal Ho Naa Ho* was released and 'It's the Time to Disco' became the go-to dance song in school annual day functions.

I spent my days listening to cassettes and nights tuning to radio stations of Delhi, which my super-cool AIWA stereo was able to catch in Aligarh. A Jamaati boy at heart, I couldn't resist Bollywood and its music.

I now began to buy Bollywood and pop albums, and get my own mixtapes done at a shop in Delhi Gate. Despite the fact he would charge me extra for 'rarely requested' songs for the mixtapes, the cassette shopkeeper wasn't ever pleased to see me as I'd make the strangest requests: 'When will *Bombay Boys* be released?' 'Can I pay to exchange my old cassette of *Rehna Hain Tere Dil Mein* for the new one with additional songs?' 'By any chance, do you have the new album by Strings or Jal?' He'd look at me with disapproval as most people just wanted easy-to-get popular numbers from *Gadar: Ek Prem Katha* or *Hum Tumhare Hain Sanam*.

I would buy cassettes of all films featuring Shah Rukh Khan. Till this time, my fascination with Shah Rukh Khan had continued. Even the Hindu boys from Kanwari Ganj loved SRK and his films. Even though my eyesight was perfect, I bought zero-power glasses from the roadside to wear them to class like Raj Aryan's character in *Mohabbatein*. Then I would get Red Tape shoes and a sweater to wrap around my shoulders. I even bought a dialogue cassette of *Mohabbatein* and memorized the dialogues. When my friends fell in love, I would quote, '*Mohabbat mein shartein nahi hoti. Toh afsos bhi nahi hona chahiye.*'

Though SRK was a Muslim who mostly played Hindu characters like Raj, Rahul and Vijay, he was nevertheless adored by both Muslims and Hindus; not condemned as an impostor hiding his nefarious Islamic designs. In the newly liberalized India, Shah Rukh Khan was a symbol that a middle-class Muslim boy from Delhi could dream of, struggle, marry the girl of his dreams and go on to rule an elitist place like Bollywood. Almost every boy and girl my age loved him. Dreams were the flavour of the time and breaking boundaries came with the package.

❧

Destiny is like a devoted postman; it will eventually locate you and deliver the message that is meant for you, be it rain or shine.

In 2002, Sayema graduated from college and gave several entrance tests at AMU, one of which was for a masters in mass communication. It fell on my young shoulders to prepare her for the admission test. A part of her preparations was an essay-style question on the recent Gujarat riots. I, and every Muslim I knew, was traumatized by seeing the dastardly images of violence. But like good Muslims must in India, we mostly kept it inside, lest our trauma became a circus for the untraumatized. What I told Sayema wasn't what I felt, but merely a compilation of what other writers or editorials in *The Hindu* had said. Like a shadow that must remain a shadow, my voice as a Muslim was non-existent.

Catapulted by her dreams, Sayema was driven and motivated. She qualified for the exam and successfully finished the course. But like destiny had written in its little secret notepad, this gave me a new goal in life. I wanted to be a journalist – somebody who would change people's perceptions of Muslims and write about people that nobody wrote about. Helping my older sister prepare was the catalyst that I needed.

One lazy evening, I came home from school and saw two young men in our drawing room, eating biscuits. 'Who the hell are they?' I asked Sayema. 'They're the sons of a distant cousin of Ammi's from Agra,' she replied. I had never even heard of their existence. 'They are here to fix my marriage to the younger brother. He is a civil engineer working in a reputed firm in Saudi Arabia.'

For Indian parents, their children's marriage is their life's mission. It's the most important event that can ever happen to someone, especially a woman, who has been encouraged to think about her wedding since she learnt to speak. 'My daughter will be the most beautiful bride ever,' Aligarh parents will say about their four-year-old. It's as if a person is born, raised, and lives solely for the purpose of being married, and then making it work. Anyone who deviates from this course is either a tragic figure or a lunatic.

For Papa, Sayema was Allah's gift, the one he raised like a princess. If he had his way, he'd have never let her go. But eventually, tradition and Ammi prevailed. He made a few phone calls to friends in Saudi Arabia, everyone said good things about the boy. But he still was apprehensive.

A common thread that ran through everyone in Farsh Manzil, especially our family, was that all of us were pessimists. We'd expect doomsday scenarios in everything. Even if something good was happening, we'd wait for something bad to happen, ruining even our happier moments in anticipation of future sadness. We'd always be waiting for incoming tragedies. Almost all our versions said that the world was going to eat us and leave us for dead. That we are good, but not good enough.

This trait wasn't just limited to our house. Almost everyone in Muslim neighbourhoods, even the successful ones, lived in anticipation of the bad times that were always around the corner. Even our hopes and dreams were suffocated by the ghetto, aspirations nipped in the bud. The ones who dared to aspire to more were considered mad.

'I will do whatever you want,' Sayema said, conveniently putting the burden on Papa. For the next few days, he spent sleepless nights and had long conversations with Ammi. Eventually, he gave his approval and a date for the wedding was fixed.

The day before Sayema's wedding in 2003, everyone was celebrating in Farsh Manzil. Women dressed up in saris and salwar suits sang traditional songs, the beat of *damru* filled our main hall, smiles lit up the evening. But tragedy struck soon. Chotti Ammi, my father's elder sister, my aunt, had passed away. Destiny, this time an envious neighbour, had plans to steal our joy.

Chotti Ammi, whose real name was Qamarunnissa and who was very excited for Sayema's wedding, had suffered a heart attack a day before. As the news of her death reached Farsh Manzil, like the anti-climactic scene in a family drama, the scenes of songs and celebration turned to tears. Everyone asked if the wedding would be postponed. But it was too late. The preparations were already in place. 'The wedding will take place as planned,' Papa said amid murmurs from the family.

On one of the strangest mornings of his life, Papa watched the coffin of a beloved sister be lowered to a grave, and a few hours later, he stoically received guests at Sayema's wedding. I don't know how he did it, but he did. I was wondering what he would be thinking about as he went into the wedding: was he thinking of him and his sister, now dead, growing up together?

From there on, Sayema's marriage ceremony went smoothly. Her wedding film was made with songs like 'Mubarak Ho Tumko Ye Shaadi Tumhari' and 'Babul Ki Duaen Leti Ja'. Bollywood was everywhere.

Meanwhile, I had continued spending my time with the Jamaat. We'd meet new people, pour our hearts out and welcome them as brothers. Like friends after a high school farewell, some stayed, some went away, lured by Shaitan.

Talking of demonic influences, I had continued to listen to music, but I was betraying cassettes for compact discs with hundreds of MP3 music files. They were more convenient. The tape reel wouldn't get caught. Also, I wouldn't need to glue broken tapes and tolerate strange sounds when the glued-over portion played between songs. As Ammi was insistent on freeing up space, I packed all my cassettes into cartons and moved them into the old storeroom. They are still probably there.

When I would become a pro at downloading music, I'd betray Bollywood music for Pakistani rock and Western music. Songs that I downloaded were tagged as 'Zed's Collection' and later found space in thousands of smartphones in Aligarh. This was the point I found that music helped me concentrate on my tasks. Now I'd only study with music in the background. I would listen to music on my Walkman or my PC as I walked, worked or shat – an obsession I would never be able to outgrow.

Everything seemed better if you added background music to it. These songs were playing in my head even during religious patrols where I taught others to be good Muslims.

# 10

# FURY

ONE OF THE most painful days of my life began like any other. I woke up at 5.45 a.m., brushed my teeth as harshly as I could, waited for Ammi to make me a fried egg, toast and tea, and stood in front of the mirror for ten minutes combing my hair. I looked like a rag on bad hair days but pretty good when the hair remained in shape.

Then I slowly walked to Jama Masjid to catch Route No. 4, the coolest school bus in St Fidelis School. It ferried the 'wild' children from Sheher – Muslims from Upar Kot and Hindus from Kanwari Ganj and other places in the old town.

On Route No. 4, childhood innocence mostly prevailed over religion. My best friend on the bus was Ankur who, believe it or not, came from Gudiya Bagh. Every day, he and I would get down together at Delhi Gate and go on to eat samosas in Kanwari Ganj, and the bill was mostly paid by Ankur. Often, we'd throw religiously charged jokes at each other and threaten to raid each other's homes during the next riots. 'Don't come to Farsh during a riot. You'll see a different face of me,' we'd tell each other. Every

Eid, he'd come to my home. On Diwali, I'd go to his home and burst firecrackers in the already polluted air of Aligarh.

The bonhomie in the bus was mostly unbroken except one time, and I was the one to test its resilience. The day before Holi, as the Hindu kids played with colours in the bus, the Muslim students sat on the back seats and judged them. 'If a Muslim plays Holi, the part of the body where the colour lands will be cut off on the Day of Judgement,' Natiq, frustrated by the noise and the ruckus, told me.

*How is Natiq so wise?* I wondered. Suddenly, Kapil, my classmate and friend, ran towards me, took out his water bottle and splashed all the water on my head. Whether I reacted from impulse or hate, I didn't know. But I got up, held his hair, pushed him back and threw him on the bus floor. Everybody went silent. The celebration was over. The next day, we buried the hatchet and were friends again.

I was usually liked by most of the kids on the bus and was, as reported by my secret sources, the crush of at least two girls. The bus took one-and-a-half hours to reach school. When you spend three hours together every day, you are bound to become friends. There was another reason the kids loved me. I was the official DJ of Route No. 4, the only bus which played music.

Every day, I would give the driver one of my music cassettes. I had a decent relationship with him and did him small favours occasionally. That also meant nobody else's musical taste would be considered. 'These are my tapes, and I'll play whatever songs I want,' I'd say if anyone had suggestions. Very few kids my age in Aligarh were allowed to buy their cassettes, and I exploited my independence to the hilt.

One of the three teachers who came along on Route No. 4 had a problem with this arrangement. But whenever she objected, the bus driver insisted that he needed music to not fall asleep while driving. What could she possibly do other than listen to the music with a frown on her face?

When we reached school, I would walk through the dusty playgrounds, reach the staircases painted brown and white to match our uniforms and climb to my class on the third floor. I sat on the last bench where I could easily gossip with my friends as the teacher taught the kids in the front row. My image in class was friendlier than Shamlan's but less friendly than my other friends, Aamir Hasan and Zeeshan.

In these times, it wasn't rare to find teenage boys crying over girls who didn't know they existed. Shamlan was somewhat popular among the girls but was mostly let down by his own overconfidence. Whenever he liked a girl, he'd become sure that the girl liked him back. In some time, he'd blame the girl for being a coward for not coming to *him* to 'propose'.

'I can feel it; she likes me but is too afraid to say anything. Have you seen her staring at me?' he'd say.

'Could it possibly be because you stare at her and she stares back because she's wondering what's wrong with you?' I'd say.

'Oh! I don't stare at her first. I only stare at her when she stares at me.'

'Didn't you say the same thing about the other senior you liked?'

'Don't talk about her. That coward couldn't even tell me that she liked me,' he'd reply. The circle would come back to where it was. Though Shamlan was kind of cute, he'd only fall for the pretty, uptight girls. He always had a thing for seniors.

My 'girlfriend' was a year junior to us. She was pretty with her hazel eyes and had been the reason for many physical fights among boys of her class. As the norm of the day, our 'affair' had started with us staring at each other during lunch break. But unlike Shamlan, I had the guts to talk to her. After that, she'd wait for me at the school tap every day during recess. Both of us would stare at each other for the entire break, smile shyly and roam around in the same area for lunch. If there were only juniors around, we'd even exchange a sentence or two. 'You finished lunch too fast today,' she'd chide me. As our 'love' grew stronger, we started meeting at the water cooler after every other period. To the surprise of our classmates, both of us would make a lot of trips to the water cooler every day.

But our romance really blossomed when we began meeting in the school's Sick Room. I often pretended to fall ill to bunk class and go there. Sometimes, I'd just vanish before the next teacher arrived without asking permission. On other days, I'd roam in the school corridors, pretending to have been sent by a teacher on an 'important task' to the staff room. And since I was a topper, I was able to exploit the 'good boy' image. And she was also like me. When I'd pass her classroom, she'd pretend to be nauseous and ask permission to go to the Sick Room. And then among kids with broken heads, acute diarrhoea and high fever, we'd sit near each other and stare into each other's eyes.

Shamlan's love life, though, wasn't as simple. Every day he'd ask me to go with him on Route No. 2, the bus on which both his current crush and ex-crush travelled. For this, I had to get off at Kathpula and walk two kilometres to my home. Every. Single. Day. But what are friends for? I'd give my life for Shamlan if he'd asked.

The owner of the bus service that ferried the not-so-secular students of St Fidelis was named Secular Travels. The name of the bus services often decided the people of which religion would use it more. To some extent, Hindus had the privilege to name their businesses like Shri Ram Satnam, Maa Vaishno Devi or Parul Travels. Muslim bus owners mostly stuck with names like Golden Arrow, Indian Bus Service, Universal Travels or neutral abbreviations like MS Travels. The name Secular Travels was probably a way to hide the religious identity of the owner.

For our school, Secular Travels had appointed Bablu to extract bus fees from reluctant students. He'd also keep track of discipline issues in the buses, often scolding me for travelling in buses apart from Route No.4. A fair, tall and heavily built man, Bablu would often get smiles from female teachers. But what perhaps diminished his prospects was that he wasn't too bright. He was so simple-minded that a fourteen-year-old boy was able to scam him.

The scam was simple but clever. To collect bus fees from the students, Bablu used to sit in a small cabin outside the principal's office. All the students were issued a card. The front of the card had the student's information. On the back of the card, a table for all twelve months of the year was printed. After receiving the fee for the month, Bablu would stamp the respective square for the month with a seal reading 'Paid'.

The junior boy (let's call him Goat) wanted to save his bus fees, which were a huge Rs 450 per month in 2002. To achieve this, Goat first befriended Bablu and became a regular visitor to his cabin. Whenever Bablu went out, Goat would promise to look after the cabin. Then he'd pick up the stamp and fill out all the months that were due. Goat would then use this money to take his girlfriend out on dates.

Of course, Bablu had another fail-safe: a register listing all the students using the bus. After receiving the fee, he'd put a checkmark in front of the respective student's name. But Goat had noticed that too. So, after stamping his card, he'd open Bablu's register, find his name and put a checkmark in front of it. Goat did this almost every month for nearly two years and was never caught. During this time, he managed to scam Bablu for around Rs 10,000, a huge sum for a seventh-standard kid. As he got confident, he began to charge other students who wanted to save their bus fees for Rs 200. Secular Travels never found out.

Unaware that he was being scammed by someone half his age, Bablu still had the unenviable task of chasing other fee defaulters. 'Please pay by tomorrow or you won't be allowed on the bus,' he'd tell someone almost every day. But everyone knew Bablu was too kind to stop anyone from boarding the bus. So even after repeated reminders, many, like me, used to delay their bus fees as long as they could.

My relationship with Bablu was always cordial. He'd mostly ignore the complaints about me going on other buses, and whenever we'd meet, we'd greet each other politely. If ever there was an issue with discipline in my bus, he'd ask me to handle the kids. I would do it and the kids would listen to me. In Aligarh, everyone needs favours from others at some point.

The exchange of favours has governed human relations since they first settled in communities. It could be anything – assistance from a neighbour in an emergency, borrowing money from a friend, using somebody's expertise to crack a business deal or political support to win an election. This exchange of selfish interests in the guise of selfless goodwill drove my relationship with Bablu.

Until the day he saved my life from a murderous mob and rose to become a hero.

That day, when school got over, I began walking towards Route No. 2 to support Shamlan once again as he tried to mentally manifest his crush coming to propose her feelings. I was one among many children moving in groups or in queues to get out of St Fidelis' iron main gate. Striking our black school shoes on the dusty ground, we were eager to go home. As I reached the bus, I saw Bablu, with a look on his face like a loved one had died. Wearing a dark blue shirt on his muscular body, his eyes as blank as the class blackboard in summer vacations, he was waiting for me.

'Where are you going, Zeyad? Come here,' he called out.

'Bablu Bhai, I will submit my bus fee tomorrow. Let me go today,' I replied.

'It's not about that. There has been a fight in Sheher – somebody has been shot.'

'It's Sheher – someone is shot almost every day.'

'It's different – this one's a Hindu-Muslim issue. You need to go on your own bus.'

'I have some important work, Bablu Bhai. I need to have some notes photocopied for the class tests.'

'Not today. You'll listen to me and board Route No. 4 right now! I will also be on your bus today,' he said firmly. I tried to convince him but to no avail. As sad as a sailor lost at sea, I told Shamlan that I wouldn't be able to go with him.

The mood inside the bus was different today. The bus was as quiet as a mosque in Asr prayers. On the way to Upar Kot, we didn't play any music. 'Not today, Zeyad,' a teacher told me, and I didn't insist. Route No. 4 moved slowly as students sat, unusually silent. When the bus crossed Kathpula, everything seemed fine. Men were going about on their mopeds and bicycles, the shops were open, and schoolkids were returning home on cycle rickshaws.

'See, I told you. Everything is fine,' I said to Bablu Bhai as Natiq and I went up to his seat.

'Just keep sitting,' he replied.

As we passed the Grand Surjit, Aligarh's newest cinema hall, the crowd thinned out a bit, but it was nothing out of the ordinary. Like hands of a clock moving around its predefined orbit, the bus made its usual stops, and students got down and walked home. We moved along, looking outside, as if our hearts were warning us of dangers that lurked in the lanes of Aligarh. When we reached Goolar Road, an area where most of our Hindu bus-mates got off, the bus became half-empty, just like every day.

However, it now seemed clear that something was different. The roads had begun to look a bit too deserted. Men on mopeds and bicycles disappeared. It spooked me. This was not an ordinary day. 'Drive slowly and keep your eyes on the road,' Bablu told the driver.

As our bus moved towards Delhi Gate, less than 500 metres from my home, an eerie quietness had begun to dominate the area. The street was too empty. Everybody was silent and glued to their seats. The air was tense like a lull before an incoming storm. As Bablu stood near the bus door, his brain working rapidly to notice any signs of trouble, the two women teachers kept looking outside.

A few metres before the Delhi Gate crossing, the first unusual thing happened. The parents of the kids from Kanwari Ganj had come to personally escort their children home much before their usual stop. Ankur looked at me and the rest of us, dejected, picked his bag, got down and walked towards his father. A reluctant look of betrayal reigned on his face. Slowly, Ankur and his father moved out of sight. Other Hindu parents also took their kids away and disappeared into the narrow lanes. Now, only a dozen kids and two teachers remained on the bus, all Muslims. The only Hindu that remained was Bablu.

As the bus began to move, a man who had been standing at the stop where Ankur had gotten down, a green canister in his hand, his body trembling like a leaf on a windy day, tried to board the bus. 'It's a school bus. Get down,' Bablu shouted.

'Please, just drop me at Upar Kot. They'll kill me if they find who I am,' he begged.

Bablu tried to get him off the bus. It was difficult to trust a stranger with a canister of unidentified liquid. 'Get out at once,' Bablu reiterated.

The man cried and folded his hands. Noor Ma'am, our computer teacher, had a soft heart. 'Let him come. We'll drop him off after a bit,' she told Bablu. At a time of great peril, an uninvited, unknown passenger had boarded our bus.

As Route No. 4 moved forward, our hearts throbbed with fear and our nerves remained on edge. A sinister quality had now engulfed the eerie quiet. The route of our school bus, which we had travelled almost every day for the last three years, now looked strange and very, very long. As we reached the Delhi Gate crossing, a mob of around fifty surrounded the bus. The driver had no option but to stop.

Through the windows, we stared at the mass of screaming, angry men, some of them drunk, some of them sober in a nefarious way, blocking the way of our bus. '*Har Har Mahadev!*' they shouted. Some had knives in their hands, others had stones. All of them had intense, hateful eyes that wanted to see blood being shed. In the gullies behind them stood more men. Some of them began trying to enter the bus. Like an elephant guarding a castle against enemies, Bablu kept holding the latch with all his strength. 'You can't come inside,' he said with pleading eyes, and they said something threatening back.

'Shut the windows,' Noor Ma'am shouted. We had been too engrossed in what was happening outside, and Noor Ma'am's voice shook us out of it.

*I should have gone by Route No. 2 today,* I thought and cursed Bablu in my heart.

Suddenly, we heard a thud. It sounded like a stone hitting a steel surface. One among the mob had thrown a stone inside our bus. Fathima, Niki Baji's cousin, someone I often picked from her home, screamed at the top of her voice. As if on cue, other girls also started screaming.

Natiq stood up. 'Zeyad, shut the windows. *Bus pe pathrav ho raha hai,*' he said.

I shut my window and latched it and the others rose and did the same. 'The window on the last seat is stuck. It won't close,' somebody shouted as more stones began entering the plastic-and-steel body of the bus. Within seconds, my survival instincts to do what was necessary to protect us kicked in. Along with another boy, I went to the back and we pulled the window with all our might, and finally, it shut. We had just done it in time. Within seconds, hundreds of stones were hurled at the plastic windows of Route No. 4.

I realized that we were in the middle of a stone pelting. The angry, emotionless mob had somehow guessed that we were a bus full of Muslim kids, and they didn't want to let no stone unturned to hurt us in whatever way they could. For the burning desire to teach a lesson to Muslims, our bus was the only available target. As other kids held onto the window latches tightly, I concentrated on the sound of the stones being thrown from all directions and hitting the plastic windows, like it was the last soundtrack being played in Route No 4.

*Thak. Thak. Thak. Thak. Thak. Thak. Thak. Thak.*

It went on for minutes but seemed endless. It was strange how a simple sound could be so scary. We weren't being fired at with bullets. Probably, it was not the stones, but the intensity of the hate dictating the mob that probably terrified us. At times, many stones hit the plastic windows of our school bus simultaneously. Then the sound would die down, but some eager rioter would start the process again, and the girls would scream again. Sometimes, the sound of the stones was drowned by the cries of '*Har Har Mahadev!*'

As I focussed on the sound of the stones, a dramatic scene was unfolding near the front door of Route No. 4. Like a lone soldier, Bablu was trying hard to save our lives by holding on to the bus door with all his might. The powerful mob was pushing hard to open the door where he stood. 'This is a school bus! This is a school bus, for god's sake!' Bablu kept shouting as he put his full weight against the door, the only thing standing between us and the mob.

It was like a Renaissance painting – an Atlas-like figure shouldering the weight of a planet and denying death, waiting outside the door, ready to snare a dozen lives.

But gods of death wouldn't give up that easily. More men were joining the mob. Some tried to climb up to the windows but failed because of how high they were. But not all the gods were against us. We were lucky that the bus we were on was new. We often had old buses without windowpanes coming in. If we had been on such a bus that day, some of the students of St Fidelis would have ended up at least with broken heads. *If we die today, will we make it to the news read at the school assembly next day?* I wondered. *Of course, we will.*

Death was trying its level best. Now the mob had partially opened the door. The teachers had now joined the screaming chorus. The screams didn't deter the mob.

'This is a school bus. Please let us go,' Bablu pleaded.

'No, you are a Muslim!' the angry men shouted back.

'I am Hindu. Look at this!' Bablu showed them his saffron-thread locket with a Hindu deity on it. Suddenly, the storm began to lull. The mob stopped pushing the door.

'The driver is a Hindu. All the kids and teachers are Hindus,' Bablu lied. The mob knew he was lying, but his being Hindu had lessened the vigour of their hate.

All of this was happening a few feet from the area police station, but there were no cops in sight. They either didn't care about our lives or were too afraid to take on angry locals. We were completely at the mercy of the mob, who wanted to unleash their anger and hurt the schoolchildren sitting inside. Most of them were young boys, but I could see middle-aged and elderly men watching from the sidelines without doing anything to stop them. Or they were making sure the young boys finished the job.

'The conductor is lying. I know that kid. He is Muslim! Get him off if you want to move ahead!'

From the crowd, I saw a finger pointing at me, scaring the shit out of me. That finger had singled me out. That finger belonged to the grandson of the neighbourhood shopkeeper, the man our family had been buying groceries from for three generations. Once, his grandfather had wanted my father to bring back Lahori salt from Pakistan. Now, his finger was pointing me out as a Muslim and calling for me to be killed.

'He is a Muslim – I know him. Get him off the bus,' he said again.

His words sank into my bones.

I could see angry eyes sizing me. *If they get their hands on me, they'll surely beat me to death*, I thought. I was now sure that I was going to die. *Will they spare me because I am cute*, I thought, but it was just my mind giving me hope.

'Get him off!' Lala's grandson kept saying. Bablu's lie had caught up with him, and the mob began to push the bus door again as Bablu held on to it like his life depended on it.

Then the mob began to circle the bus like vultures in a graveyard. Like hounds desperate to attack their prey, they pointed at Noor Ma'am and someone shouted, 'That teacher is a Muslim – I know her!' They didn't know that all of us were Muslims but were convinced that two of us were. It didn't mean that the rest were safe, but it was sure I and Noor Ma'am were the primary targets for the mob.

'I won't let you get into the bus. I will lose my job, and the police will arrest me,' said Bablu, using all the strength in his body, pushing with all his force. He now had support from the conductor in stopping the door from being opened. 'Do you know what the Muslims did? They didn't let a funeral procession pass through their graveyard; they also beat us,' someone from the mob shouted, his eyes red with tears of anger.

'These kids and teachers are my responsibility. Before you kill them, you'll have to kill me,' Bablu said with tears in his eyes, holding the door with all the might inside him, still the only thing standing between us and death. On seeing Bablu's insistence, some elderly men finally stepped in. The boys temporarily stopped pushing at the door and discussed something among themselves. The minutes they were talking were probably the longest of my life.

Suddenly, the impossible happened – the mob that was blocking us cleared a path ahead. Lala's grandson looked even angrier now, his prey was getting away. The bus driver started the bus and drove away from the Delhi Gate crossing. And so, with his persistence, strength and conviction, Bablu had saved our lives.

The bus passed the deserted police station a few feet away, and then the mixed population area where ironworkers lived and got on to the slope that led towards Jama Masjid, our bus stop. As we threw away the stones out of the bus, the man with the green canister, who had sought refuge in our bus, got down and ran into one of the lanes. Most of our parents were waiting for us at the stop, and they thanked Bablu for getting us home safe.

As police stood outside Jama Masjid, we got off the bus and began walking towards our homes after what was probably the most traumatic event of our lives. No jokes were told on the way home that day. St Fidelis was closed for a couple of days and then reopened. We told the other kids of Bablu's bravery, and they listened to it with intent and were impressed with his act. 'I always thought of him as a fool, but never thought he was that brave,' one of them said.

Soon, we began to concentrate on our exams and Bablu went back to hounding kids for bus fees. He didn't get a bravery award or even a mention in the school assembly for his act of heroism. Nobody from the media reported on this, no teachers congratulated him and few came to know about it. We, the people of Route No. 4, also wanted to forget the trauma and move on with our lives. Bablu, the uncelebrated hero, the Atlas who had saved our lives, kept sitting behind the cash counter, probably still being scammed by Aligarh's kids.

Days later, when I told Ammi how Lala's grandson was among the mob and had identified me, she was surprised and angry. 'I always knew these people were communal,' she said. For a month, I didn't go to their shop. But a month later, Ammi sent me to their shop to get some groceries. 'Everything is fine now. They sell the best stuff, after all,' she told me.

The boy who had wanted me to be killed was sitting at the shop. I gave him the paper with the lists of groceries. He took it, looked at it and then began to take pages out of a notebook and pack spices in them. His father asked how my father was doing. I told him Papa had been well.

In Aligarh, everything was back to normal. Until the next time.

# 11

# THE MODERN NEEDS OF A MODERN FAMILY

I T'S NOT AS if Farsh Manzil hasn't changed with time. Though constructed almost perfectly by my grandfather, my home had been reconstructed more times than was required. Expanding families, space constraints and hygiene reasons led to these modifications.

Like a high-nosed old man, I have detested these changes with all my heart. But unlike me, Papa and Bade Papa didn't value the aesthetics of the house their father built with immense passion. Like a curse that returns at regular intervals, these crimes against architecture have always been committed after a gap of ten years.

The first reconstruction, likely dictated by a pandering to Western aesthetics, took place in 1985 (before I was born). We always had a baithak, the Indian version of drawing rooms, but that had now become Bade Papa's room. So, the spacious *gok*, or balcony, behind the main hall in our portion was turned by Papa into our drawing room – a modern need of our modern family.

Probably Papa knew in his heart of the blunder he was committing, so he convinced the workers to match its design language with the old construction. A century-old sheesham door was sacrificed – it was cut in half and used for the windows. A sofa set, a green, fluffy carpet, a *diwan* and a glass showcase arrived, giving the new room a faux-royal ambience (it would also be where the bulk of this book would be written). It would later become the haunt of Papa's political friends, where they'd sit for hours, smoke, drink tea, discuss university politics and laugh so loudly that even the Hindus down the slope could hear it.

In this revision, of the eight doors in the main living room, the heart of the Farsh Manzil, two were closed. One was converted into a wardrobe for the children, the other was permanently shut and covered with plywood. Everybody loved it, except my grandfather's ghost.

After Daadi's death, Bade Papa told Papa that they wanted to occupy some portion of the living room. 'My two sons are now grown and need their own space,' he said. My father, the people-pleasing youngest of the nine siblings, agreed. So, a bit less than half of our aesthetic living hall was made into a temporary, yellow, ugly wooden room. My childhood was spent seeing this caricatured version of the main hall.

The worst was yet to come. The year 1995 arrived like a devil, took away Farsh Manzil's soul and turned it into a caricature of the past. The Indian economy had been recently liberalized, and people had more disposable wealth than before. Bade Papa had been living in one room across the courtyard with his wife and three children. Because he'd gone for a love marriage against Daadi's wishes, they'd been consigned to the erstwhile *baithak*. As more space was required for their growing family, Bade Papa decided to construct a room in the courtyard, another modern need of a modern family.

Like a pillow-murderer, this revision would smother into submission Farsh Manzil's rustic charm. Many things would go:

the huge brick-laid aangan, the old basement toilet, the bathroom
with an open pipe for a shower, the adjoining red water tank where
Ammi cleaned the dishes of her messy family. What broke my
heart the most was that the construction will destroy the small
garden on the left, something of a rarity in Upar Kot. Another
obliteration that hurt me personally was a century-old tin shed
supported by superbly carved sheesham pillars, where our cousins
parked their bicycles.

But like every beautiful thing in life, they had to go because our
family chose utility over beauty.

Now, Bade Papa had a second room, complete with glossy
enamel paint, telephone and air conditioning. Inspired by elder
brother, Papa also jumped on the bandwagon. The old kitchen
where Ammi had cooked for decades was broken down and
expanded by incorporating the erstwhile bathroom.

We also got a separate toilet, where I could shit without fearing
the dozens of lizards, regular visitors to our older toilet. This was
the only thing that made me happy: scores of lizards, of which I
had a phobia, ran away (or were killed) during this construction.
Our toilet was built where the tin shed adjoining the main hall
once was. It meant two more doors from the main hall had been
closed. Of the original eight doors in this room, only four now
remained.

One more thing was gone: the toilet for the family of Noorjahan
Apa, our tenants. They now had to poop in a toilet on the terrace,
which only had a curtain for a door. Noorjahan Apa saw it as Bade
Papa's plan to trouble them. 'They want to push us out of the
house,' she told Ammi. A new terrace alongside Noorjahan Apa's
portion would also take their privacy away. Badi Ammi's privacy
was also gone and along with it, two windows in the lobby of her
portion. 'My father constructed this house with such love. Look
what his sons have done to it!' she'd say.

Ten more years passed. They were kind to Bade Papa's family. His sons, whom we had tolerated playing Michael Jackson and Queen songs from their temporary wooden room in our main hall, were now earning. The elder one, Tariq, was a management executive in Delhi, while the younger one, Naved, was a software engineer settled in the USA. They'd invest this money in improving their home and standard of living.

In 2004, Tariq began dating a girl from Syana, a tehsil in the neighbouring town of Bulandshahr. After facing parental disapproval initially, he convinced them to talk to her parents and get them married. However, there was one minor issue: where would the soon-to-be-wedded couple live? And so, after decades of mutual coexistence between the two brothers, the moment of reckoning had arrived – the word 'batwara' was finally uttered in Farsh Manzil.

Batwara, or partition, has brought catastrophe into the lives of Indian families for millennia. Dividing property among inheritors is mostly never an easy process – it involves family quarrels, compromises, decades of animosity, emotional blackmail, murder, and if you are powerful enough, war.

The Mahabharata, the greatest Indian war, happened because of a succession dispute between brothers. In the Ramayana, Lord Rama was exiled at the insistence of his stepmother, who wanted Ayodhya for her son Bharata. Even in medieval times, many Indian kings, Hindus and Muslims alike, had to kill their brothers, stepbrothers, cousins, fathers, sons, and sisters to establish their rule over their kingdoms.

Many Indian families have a horrific story of how they have been cheated out of their property in the past. Many people's entire lifetimes are spent conspiring to either get back their own property or usurp someone else's. When a home or land is divided among brothers, it is also an emotionally traumatic moment for everyone involved. Ties that have stood the test of time often wither during these times, leading to animosity between siblings, tears being shed, and decades-long arguments which often end up in courts.

Many see the Partition of India as a property squabble between brothers. 'The Hindus are the elder brothers, the Muslims the younger. You wanted your own land; we didn't want to give away ours. This was what led to fights,' I heard my father's Hindu friends telling him more than once.

In our Muslim household, what would die in this separation was decades of symbiotic coexistence. Papa and Bade Papa had always been more like friends than brothers. They had common pals, spent a lot of time together and respected each other's boundaries. But none of that could now delay the partition of Farsh Manzil. 'Can I really bring my daughter-in-law into the two rooms we have?' Bade Papa asked when he brought it up.

Like an outdated coat of a dead parent, Papa's heart belonged to a time that didn't exist anymore. His elder brother was asking for his home, where he spent his childhood and adulthood, to be broken down and overhauled. It tore him up inside. But after consulting his friends and brothers-in-law, he agreed. 'You don't want your children fighting over the property after you die,' Achhe Mammu told him.

Farsh Manzil was now set to be broken up but dividing a hundred-year-old house into two parts, was a humongous task. It was built for a joint family who'd live, eat and die together, but an alien concept of nuclear families would break this dream. 'My father hadn't anticipated how *bemurrawat*, how inconsiderate, the next generation would be,' Badi Ammi told me when I brought her supply of eggs and bread.

The lawyer that Bade Papa had consulted suggested that we didn't need to divide the land. 'A mutual agreement between the two brothers is enough,' he told Bade Papa, who then repeated the plan to Papa. So, the eventual division was haphazard but consistent with the needs of the two families. The section under Papa's bedroom went to Bade Papa as they had already made it a garage for their Maruti 800. Badi Ammi insisted that her portion would only be given to Papa after her death. 'The upper story was built for the sisters. Only your family can have it after I'm gone,' she told Papa. Noorjahan Apa's portion went to Bade Papa. The remaining courtyard, the foyer and entrance spaces remained common.

The construction began and our lives were tumultuous for months. Like an invading army, labourers arrived with hammers and anvils to bring down old walls brick by brick. The quiet of Farsh Manzil was broken by the grinding of cement mixers and labourers hammering away at its unusually wide walls. 'It's easier to break newly built houses. These broad, limestone walls are the strongest I've ever seen,' said the mason as he negotiated a higher price for his work.

Along with the walls of Farsh Manzil, the friendship that the two brothers had enjoyed, despite their wives not liking each other, was breaking down. Like smoke enveloping a room, an invisible hostility was rising between the two families. I could see Bade Papa's family's love for me waning. They were now not as welcoming when I went to read their newspaper. New rules were being defined in the house. Spaces were being exchanged. In the middle of it all, Papa felt abandoned.

Abandonment is not the same as rejection. The pain of being rejected by those we love, those we call home, stirs abandonment. In the world we inhabit, parents have left newborns outside orphanages and kids have left old parents on the road. Friends have abandoned friends, and lovers have abandoned their beloveds. Abandonment experienced as a child leaves trauma lingering in the shadows. Perhaps they are not worthy of love? If parents can leave, why would a lover stay?

Not all of these abandonments are physical. People can mentally abandon others in their heads, and it hurts the same. Some wait endlessly for those who have abandoned them. A few wait for it to happen and ruin their lives in the present. In unhealthy relationships, it becomes a race. Who will abandon whom first? Some abandonments come from a lack of self-worth: 'What if they stay and find nothing worth loving?'

As Farsh Manzil was being transformed, so were the feelings of those who lived inside it. For decades, Papa had been parking his scooter in our foyer. As construction began, the scooter was dented by a worker. The next day, he parked it in our garage, which according to the agreement, lay in Bade Papa's portion. As hurtful as a knife through one's heart, objections were raised to it. 'We find it hard to park the car,' Badi Ammi told Ammi.

'Saad, please remove the scooter from their property,' Papa told my brother. He did it immediately.

A week later, Papa called some labourers and had the temporary wooden walls removed from our main living room. This was the first time I had seen the architectural beauty of this room. But even restoring that room couldn't heal Papa's heart. He was failing to preserve the relations he had spent his life protecting.

The walls had now been broken. The dust had settled. The debris of a hundred-year-old house was picked up by sweaty workers and thrown into the garbage. Brick by brick, new walls began coming up, complete with modern amenities but without any beauty. But like a promise made to a dying lover, it had to be done. Tariq Bhai's marriage was on the cards.

There was something else that had to be done. Somebody had to tell Noorjahan Apa to leave the house where she had lived all her life.

# 12

# NOORJAHAN APA

NOORJAHAN, THE TWENTIETH wife of the Mughal emperor Jahangir, was one of the most powerful women in Indian history. I found out about her through a show on Doordarshan, India's state television. A shrewd planner, administrator and an ace marksman, she spent her spare time hunting tigers. She is said to have exerted equal, if not more, influence as the king, passing decrees and taking political decisions that protected her lazy, drunkard husband's rule. Such power in the hands of a woman at that time was revolutionary. One of the most famous stories about Noorjahan is about how she rescued her husband from a battle in which he faced certain defeat and death at the hands of his enemies.

In my life, I had my own Noorjahan, sort of my nanny, who was as responsible for raising me as Ammi. Whenever Ammi and Sayema went out shopping in Penth, they left me with her, and she took care of me as if I were her own child. I didn't have enemies like Jahangir had, but my Noorjahan rescued me from Ammi's anger, bad food and attacks from packs of monkeys that thronged our terrace. On one occasion before my birth, she manifested her inner Mughal queen she was named after and single-handedly saved Farsh Manzil from being burnt down by Hindu rioters.

Noorjahan Apa's family had been our tenants for forty years, since my grandfather's time. Her family of four occupied the portion directly opposite Badi Ammi on the first floor. Unlike the Noorjahan on Doordarshan who wore expensive jewellery, she wasn't rich or powerful. She was a loving old woman with grey hair and sharp features. Her face bore testimony to the hard times she had seen.

She lived with her husband Ghaffar Bhai, a lock worker, and her two sons, Aslam and Ballu. Ballu's real name was Salahuddin but I never heard anyone call him that. 'Until I grew up, I didn't know you people were not my blood relatives and that we were your tenants. It was the biggest shock of my life to find out that this was not our home,' Ballu Bhai once told me. Even I hadn't known for years that they were not our blood – until this fact was rubbed against their pride with sandpaper.

Noorjahan Apa's portion was separated from Badi Ammi's by a small passage. A small lobby opened in a longish room where the family of four slept on a double bed and two charpoys, under which their belongings were mostly kept. The large window at the end of the room overlooked the entrance and brought in the azaan from the mosque five times a day. 'We are lucky that we can hear the azaan so closely,' she'd say whenever the muezzin called.

When she wasn't reciting duas on her green rosary, Noorjahan Apa was cooking on her stove in a small courtyard shadowed by an adjacent neem tree. If between her prayers, gangs of monkeys came to steal food from her kitchen, she'd take out her stick and scare them away. Her veranda-cum-kitchen was partly covered by a canopy under which were placed the family's assortment of clay pots, regularly filled with water. They could never afford a refrigerator even when it became a common thing.

Her elder son, Aslam, had studied till high school and worked in the Nawab of Chattari's office. Ballu first worked as a lock worker like his father but then sold children's clothes from a pavement shop outside Jama Masjid. Both Ghaffar Bhai and Noorjahan Apa helped the rest of Farsh Manzil in whatever they could. Whenever one of her sons wasn't happy with what she had cooked or she wanted to get something off her chest, she called out to her best friend, my mother. 'Dulhan, Dulhan! Come up after you are done,' she'd say from the balcony overlooking our courtyard.

Whenever Ammi didn't cook something I liked, I'd make my way to her peaceful home. Every time, she'd give me food that was delicious. Little did I know that eating one of their rotis meant one less for them. 'Why don't you make rotis keeping Chotta Bhaiya in mind too?' Ballu Bhai would often say angrily.

When I was five, Noorjahan Apa found a girl for Aslam Bhai, and a wedding took place. The only memory I had of the wedding was coming back on a bus from some very deserted place. But like every household, the fights between Noorjahan Apa and her daughter-in-law began soon after. Both came to Ammi to tell their own story and 'convey something' to the other party. Our new 'sister-in-law' sat in our house every day, complaining about the travails of living with a family of five in a single room. 'They have separated our portion on the side, but can I live here forever? Aslam and I can't even have a conversation,' she'd grouse. Noorjahan Apa came to complain about how she was disrespected every day.

Ballu Bhai also came home to joke around with us and escape the tense situation in his own home. With every passing day and every fight between his mother and his sister-in-law, his anger against his brother kept growing. 'I know how much hardship our mother has suffered to raise us. If she can disrespect her like this and Aslam can't say anything about it, then let this tradition of marriage go to hell,' he'd say. As the fights kept escalating, the egos of the two brothers became too big to handle.

The ego is like an angry animal hidden inside, prodding you to fight for yourself, but also a prison that limits you. It reduces people of warmth to empty shells of concocted confidence and hinders their souls from blooming. It makes them afraid of facing the nuances of the world. Ego divides people from inside and outside – you think you are controlling your life but in reality, being controlled by your fears and pride.

In the fight between the brothers, I was on Ballu Bhai's side. Whenever I went past his stall on the way to get vegetables, he'd get me a lemonade or a sweet *paan*. At Farsh Manzil, he'd bring us *lassi* and crack jokes that he'd heard from the hawkers near Jama Masjid.

I had my reasons to dislike Aslam Bhai. One evening, when I was playing on the terrace, he got angry at me for no reason. I was only five or six. 'Why are you playing here during *Maghrib*?' he asked me furiously. I didn't pay him any attention and kept on playing, which agitated him further. 'You are *still* here? I'll teach you a lesson now!' Before I could run away, he picked me up by my legs and dangled me upside down from the terrace. I could see Sayyed Baba's grave directly beneath me. I was immobilized. 'Should I throw you off?' he shouted and dangled me further out.

I gathered enough courage to plead with him. 'I promise I won't come here in the evenings,' I said, my tears falling on the upside-down grave three stories beneath me. He pulled me back and let me go. 'Don't tell anyone or I'll definitely throw you off the next time,' he said. I never said a word.

Over time, the tension between the two brothers kept growing and one day, the inevitable happened. The sound of Noorjahan Apa screaming came from their home. As I ran above, I saw Ballu and Aslam in a physical fight in the small lobby of their home. As both kept pushing each other, Ballu held Aslam's face, a scissor in another hand, while Aslam held Ballu's torn shirt. It was only after Ammi intervened that they let each other go. Aslam went to wash his face, and Ballu went to his shop wearing a torn shirt. This was the opportunity the couple was waiting for. Within a few days, they left. Aslam talked to his employer, the Nawab of Chattari, and moved into one of the many empty rooms in his *haveli*. He would avoid his mother for long.

Women in Farsh Manzil often told stories of how beautiful Noorjahan Apa was when she came to live here as a young bride. 'The people of the mohalla constantly talked about her dusky colour, sharp features and how lucky Ghaffar Bhai was,' Mehro Phuppo once told me. But it wasn't until Ammi told a nearly forgotten story that I realized Apa was also as courageous as the Mughal empress she was named after.

To understand how this Noorjahan saved our home from rioters, you would first need to hear the story of Bhura Pehalwan.

In Aligarh of the 1970s, Suresh alias Bhura was a renowned wrestler: he was immensely powerful, had bulging muscles and incredible fighting acumen. Like every boy in Aligarh, he too wanted to be a strongman, someone everybody was afraid of. That he was also good with knives drove him towards petty crime. The kingpin of the infamous Golden Gang, he was often on the wrong side of the law for extortion.[1]

In those times, Seema Talkies was one of Aligarh's most popular cinemas. Aligarhians were so fond of Bollywood that they'd use inside sources to get tickets to watch the first shows of latest blockbusters on the big screen. There was always a rush outside all cinema halls, including Seema Talkies, sometimes leading to quarrels outside the booking window. That was why the cinema halls resorted to hiring roughnecks to manage Aligarh's rowdy crowds.

Bhura was in charge of maintaining peace at Seema Talkies. Aligarh being a den of envy, not everyone was happy with his influence. On 3 October 1978, a rival gang gathered outside Seema Talkies, overpowered Bhura and stabbed him. Two days later, he died in a hospital and all hell broke loose.

Though the reports found that Bhura was stabbed in an inter-gang rivalry over the influence in the area that had no communal overtones,[2] the rumour that had spread in Aligarh was entirely removed from reality. It was said that Bhura was stabbed because of a wrestling match at a fair on the outskirts of Aligarh a month ago. In the rumoured fight, he had faced a Muslim wrestler. The Hindu version of the rumours said Bhura had won the fight, while the Muslim version said the Muslim had won. In both, the match ended with communal resentment, which then led to Bhura being stabbed in revenge. After news of Bhura's death broke, communal mobilization began in full swing. Soon, widespread riots broke out in Aligarh. It was called *Bhura Ka Jhagda*, the riot of the dusky man.

Men with evil in their hearts came out on the streets, looking to shed some blood. What often protects the image of such men is they don't always go around hurting people. They carefully select those they can hurt in secret and those in the open – that's how they get away with it. But if someone knows they can do bad things to you and get away with it, chances are they'll do it again. They wouldn't even know they were doing a terrible thing. They believe that some people deserve the pain they cause them. Somehow, this time, it was our family.

On 5 October 1978, the fires finally reached Farsh Manzil. After Bhura's funeral, the attendees attacked Muslim homes on the Farsh, and a brisk fight ensued. The Hindu mob was angrier and stronger than before, and they decided to quench their anger by burning down Farsh Manzil. First, they began to burn down the cycles on the slope and then moved towards our basement-cum-ground floor where my grandfather once sold his medicines. Somebody took out a petrol can, and it was set on fire. Later in the riots, PAC opened indiscriminate fire on Muslims, killing many of them, on which India's minority commission expressed apprehensions in a report.[3] Even before I was born, my town only made headlines because of violence.

Ammi was a young bride then, and this was the first riot she was experiencing. Sayema was just a few months old. Like everyone else, they also went to our neighbour's house to avoid being burnt to death. However, one person remained in Farsh Manzil – Noorjahan Apa, the bravest among us.

On hearing the mob outside the house, trying to burn down the place she'd lived most of her life, she came out on to our terrace. At first, she began throwing stones and bricks at the rioters. When it didn't deter them, she went to her courtyard, gathered all the pieces of firewood, lit them up and began throwing them at the rioters. By now, the basement door had been burnt. The Hindus were not giving up, but they had underestimated Noorjahan Apa's perseverance.

She went back home and collected all her old clothes and bedsheets. One by one, she dipped them in the kerosene meant to light her lamp. Targeting the rioters, she threw those burning clothes at them. Most likely (and hopefully), somebody caught fire and so the Hindus realized that this old woman would keep returning, time and again. They retreated, and soon, our Muslim neighbours came and doused the fire. But the front door and some part of a staircase had been burnt. Our house was saved only because Noorjahan Apa had stood like a rock against all odds. Single-handedly, she had fought against an army of angry men and eventually sent them packing.

And one fine day, her grand sacrifice was discarded just like flowers in a trashcan. Decades later, she was thrown out of the same house she had saved. The reason was Tariq Bhai's impending wedding and the expansion of Bade Papa's portion. Noorjahan Apa couldn't believe it when she was told her family needed to leave. 'Dulhan, can't you make them see that we can't live anywhere else? I have little life left, and I want to die here,' she said, trying to convince Ammi to convince Papa to talk to Bade Papa and cancel the construction plans. Of course, that didn't happen.

To remind her that she was a tenant, the issue of the monthly rent, the negligible amount of Rs 100, was brought up. 'What can we do with 100 rupees?' she was told. After that, she was made an offer that she couldn't refuse. 'We'll give you Rs 50,000 to vacate the home, and you can buy a new home,' she was told.

This money was thought of as compensation for vacating a home where she arrived as a young bride, where her two sons were born and grew up, where the smoke from the stove nearly took her eyesight, where she married off her son, and where her hair turned from black to grey. For the 'settlement money', she had to leave the place she wanted to die in. 'Please don't let us go,' she begged everyone. But like a funeral procession for a loved one, it was something that had to be done.

On the day she and her family left Farsh Manzil, a rickshaw waited to ferry their belongings to their new home somewhere on the outskirts of Aligarh. Everyone from Farsh Manzil had assembled, some of them crying like children but toothless to do anything. I hated everyone, but what did I know about the world? 'I will come and meet you in your new home, Noorjahan Apa,' I said, making a promise I wouldn't fulfil.

That night I had one of the most horrible dreams of my life. A witch had come to live in the courtyard where Noorjahan used to cook. She wore a black sari, was the ugliest person I had ever seen and descended from the nearest peepal tree. When I went there to retrieve a cricket ball, she locked me in Noorjahan Apa's courtyard, now deserted. 'Now, everyone will forget about you and will not even come to find you,' she told me. I kept screaming for help, but nobody heard my screams. 'I am not going to leave until I kill everyone in your family,' she said. And then she did. And I just sat there, watching her casting spells on my family and slowly killing them.

Death is the enemy always lurking at your door, sometimes knocking softly and sometimes loudly. It waits for you at crossings with malfunctioning traffic signals, in slippery bathrooms, in filthy hospital beds and in unknown diseases lurking inside your body. At times, it chooses another human being as its conduit, who has become angry and emotionless because of the vagaries of life. Death, the ultimate fear of our hearts, has happened to everyone who has ever lived. One way or the other, sooner or later, savagely or slowly, death finds its way to you.

Within a couple of years of leaving Farsh Manzil, Noorjahan Apa found death. She passed away in her bed because of a cardiac arrest. 'There wasn't a day she didn't talk about Farsh Manzil. She asked me to forgive you and not to be angry with you,' Ballu Bhai told Ammi at her funeral in a graveyard near her new home. Within a few months, Ghaffar Bhai also followed his wife.

Ammi was one of the few people from Farsh Manzil who went to meet her before she died, and that day, Noorjahan Apa gave her an important responsibility. 'Dulhan, if something happens to me, you must get Ballu married,' she said on her deathbed. However, Ballu's anger at his brother and sister-in-law for treating her mother unfairly meant that Ammi wouldn't be able to fulfil this promise. For years, she tried to show him prospects in Upar Kot, but Ballu wouldn't budge. 'Where would I bring her when I don't even have my own home?' he'd ask, one of his many reasons for not marrying. With sad eyes, remembering his brave mother, he sat every day at his pavement shop selling kids' clothes. Ammi eventually gave up.

For years, I tried to avoid going past his shop because of my shame at being unable to stop them from leaving. One day while buying vegetables, I gathered the courage to face him. He welcomed me like a younger brother and gave me a sweet *paan* like he always used to. He was, after all, Noorjahan Apa's son, and my brother. Few years later, he told me why he left his job as a lock worker and moved to Penth to start a cloth shop.

At that time, fresh out of school and not being able to afford college, Ballu Bhai was working at a lock factory on the outskirts of Aligarh, and he was paid quite well. Noorjahan Apa didn't like him working in a Hindu-majority area because often, it was the workers caught up in enemy territory who bore the brunt of the riots. But Ballu Bhai wanted to make a career as a lock worker and didn't heed his mother's advice. All that changed after an incident at Guptawali Gali, a two-minute walk from the border of Upar Kot.

'I was at the workshop when I heard that a riot had taken place in Aligarh,' Ballu Bhai told me years later, during the writing of this book. Hearing the news, he remembered his mother's words and left the workshop with a few other Muslim workers. The only way to reach Upar Kot was through Hindu areas, and Ballu and his friends chose to walk together on Railway Road to reach the U.K. 'The road was deserted, and all the shops were shut. But as soon as we reached Abdul Kareem Crossing, there was chaos. Just a few minutes earlier, three boys were "snatched" away by a mob of Hindus in Guptawali Gali. Two were injured, and one just disappeared,' he said. 'If we had reached there five minutes earlier, it could have been us.'

As soon as he got home, he told everyone about the incident, including Papa. 'Your father became very agitated because Saad was due to come home from school at that time. He ran without even putting on his slippers shouting, "My son! My son!" Saad arrived home unharmed, but Papa became the butt of jokes for running out like a madman, the cowardly dad who kept his sons soft.

Three days later, a body was found in a drain nearby, the face bashed beyond recognition. The police came up with a novel idea to find the family. 'Looking at the label on the shirt the body was wearing, they went to the tailor's shop it belonged to. The tailor asked around and found that a boy from his neighbourhood was missing,' Ballu said. Thus, the dead body was buried by his family instead of being cremated namelessly in a public morgue, all thanks to their family tailor.

However, this incident changed Ballu Bhai's life forever. 'Amma made me promise I would never work in the factory again, and I quit the next week.' Soon, he found a spot at Penth outside Jama Masjid and became a street vendor selling children's clothes, giving up his dream of becoming an expert machine-man at a lock factory. For the next two decades, he would sell clothes at the same exact spot because of his mother's fears.

Ammi often tried to make us feel guilty for not loving her enough by telling us how Ballu Bhai respected not only his mother but ours too. One of Ballu's shopkeeper friends told this story during one of Ammi's regular shopping sojourns to buy clothes for Sayema's daughter in Saudi Arabia. 'His friend told me how I am the only person in the world Ballu is afraid of. A few weeks before, when I passed by his shop, Ballu was smoking a cigarette. Seeing me, he quickly hid it. In his hurry, he couldn't stub it out properly and it burnt a big hole in the mat of his shop.'

But the hole in Ballu's heart was much deeper than the one in his mat. Ten years after Noorjahan Apa's death, he came to Farsh Manzil and asked to meet Bade Papa. They weren't happy to see

him after so many years but came to their baithak, now rarely
unlocked, to meet him. Ballu took out a bundle of notes totalling
Rs 50,000.

'Amma died carrying the burden of this money on her heart.
I don't want to take it to my grave. I want to fulfil my promise to
Amma, please take back this money,' he said as he left the notes
on the glass table. As tears flowed down Ammi's face, Noorjahan
Apa's younger boy, my brother, separated only by blood, left the
foyer of Farsh Manzil and went back to his pavement shop to
sell children's clothing. To this day, he hasn't fulfilled the other
promise he made to his Amma: he hasn't found the money to get
married.

# 13

# THE BATTLE

F OR MANY YEARS, public taps, locally referred to as *piyaoon,* have
been erected in Aligarh as a public service, but as is the fate of
most things in Aligarh, they mostly end up as places to exchange
community gossip. The piyaoon in Dahiwali Gali, a market area
where half of Aligarh bought their vests, bras and underwear, was
built in 1940, after local Hindus wanted a temple on a piece of
land alongside a mosque. Naturally, sparks flew. To stop them from
turning into a raging fire, community leaders decided to construct
a public tap, a neutral structure, on the disputed land.[1]

For decades, it was a source of water for lazy shopkeepers and
passers-by on hot summer days. Then it became a reason for war.
In 1978, like a recurrent nightmare, the conflict rose again when
a Hindu group decided to build a temple alongside the tap. When
the mosque management objected to the demand, a brawl ensued,
turning into a full-blown riot. Shops were set ablaze and a curfew
was imposed. The matter eventually went to the courts, which
ordered the status quo to be maintained.[2]

This riot resulted in the killing of a six-month-old girl. Angry at
all Muslims, the Hindus attacked her family. Their animal instincts

dominating their conscience, they stretched her body in half from the legs. In the fight between grownups, a child lost her life.

'Life is nothing but a battle. It is what defines us and shows who we are underneath,' Papa would say. It always made me wonder what I would turn into when the stakes were against me. Muhammad, Ram, Churchill, Hitler and Gandhi are known for the battles they picked up and the way they fought them. In the modern age, the toughest battle for most of us, though, is simply to discover our battles.

Feminists say the battle lay between women and patriarchy. Marxists claimed it to be between the capitalists and the proletariat. Philosophers theorize that it was between man and nature, good and bad, order and chaos, and most importantly, selfishness and selflessness. The battle that eventually reached my doorstep, as expected, was one between Hindus and Muslims.

Beginning in April 2006 like a plague that afflicts people's hearts, it metamorphosed into months of violence, in which Aligarh's market areas became a battleground.

Markets like Dahiwali Gali have always played a role in deciding relations between the two communities. In this battleground, only your merchandise mattered. One could buy an imported perfume for their wife, a garland of banknotes for the neighbour's son's wedding or rusks that their uncle savoured. 'Always buy stuff from Hindu grocers, it is cheaper,' Ammi would tell me if I bought stuff from Muslim shops.

Markets were where the trust between Hindus and Muslims operated based on financial gain. It was also where it was shredded to pieces – most of the communal violence took place in these spaces. Muslim shops where Hindus would line up on slow afternoons would be burnt down at night during riots. Stray incidents took place in residential colonies too, but like a pack of coyotes, most evil men liked to hunt a bit away from homes. Killing someone near your home brought with it the risk of a police informant giving you up.

The markets provided the anonymity to kill. It was where mobs could hide in narrow gullies and shoot down passing motorcyclists or bearded businessmen – easy killings, less trouble. Like a sinner looking for penance, the markets were also what brought normalcy back. In Aligarh, the financial dependency that Hindus and Muslims have on each other is a kind of safety valve. When traders suffered losses during curfews, they forgot about revenge and the wounded town limped back to normalcy.

The markets that turn into battlegrounds in a riot are generally full of people going around their business and living their lives. An obedient son, a careless worker, the girl walking home in her blue salwar suit, a people-pleaser, a clever child, the braggart who tells everyone about how great he is, the patient helpful listener, the woman carrying groceries with her children, the gossiping men, the girl selling *sheermal* to support her family, the arrogant shop owner who'd listen to you only if he is sure of a potential sale, happy young people, the slightly sad middle-aged couples and the many, many defeated old men.

On 5 April 2006, some Hindus decided to break the promise their ancestors had made about the tap in Dahiwali Gali. On Ram Navami, Lord Rama's birthday, they assembled in the market to organize public prayers on the disputed land.[3] At first, the Muslims watched from the sidelines like a crowd gathered to watch a street circus. A feature of such conflicts, mostly planned, was political thugs trying all tricks to provoke Muslims into a fight, and then have them gunned down by their armed men or even the police or the PAC.[4] Hindus died too but in fewer numbers than the Muslims – small sacrifices to achieve larger goals.

When the Muslims didn't react to the public prayers, a loudspeaker was brought in. The mosque staff objected, and it soon turned into a brawl. Soon, politicians robed in saffron arrived like moths after a rainy day. 'This is not Pakistan, this is *our* country,' they declared amid the chanting of religious slogans.

Like an uninvited guest, chaos was back on the streets of Aligarh. Shutters went down, stones were hurled, bricks landed against the jaws of men. Women ran from the market area, not customers but *enemy women* now. For over two hours, hate reigned on the streets. Three Muslim shops were looted a few feet from the police chowki. On Railway Road, rioters ransacked a century-old watch company. The bonhomie, which generations had tried to preserve, was shattered like the glass window of a poor man's shop.

The slow dance of religious hate continued until the cops arrived. Nobody died but bitter feelings remained. 'If the police hadn't arrived, Muslims would have sent the Hindus running,' Ballu Bhai told us, repeating the version he'd heard from his friends. Little did he know that revenge, in all its smouldering sway, was on its way.

The next morning was calm like an ocean before a storm. Hindu shopkeepers refused to open their shops. 'They might be up to something,' said Siraj, my friend from Tablighi Jamaat as we went around taking stock of the situation. 'They won't try anything after what happened to them yesterday,' said Shadab, the perennial joker of the group. His friends and family had advised him not to open his sugar candy shop in Kanwari Ganj, but he did anyway.

Like Siraj and Shadab, our mohalla was divided into people who thought the trouble was coming and those who thought it was a rumour. 'Why should I close my shop? It's just another day,' said Ishrat Bhai to those who advised him to shut down. Like any other day, Papa went to his office at the University. At home, Ammi kept circling the balcony at every little noise, like a sniper on the lookout.

'A Hindu mob is coming from Abdul Kareem Chauraha!' a boy suddenly shouted.

'They are coming for idiots like you,' Ishrat Bhai mocked him, but he slowly slid a few toffee jars inside – just in case.

'The Hindus are coming. They have guns,' declared screams from beneath the Farsh. Ishrat Bhai moved the chocolate counter and the milk buckets inside. Muslim boys assembled at the upper end of the slope – just in case.

Ishrat Bhai was in the middle of locking up his shop when the Hindu mob began to climb the Farsh. 'We will show you what happened in Gujarat!' shouted the Hindus from under my balcony, pouring petrol on a car. The battle had begun, in its all nakedness, the first time I was witnessing it around my house.

First the mob set on fire a jeep, Rasool's son's prized possession. Some rioters tried to get into their home, but its doors were firmly locked. From their windows, screaming and crying, the family saw their jeep burn to a cinder. By then, a Muslim mob had assembled too. They had found bricks from an under-construction home and began raining them down on the Hindus. But like rotating characters in a play, the frontline stone pelters backed out and the armed men among Hindus took centre stage. Stray shots began to be fired like invisible arrows at the boys on the top of the slope. The sound of religious slogans was marred by muffled gunshots.

'Where *is* the police? Aren't the rioters afraid of the cameras?' said Saad, as bricks landed in our balcony, breaking Ammi's pots. The district administration had installed CCTV cameras on the main crossing. But like a surgeon operating with intense precision, before heading towards the Farsh, the mob covered their faces and broke the cameras with stones.

Saad, assessing the danger outside, came back five minutes later. 'They are firing bullets! One went past my ear!' he said. It was clear we were in the middle of a coordinated attack. 'The Hindus are shooting at Muslims from their terraces. Somebody is firing from the top of the bank,' said one of my many cousins.

Inside our tense home, Sayema was terrified. She had come home from Saudi Arabia to give birth to her first child. Helping her eight-month-pregnant daughter escape was Ammi's biggest worry. 'Stones are entering our courtyard,' shouted Nadeem Bhai from Palle Ghar. By now, people were firing bullets at our home – they will remain embedded on our terrace walls for months. Like a sign of impending doom, black smoke from the burning jeep was entering our drawing room. I went to check if our home was on fire. It wasn't yet.

'Har Har Mahadev!' The chant seemed to descend from the skies. Sayema kept crying, and Ammi finally began to lock up our home. As we slowly walked outside amid the screams of women and bullets, I began to imagine the worst – a bullet entering Saad's head and a stone hurting Sayema's unborn baby.

Though the lane that we had to enter was just a few metres from the entrance of our home, trying to go there amid the chaos outside had its dangers. Men were screaming and running around, bricks were pouring from the sky, and the sound of gunshots were ringing our eardrums. We surrounded Sayema and walked slowly to the lane just outside the mosque, the terrace of which had become a battlefront.

'This way, this way!' shouted women from the lane as their children broke old walls for more bricks. This wasn't time to be neutral. It was only after we entered the narrow lane that we felt secure. We waited for a few hours at a family friend's home near Jama Masjid, comparatively safe but not entirely out of harm's way. 'They must have broken my pots,' Ammi kept saying, shocked.

When we reached home after a few hours, blood was splattered everywhere on the pavement like it had rained from the skies.

I asked Siraj who was still lurking around in the mohalla. 'After you left, the cops came from behind the Hindus and began firing at us. They were only waiting for that,' he said. Some reports said nearly fifty people had been shot by the police, all of them Muslims.[5] Overall, eight would die in violence – one of them was Shadab.[6]

'A police bullet entered under his neck,' Siraj told me without a hint of tears. I didn't believe him at first, but I realized he wouldn't lie about such a thing. Shadab, the joker of our prayer group was gone, shot to death, never to come back.

I had met him in the morning. He was smiling his usual smile, as if the world around him was a joke only he understood.

In Islam, death is a time for solemnity rather than mourning. It is also a reminder to the living, asking them to reflect on the fleeting nature of life. Some say when a person dies, their soul remains but exists in a realm invisible to us. Probably Shadab was around, with his mischievous smile in an alternate realm, cracking a joke to make the angels laugh.

'It's God's will. What can we do?' Siraj said. Like many Muslims, he saw death as a predetermined event that every soul will experience. It led me to ponder. When Shadab found his end in a police bullet, was the bullet forever waiting, loaded in the cop's rifle to enter his neck? Was the cop responsible or was it Allah's will? I looked at the cops, standing with their rifles, lost in their own thoughts.

'What can we do for his family?' I asked Siraj. 'Nothing. You can't bring back their son. Let's go to our mosque and pray for him,' he told me. It made sense. A prayer for Shadab would be the best tribute.

We entered the mosque, took off our slippers and went for our ablutions. Cold water poured out from the tap. I thought about Shadab and his wudhu jokes. When I forgot the sequence of doing wudhu, he'd say, 'You should take Dimagheen tonic every day, Zeyad Bhai, so that you don't forget things!' Instead of telling him that my long-term memory was sharp, I'd follow him in the ritual and then wait for him to lead our prayers.

I came back to the present, where now his best friend was leading the prayers for his death. Some other boys had joined, like us, finding solace in the mosque.

'*Allahuakbar!*' Siraj chanted, bringing his hands to his ears. We followed Siraj's chants throughout the *Nafil namaz*, but our mind was somewhere else. '*As-Salam-Alaikum Warahmatullah*,' he said twice, ending the prayer, once facing the north and once the south. In our dua, we prayed for the salvation of Shadab, Naved, Sarfaraz, Azam, the four boys who had died outside my home, blood from their bodies still fresh on the tarmac a few feet away. There was nothing else to do.

Later, all of us Tablighis went to Shadab's home. As neighbours gathered outside their door at the intersection of the lane, we heard the wailing of his mother echoing in the silence of a curfew. 'My son! My son!' she kept crying, remembering her nineteen-year-old boy. As the men of the family looked at her with blank eyes, the women tried to console her in vain. How does one console a mother whose son had died?

Like the Tablighis often do, we gathered outside the door and offered a dua, as other men joined us. The sound of Shadab's mother's wailing faded from our ears as we left the narrow lane and went back to our own mothers.

'Where is Shadab Bhai now?' a kid asked us. I kept looking at the doors in the lane of the barbers. Umar, a Tablighi kid too mature for his age answered: 'He is now in heaven, joyful for having found a place so close to Allah. All those who saved us are our martyrs.' Nobody contested that: the image of Shadab making merry in paradise was all we needed to carry on with our lives.

⁓

The end of the violence wasn't usually the end of the conflict. After the deaths came the arrests. Cops gave the arrested boys the option of either being implicated themselves or providing the names of Muslim 'troublemakers'. It sent the rumour mills working overtime. 'There are police informants among us,' said my cousin Shakeel Bhai.

After every round of riots, rumours of who was an informant would hover in the air like houseflies on a drain. 'I think Azeem is the mole. He drinks and hangs around with the Hindus and the police,' somebody would say. 'My suspicion is on the guy who runs the electrician's shop. Nobody knows where he gets his money from,' another would say, naming a social outsider. Like a game of snakes and ladders, the rumours of who was a police informant were not just a fun exercise to kill time. Men suspected of being informers had been found dead under mysterious circumstances, their bodies fished out of drains.

The curfew was a gala time for most in the U.K., especially for kids. Everyone spent time with their families and solved old family conflicts or in some cases, discovered new ones. I was happy to see the news of the Aligarh riots on news channels. 'You saw the burning jeep on the news? The yellow wall behind it is my home,' I would proudly tell friends who telephoned to check on our well-being.

At this time, Ammi's only concern was to stockpile milk and groceries as prices would soon skyrocket. The policemen sitting in our mohalla shouted or used their batons freely if an adult man came out, but ignored the kids. I was now a teenager who looked like a child. 'Zeyad, I heard milk is available in Sheikhan. Please go through the gullies and get some,' Ammi asked me.

'What if they shoot at me and I die?' I replied, suppressing my excitement to go out on this adventure. Until recently, only Saad would go outside to find vegetables, milk and meat in the middle of a high-security curfew. 'Is there anything anyone else wants? I am going out,' I would ask all the homes in Farsh Manzil, who'd marvel at how brave I was.

After a few days of restrictions, the cops got bored of stopping people from getting out. They'd act friendly with the locals and smile at kids passing through. Even adults would come and go, and they'd look the other way. Tired of staying in their homes, boys began to organize cricket tournaments on the empty main roads. Everywhere in the U.K. was a cricket ground now.

Seeing the blatant violations, the police began to ease the curfews for a few hours at a time and then for most of the day. The major safety checkpoints for Muslims during the time of on-off communal tension were Maal Godaam and Rasal Ganj. Families living here worked as lookouts for other Muslims and in case of trouble, assembled outside their homes to warn people passing by. 'Don't go ahead, a riot is in progress,' they'd say.

Even in these times, Papa would go to his office and return late at night after meeting friends. This was a sore issue between Ammi and Papa. 'Why can't you come home early? I can't sleep when I think of you coming back from Railway Road,' she'd say. '*Arre*, nothing happens in the night. Everyone is asleep and the road is deserted. I always keep an eye out,' Papa would reply.

Aligarh was limping towards normalcy, or we thought so. However, it was just the intermission. The Muslims wanted their revenge too, and it was straight out of a Bollywood film.

Three masked gunmen on a motorbike went around killing the Hindu political leaders alleged to be behind the attack on the Farsh. It started on 19 May 2006, with Raju Kumar Samosewala, a BJP leader who had a chaat shop in a mixed locality in Usman Para. As the local story goes, two men came to his shop and began talking to him about the riots as they ate his snacks. 'Have you heard of the men looking to kill the Hindu leaders responsible?' one of them asked him, as Raju waited to close his shop.

'I am not afraid. I have been living here for years,' Raju replied.

'Would you be afraid if I took out a gun and shot you?' the customer asked, gulping down a piece of chaat.

'Do it if you have guts,' he replied, laughing.

The man and his companions threw their plates in the dustbin, and instead of taking out their wallets, they took out masks and a gun. They came back to the shop, put the gun at Raju's temple and blew his brains out. As the other customers ran away, they leisurely started their motorbike and soon got lost in the lanes.

On 23 May 2006, another Hindu leader, Raman Gupta was shot in a similar way. A list of Hindu leaders, who were future targets, was circulated and reported in newspapers. A prominent name on the list was O.P. Gupta, a rich businessman. Fearing for his life, he stopped sitting at his wholesale shop in Kanwari Ganj, from which he supplied soft drinks to a large part of the city. On 28 May 2006, three men came to his home to place an order, and Gupta allowed them inside. In the middle of the discussion, one of the men took out a gun and shot Gupta in the head.[7]

These three killings shared many similarities. All three victims were shot in the temple of their head using a country-made pistol, and died on the spot. The murders always happened around 9 p.m. around their shops. There were three murderers, who used a bike to reach and flee from the scene.[8] In the many conspiracy theories that were bombarded, some said the shooters were trained terrorists from Afghanistan, some believed they were contract killers, while others believed they worked for India's intelligence agency.

On the night O.P. Gupta was killed, the hell broke loose again. Men were ready to shed some more blood. A Hindu mob took out their anger on Muslim passers-by on Railway Road. Boys were dragged in lanes and stabbed; lock workers working shifts in Hindu areas were beaten with rods. The mob was ruling the streets of Aligarh again.

Being part of a mob replaces everyone's individual identity. It didn't matter whether their target is innocent. In that moment, they just need a punching bag to express their inner anger and frustration. Instead of being repulsed by the pain caused to the victim, they enjoy it. It makes them feel like gods for the moment. It stimulates them. It gives them the power they secretly desire but can never achieve in their normal lives.

Everyone in a mob is not equal. There are the queens and kings of the mob. These leaders often have intense childhood issues, which makes them unable to empathize. As adolescents, they were probably antisocial and lacked close family bonds. The mob gives these leaders a social identity – they are a gang, a set of people who validate each other.

Then there are the followers. They are often weak-willed people pleasers. They thrive on approval from the world, especially from the more powerful. They want to please their leaders at any cost. The more they want to be part of the group, the more likely they are to lose their identities. In secret, the followers are sometimes horrified by what they're doing in contrast to remorseless leaders. But they are easily manipulated and controlled by them.

Being in a group seems to make some behaviours acceptable that would otherwise not be. It also takes away accountability. It becomes easier to say 'Everybody was doing it' as if that makes the terrible action right. The bigger the mob, the greater the dilution of individuality. The mob attains its own character as people lose their identity. The target becomes the medium of their anguish.

I wondered what makes people's hearts so dark that they are willing to slaughter children. Was it constant rejection or an intense desire to prove themselves worthy? Do they want to punish someone for their misery because hitting their fathers, wives and children would make the world see them as bad men? But if you kill a Muslim, only adulation will follow?

This mob took the lives of three people, all Muslims. The temporary bonhomie was over. The season of violence was back in Aligarh.

Over the next few days, stories of barbarity began to fly. 'You know what happened to the Muslim couple travelling on Railway Road during the riots? The Hindu guy, one from whom we buy ice cream, took out a gun and shot the boy in front of his wife,' Shakeel Bhai, my cousin from Palle Ghar, would come and tell. 'They had gone to watch Aamir Khan's new film. Fanaa *dekhne gaye the, khud fanaa ho gaye,*' Nadeem Bhai, Shakeel Bhai's younger brother, said to the sly smiles of everyone around. There was an implicit blaming of the victims in that assertion.

As the battle rages, it infects everything. I began to notice things I hadn't before – the dangers that lurked at milk shops, grocery stores and chaat stalls. Now when I looked at the horizon, I began to organize homes around me as Hindu and Muslim homes. I also noticed the homes at the cross-sections of Hindu and Muslim areas. As you walk in a Muslim lane, there would suddenly be a door with a swastika and lemons and chilli, proudly proclaiming them as Hindus. Similarly, there would be Muslim signs outside other doors.

The story of the religious divide was most often seen through names of shops. Though the boards of shops in the interiors of Muslim mohallas will say Faizan Tailor, Ansari Medico or Khan Mobile Repairs, the ones in Hindu majority areas would become National Gun Shop, Alpha Chemist, Hindustan Watch Company or Lucky Dry Cleaner. There was even a Saxena Brothers owned by a Muslim, who wanted to preserve the original Hindu name of the shop due to its goodwill. I have never known a Hindu shop owner in Aligarh who retained a Muslim shopkeeper's name. They would name their shops Soni Cloth House, Shri Laxmi Prasad Maharaj Sarraffa Brothers or Jai Shiv Puri Bhandaar.

Even when riots are a distant dream of the past, everything changes when Muslims move to Hindu areas in Aligarh. The same happened when Hindus came to Upar Kot. The atmosphere changes. People's stances change. Their expectations change. The tenor of their voice changes. Their voice becomes low, they behave like decent and mannered human beings and mind their own business.

I would be picking up fights and arguing with Ishrat Bhai if he gave me a rotten egg in Upar Kot. But as soon as I entered Hindu territory, I would become the nicest boy in the world. I would walk with my head down in a straight line. I wouldn't shout. I wouldn't argue with shopkeepers even if they cheated me or charged extra for comic books. They also knew this. Some took advantage, some didn't.

Before it occurs in the physical realm, ghettoization begins in the minds of men of women. This is like a self-imposed exile, that makes communities living in harmony with each other for centuries, insular and uninviting towards each other.

Human habitats become segregated based on your faith. The cross-community trust collapses like a house of cards. The other becomes like an alien, without a heart and without an iota of humanness.

It is from this ghettoization, in the real world and in people's minds, that violence emerges. It is from these constrictions of the heart battles emerge and boys like Shadab often pay the price.

# 14

# WOLVES

THE MUGHALS RULED India for over three centuries, celebrated by secularists for their inclusive approach but reviled by fundamentalists for the same thing. The third and most popular king of the family, Akbar, even attempted to start his own cult by combining Hinduism and Islam. Like a punctured hot air balloon, it was never able to take off despite Akbar's patronage.

His son and next emperor Jahangir, however, wasn't that much into religion. He drank all day, was an opium addict, wrote poetry and was more into arts. He claimed himself as an animal lover but was too weak to give up his love of hunting them as a sport. Though his forefathers were mainly into hunting deer and tigers, Jahangir liked to prey upon something else – wolves. For these expeditions, the places he chose in his huge kingdom were the forests of Kol.[1] Centuries later, the forests of Kol had given way to the concrete jungles of Aligarh, but one thing remained true: wolves still roamed here albeit in the disguise of human beings.

In my eleventh standard, I came to know about this side of Aligarh when I left my sophisticated convent school to join the senior secondary school of AMU, an all boys school. It lay across the Kathpula in Civil Lines – a universe apart from the U.K.

Civil Lines was as different from Upar Kot as the contrasting pole of a magnet. Here lived the posh people of Aligarh, AMU professors, clerks, doctors, engineers, judges, policemen and traders. In Civil Lines, Aligarh was a town of over a hundred grand havelis, where rich zamindars and nawabs lived. Trees and British-era architecture lined broad roads. Streetlights were everywhere. Roads were without potholes and the drains were nearly invisible. There were fancy apartments and well-maintained colonies. Even the hate here was decent: Hindus and Muslims lived close without killing each other. 'The riots don't happen here because people are civilized,' everyone said. In reality, they were as civilized as chameleons camouflaging themselves in whatever colour is around.

Here, every other person is a character – most of them controversial, competitive and snobbish. More than actual knowledge, there will mostly be a facade of knowledge – everybody is entangled in a culture of exhibitionism and sycophancy. 'People of Civil Lines will do everything to prove that they know more than you, even on topics you might be an expert in,' my friend Shahrukh often says. If Neil Armstrong would have stepped into Civil Lines rather than on the moon, he'd have definitely run into Aligarhians giving him lessons on 'good astronauting'.

The people of Civil Lines are addicted to drama. If there are no conflicts around them, they will create it out of thin air. They will be involved in matters they have no business being involved in. This is one of the reasons most AMU alumni are connected to Aligarh decades after passing out, wherever they are settled in – the US, Libya, Dubai or Nicaragua. There are few places as dramatic on Earth as Aligarh.

This idea of forcefully dramatizing real life is reflected in the nicknames that are given to people in Civil Lines and in the university campus. These names would reflect the simplest aspects of a person or their eccentricities. 'Let's consider a student who likes walking around the campus a lot. After some time, he will be named *Salman Paidal*. If there is a professor who doesn't have a car and would use *Tirri* - half rickshaw, half motorcycle that ply in Aligarh - he will be called *Tirri*,' Shahrukh told me.

Then there are teachers or students named after animals they look like: Batakh, duck, because of his lips; Cheel, eagle, because of his baldness; Bakra, goat, because of long ears. Other animals/ professors are Rabbit, Lomdi, Haathi. Some are named after physical attributes they can be reduced to *Anda, Kaala, Maila, Tunda, Langda* and *Rumaal*. Some are known by the objects or vehicles they use: *Beedi, Yamaha, Boxer, Chooran, Tamancha, Katta, Shooter, Chatni, Maachis, Chappal*. A professor, who had never gone to Hajj was named *Haaji*, because he was unnecessarily self-righteous.

Then there are professors named *Dhobi, Jaadugar, Qawwal* because students thought they looked like these professionals. And of course, there are the crazy nicknames: *Mental, Pipe, Chaatu, Baawla*. Pipe and Chaatu are extensively used for the ones who talk too much. The female teachers are named mostly after heroines: Madhuri, Juhi Chawla, Sridevi. If anyone is too irritating, they are called things like *Chipkali* or *Lakdi*. Most of these teachers and students know their nicknames. They became so prevalent some had to introduce themselves by their nicknames. 'Which Aarif?' if somebody asks on the phone, the person might reply: 'Oh, it's me Aarif Chappal from AMU.'

As is clear from their dominance in the nickname game, the central characters in this university town are the professors and the students. Most professors have an ancestral connection to nawabs, zamindars or rich families. Only a few have risen in ranks coming from underprivileged backgrounds. In a town where every other boy thinks of himself as a goon, some of them create harsh boundaries and live an isolated, or dare I say, insensitive life. There are countless stories of professors using their powers to exploit students and have them bring groceries, pick up their children from school or pay their electricity or telephone bills.

Most are very anti-student and part of regional lobbies from Bihar, Azamgarh, Gorakhpur, Sambhal, Bahraich, Mewat, among other places. In AMU, if you don't pander to the lobbies, you can easily be made a scapegoat for something or the other. Occasionally, there are professors who become goons themselves and carry country-made guns in their pockets. Like professors, the non-teaching staff, usually seen lounging or debating in their offices, will have their own political circles and lobbies.

Most professors and university officials live in posh colonies around the university: Sir Syed Nagar, Zohra Bagh, Dhorra, Kabir Colony, Marris Road, Badar Bagh etc. Around these colonies will be the markets like Zakariya, Shamshad Market, Amir Nishan, where students will have countless cups of tea, eat, shop, buy stationary or Xerox notes of their friends.

Like Upar Kot, Civil Lines also has many sides (which someone who comes from there should someday write about). It is also Aligarh, but the essence is different. Here, Aligarh is a girl in the cloth market of Amir Nisha Market trying to haggle with a *rickshaw-wala* for the best fare. Amir Nisha is a sea of women. It seems as if the women are happy only here, shopping for themselves and their families. They come with their closest ones, friends, sisters, daughters, and mothers, laughing at each other and arguing with the shopkeepers. They speak like they mostly can't in their homes, and they're sharp, witty and playful. They assemble in shops, inspect clothes and take home some happiness.

Aligarh is also a group of men standing around the Amir Nisha Market with passive-aggressiveness that marks gatherings of middle-aged men. A tailor who enjoys women lining up outside his shop and gives them unsolicited fashion advice. The professor's son showing off his expensive gadget, trying to seek the phone numbers of girls walking around. Teenagers who stand in the lanes to stare and stalk the women. An old man trying to sell coloured slippers to people whizzing past on motorbikes. The *rickshaw-wala* noticing all of them and their antics, trying to find a ride so that he can feed his family of four at his home.

Like a secret world within a world, poor people exist in Civil Lines too. Living in areas like Jamalpur, Jeewangarh and Manzoorgarhi, their cramped ghettos and slums bustle with the rhythm of daily existence. Their weathered faces and tattered clothes are a stark contrast to the officers and civil servants they spend their lives pleasing. Like Upar Kot, their children play barefoot in the narrow alleys, their laughter echoing through the labyrinthine maze of poverty. But unlike their rich neighbours whose hearts narrowed as their wealth grew, they persevere with dignity in their hearts.

However, like every university town, the central characters here are the students. They come mostly from small towns in Uttar Pradesh and Bihar and live in havelis which are now hostels. Others are sons and daughters of professors, traders, clerks, officers from Aligarh or other towns in north India. Then there are engineering and doctor aspirants who detest boys who sit at the dhaba – they spend their nights at the library, burning the midnight oil to become something their parents can be proud of.

In Spartan culture, when children reached adolescence, they are said to be left by their parents in a forest on their own. Aligarh parents did the same when they got their children admitted to AMU. This forest was full of animals of all kinds, scary, wild but full of lessons. 'If a child survives here, he/she would be tough enough to handle anything,' Papa would say. I disagreed. I thought Aligarh also limited its inhabitants in many ways, making them feel like rulers of this mystical forest, content but far from the realities of the outside world.

In this competitive forest, every animal is trying to prove *they* are the king. For this, one would become a mullah, someone would become a doctor or engineer, another would become a musician/ artist/writer, while someone else would become a *neta*. The last category, the student politician, is more populous than others. Clad in a *sherwani*, they are generally seen making speeches at roadsides or at dhabas, their eyes dreaming of delivering speeches in the Indian Parliament. 'Politics runs in the veins of people of Aligarh as countless cups of tea,' my friend Kaleem would say. Like professors, many students are also part of regional lobbies in AMU.

Closely associated with politics is the idea of *badmaashi*. Every other young boy in Aligarh is or hopes to be a badmaash, a petty goon. I have met all kinds of badmaash – sophisticated, unruly, rich and poor. Most turn to goondaism at the drop of a hat, others seek the help of goons only because of the quirks of fate. It is rare to meet a teenage boy here who doesn't dream of becoming a strongman someday. This desire unites Hindus and Muslims, regardless of class. In fact, criminal groups are among the few spheres where religion takes a backseat for something more primary – the timeless, omnipresent lust for power.

When life and limb are at stake, men will go to extreme lengths and seek the support of even those they consider inferior. In that process, they come across people from other faiths. It is these power equations that lead to the emergence of the stereotype of a Muslim sidekick – the bearded, loyal guy from Bollywood films who does everything to protect his Hindu master/friend.

'The only way to defeat a badmaash in Aligarh is by putting him in front of a bigger badmaash,' Shahrukh once told me. He was talking about the 'bhai culture', the complex chain of goondaism prevailing in the city. It starts with the petty goons, schoolboys and mohalla thugs, who listen to the bigger goons, college boys and local neta, respectively. They, in turn, answer only to the regional crime boss, who, eventually takes instructions from some official higher-ups or a politician. Through this chain, many boys become part of the all-pervasive mafia. At the top is always a minister or a political bigwig – the reason it is impossible to separate Indian politics from its criminal nexus.

An eleventh-standard kid, I was utterly attracted by this new world. The power trip of youth was working its charm. As my friendship with Papa withered away like freshly cut grass on a summer afternoon, friends were becoming the centre of my life. In the snake-filled swamp that Aligarh was, teenage friendships were the pathway through which we navigated the complexities of adolescence. The boys at school were not just my partners in crime, but my window to the world, something that my family was always trying to protect me from.

This was probably the reason, I became a part of a boys' gang, mostly consisting of my classmates from St Fidelis. It started as means to avoid being bullied or physically abused by other boy gangs, and then it became a part of me. I realized I was drawn to the dark, rebellious, and chaotic ones, finding the sorted ones unexciting. It was as adventurous as the world of comic books. Soon, I learnt the ground rules of Aligarh badmaashi, which were:

1.  In a fight, always strike first as it gives you a starting advantage.

2.  Always show your seniors respect. Every goon has an intense desire to be honoured and being able to do this can save your ass when trouble finds you.

3.  Never be afraid of the cops. Stand your ground and pretend that they need to be afraid of *you*. They'll go away.

This gang also gave me a chance to expand my social circles, something I found utterly liberating. To understand this phase in my life, one should have an idea of Aligarian slang. A *'barua'* is a guy who wastes entire days sitting with his gang on the roadside – something I would grow up to be.

*Kaptaan*, an Urduized version of Captain, is a leader who sits around with twenty boys on a dhaba, showing his power. On good terms with goons and influential people alike, he is a source of security and pride for his followers. He will also likely be the guy who'd harass a professor to get extra attendance for his friends, sometimes beating them up or putting a gun to their face – not a rare occurrence on the campus.

Often, Kaptaan is a narcissist put on a pedestal by junior boys for favours, but deserted when he is no longer valuable. Sort of like an intellectual counterpart to Kaptaan, Cheetah is someone who is cleverer and more talented than the others. In an approval-seeking society, most boys at AMU and living in adjoining areas spent their youth proving they are a Kaptaan or a Cheetah.

The Kaptaan or Cheetah will have in their court a *'dealer'*, a shallow guy who says senseless things with utter confidence to prove his unquestionable wisdom. The dealer will make a lot of false promises. In words of Shahrukh: *'Dealer hope deta hai aur last me ghonp deta hai.'* Moreover, the dealer will pretend to know everyone influential, including the vice-chancellor, the proctor, mayor or big traders. In moments of need or when a fight breaks out, however, the dealer disappears like a ghost on Lal Diggi.

Apart from this, there is a long list of Aligarh terms. Among the prominent ones are 'Karra', which means terrific or 'Farzi', which translates into a pretentious person. Shias are *khatmals*, or bedbugs, and the Sunnis are *machhars*, or mosquitoes.

For everything that might be wrong with Aligarh, it's a place of intellectual enquiry and lots and lots of conversations. A place where a person is respected for the humorous stories he/she has, everyone learns to talk. Everyone here is a storyteller. It's like a close-knit community, where everyone knows everyone, and lifelong friendships are forged. Moreover, as it has students from across India, it is a melting point of culture, language and traditions.

However, this liberty is enjoyed more by boys as compared to girls. Most young girls in Aligarh are controlled by conservative families and hostel wardens to stop them from becoming wayward and immoral, by mostly keeping them inside their homes and hostel rooms. Boys, like in almost every small Indian town, are free to be whatever they want. While talking about girls, slang (mostly popularized by students from all-boys schools) is restricted to their physical beauty. 'Bataa', 'Maal', and 'Kancha' all refer to a beautiful girl. 'Saaman' means her bosom and 'Balti' means her ass. 'Harrafa' is what you would call a slut or a cunning woman.

Coming from a semi-joint family where women far outnumbered men, I wasn't used to objectifying women. I didn't join in when other boys made lewd comments or quoted Urdu verses when girls walked past them. Ever since my St Fidelis days, I had as many friends who were girls as there were boys. If I met a girl from school, I'd go up to her and have a conversation, and it surprised most boys around me.

The badmaash boys, however, had their own share of female attention. Some had separate hours at night to phone each of their three girlfriends. Others lied to pretend they were wealthy. 'I am in Hong Kong for a business meeting, *jaan*! Can't wait to come back and see your lovely face,' an older boy said on the phone while sitting at a dhaba in Aligarh. His father ran a small shop, and he rarely even went to Delhi.

Like a lazy toad floating in the pond, I was more interested in *baruapanti*: wasting my days at street corners and on dingy staircases. A barua spends at least five hours a day on this passion (some even dedicate up to sixteen hours!). They spend this time joking around, smoking cigarettes, chewing *paan masala*, staring aimlessly at passers-by, bragging about their fights and girls' interest in them. Once in a while, someone would come up with a shady way to earn money, and it spread like wildfire. Baruas also have another superpower: they can sleep anywhere, be it university lawns, dhaba chairs and in some cases, air-conditioned ATMs.

I was now ignoring my old friends from St Fidelis for my fellow baruas: Atif Mungeri, Chottu, Dadda and Ankur. Dadda was one of the few Hindu boys spoiled enough to be a barua, Ankur was my former bus mate from Gudiya Bagh, and Atif Mungeri was a hosteller from, of course, Munger in Bihar. Dozens of Atif's hosteller friends joined us with full vigour to practically do nothing. Living like the world belonged to us, we lived in the moment, bunked classes, skipped exams, gatecrashed weddings, screamed proxy attendance for absent friends, played carrom during Chemistry labs and hung around with 'boys with connections'.

The unofficial leader of this group was Chottu/Amir. Slim as a fox, he wasn't physically imposing but courageous and forever eager to start a fight with anyone – a trait that made boys respect him. His younger brother Honey was brave like him, but unlike him, huge. Every boy in Amir Nisha, Aligarh's biggest ladies' market and a regular haunt of most gangs, knew the two brothers. Honey was once nearly killed by a rival, who fired upon him in the middle of the road. The shots missed, and a compromise between the two parties was reached after their parents got involved. Surviving a bullet hit only cemented his status as a legend.

In his eleventh standard, Chottu moved to Delhi to study at Jamia Millia Islamia. So, it was I and Dadda who spent the most time together. Every day, we reached school late, climbed the school boundary wall from the nearby graveyard, looking for teachers crazy enough to hide in the bushes to catch us. In the chemistry labs, we would behave like mad scientists, mixing all the chemicals trying to generate an explosion. But we were *that* bad at chemistry, it only simmered and never exploded. Our bald chemistry teacher (nicknamed, of course, Cheel the Eagle) was so engrossed in teaching to front-row students, that there was plenty of time for us to jump outside the window after taking our attendance.

The strangest among our teachers was Abid Sir, the sherwani-clad physics teacher with a long, brown, henna-dyed beard. To exhort the boys to study, he'd appeal to them in the name of Allah. Dadda was Hindu and my conscience was nearly dead, and so we came up with a plan to take advantage of his religiosity. Abid Sir would never say no to students wanting to go drink water as it was considered forbidden in Islam. After getting our attendance every day, we'd ask to go to the water cooler. The other kids would return, but I and Dadda would go to play carrom in the sports room. In a class of seventy, Abid Sir wouldn't know who came back and who didn't.

But like dogs who just scored a bone, we became cocky and began bragging. Soon, other kids joined us. One fine day, nearly half the class didn't return after leaving to drink water. Of course, Abid Sir noticed. All these rowdy boys were instructed to bring their parents or local guardians to meet him. 'Until I meet them, you won't get your attendance,' he said to the shock of the class. Within a week, almost everyone had brought their guardians in, and the only one who remained was me. I didn't want Papa to see this side of me. But losing attendance meant I could lose the year.

After much thought, I decided to find a 'fake father'. I first tried to convince a rickshaw puller into this role, but he didn't trust his acting skills. Then I brought a shopkeeper at a chemist shop as my 'elder brother'. But the day we got to school to meet Abid Sir, he was shouting at a student in the physics lab. It scared my 'elder brother' so much, he decided to make a run for it. The future now looked dark. *Should I tell Papa and fall in his eyes forever?* I wondered.

Like a firefighter saving victims from a burning godown, Dadda came to my rescue by taking me to his friend's billiards-cum-cybercafe at Medical Road. The manager here was a middle-aged man everyone called Saddam Hussein because he looked *exactly* like Saddam Hussein. Nobody knew his real name. 'Papa has gone abroad to meet some relatives, and I can't ask him to come,' I told the Saddam lookalike. After much persuasion, he agreed to pose as my father.

That day, fortunately, Abid Sir was quietly sitting in a corner of the lab. 'Sir, Papa is here,' I introduced the two and left the room. For the next five minutes, they bonded over saying bad things about me. 'He is intelligent but doesn't study,' Abid Sir said. 'I know. He doesn't even listen to his elders now.' I could hear the lookalike saying angrily. He *actually* thought he was my father, and my teacher was impressed.

When I thanked the Saddam lookalike for his help, he remained in his role. 'Respect the opportunity that you have – many don't get it,' he told me. Not wanting to break the rhythm of this drama, I promised my fake father that I would be a good boy, and I kept my promise. I began to study and scored good marks in physics, making the same teacher an admirer. But the story didn't end here.

A few months later, I was taking my real father to a doctor, and while we were on Railway Road, I saw my physics teacher walking towards us. By this time, I had totally forgotten about the fake father episode. When I saw him, I was delighted. *Sir will praise me in front of Papa! What a good opportunity to earn brownie points!* I thought. As we approached Abid Sir, I suddenly *remembered*. Thankfully, he was looking the other way and I had a few seconds to come up with a plan. I suddenly held Papa's arm and dragged him to the nearest shop. 'I have to buy something here, Papa,' I told him.

'It's a ladies' cloth shop. What do you want to buy here?' he said, perplexed.

I pretended to be confused until Abid Sir passed by. 'Oh, wrong shop!' I glibly replied, having narrowly saved the day.

We used Saddam and his billiards-cum-cybercafe once more. One day, Dadda lost his most precious belonging: his Reliance phone. Dadda was heartbroken and kept calling his number. Few days later, somebody picked up. 'I won't return it for free. Give me 800 rupees or I will throw it in a drain,' said the greedy voice on the other end.

Dadda agreed at once. The greedy voice on the other end was based in Atrauli, a village near Aligarh. 'Meet me at the Atrauli bus stand tomorrow afternoon. Don't pull any tricks,' he said. The next day, Dadda took me and four other boys with him in case the exchange turned into a fight. He was disappointed when he met the Atrauli boy. 'I didn't bring the phone here. You'll need to come to my village to pick it up,' the smart-ass said.

Of course, I was hesitant to go to Atrauli for the fear of being killed and buried on a farm. But Dadda didn't back down. 'Get on my bike, we can go together,' he agreed. On the way, Dadda told him he was a Brahmin Hindu. The caste/religion card impressed the Atrauli boy. 'Bhai, I only have 500 rupees, the other 300 are with a friend on Medical Road. Should we pick it up on the way?' Dadda asked him. Blinded by the lure of money and Hindu solidarity, he agreed. The other boys, including me, followed on another motorbike.

Dadda took him to the billiard-cum-cybercafe managed by Saddam Hussein lookalike. As soon as they parked, dozens of boys came out and dragged the Atrauli boy inside. Like villain's henchmen in a Bollywood movie, Dadda and others kept beating him for over an hour. Scared of the trouble, I went home. The next day, I asked Dadda if he got his phone back.

'*Phone?* After the thrashing he got, we made him call his gang to come with the phone and 200 rupees as a penalty for our trouble. Since we were tired after beating him up, we also told them to bring along some Pepsi,' he told, brimming with a sense of victory.

Dadda had been exploiting everyone he could since his school days. He'd keep extorting money from his father, a simple, middle-class, Brahmin man. 'I told Papa that my fees for one year at AMU is Rs 15,000, while it's just 3,000,' he'd brag. At other times, he'd ask for money to buy expensive books but ask friends to lend him photocopies. 'In his eyes, I am studying very hard for my engineering entrance exams at AMU,' he'd say, making smoke rings with his mouth. Somehow, he even got through engineering.

Dadda also introduced me to a 'free samosa' shop near our school. Run by three brothers, its owners were so engrossed in family troubles that they forgot to implement the first rule of running a shop – asking customers to pay the bill. They seemed more interested in proving points to their siblings than getting paid for their samosas. 'It's your fault that the shop is not doing that well,' they'd say and keep arguing. We, obviously, took advantage of the quarrels. Every day we ate our samosas, greeted them politely and confidently moved out of the shop without paying.

'How can someone not realize that we have been coming here for weeks, saying "As-Salam-Alaikum" every day but never paying them?' I once asked Dadda. 'I have been doing that for a year now. And would you keep your voice down? Eat the mangoes and don't count the trees,' Dadda replied.

Unlike Dadda, I never actually fought anyone physically. Like all the groups I'd later be a part of, I felt like an outsider. I came across to them as lost and disinterested, as I mostly hung around for protection. Not being part of a group in Aligarh is a surefire way to get yourself emotionally and physically abused. I was bullied inside the group once in a while, but it was rare and not too serious.

When others were exhibiting their social domination, I was busy writing Orkut testimonials for girls. In the 'About me' section on my own profile, I was a Jason Bourne-like amnesiac spy waiting for his beloved, Claire, a girl he couldn't remember fully. In real life, I wasn't that exciting and far too shy. But somehow, I found the first girlfriend of my life, my puppy love (I am not counting the girl at school who I had engaged in a mutual staring contest every day near the water cooler). In the dreamy world that only youthful love could create, life looked like a bed of roses. We will marry each other, have children, grow old and die in each other's arms. What could possibly go wrong with that?

Like young lovers we were, both of us kept talking to each other for hours. I bought a Reliance phone and recharged it every month with unlimited calls, and we talked all night. Even when the substandard phone became heated because it was being charged all day, we kept talking about our insecurities, hopes, studies, books, music, stories of our common friends and our future together.

In the madness of the love and power trips of my youth, I didn't notice that Papa was getting weaker and weaker every day.

# 15

## CANCER DAYS

LIKE ICE CUBES in water, youth dissipate into oblivion fast. But at its prime, it makes you feel immortal. Death, disease and disillusionment are still far removed from your consciousness. Betrayal, heartbreak and responsibility haven't stained your heart yet. But with time, lovely faces turn into wrinkled caricatures of themselves. You are not the rising Sun any more. The world has more regrets than hopes. Life is not giving you new things anymore but taking away what you already have. People who once admired you, including your children, now try to stay away.

Work had always given Papa's life purpose. Even after he retired when I was in my twelfth standard, he kept going to the university to meet friends, but the power that came from his official role was gone and with it a bit of the respect. Aligarh and its university became a mean place. 'You are too old now to come here. Why don't you go home?' his friends would say to him.

'Remember this always, people show their true colours only when you don't have anything to give them,' he'd come home and tell Ammi.

He had always had a thin frame, but now at sixty-two, he looked weak and fragile. It made Ammi super anxious. One afternoon when I was preparing for my semester exams at the school, Papa went to the regional transport office to help a friend get a licence. An hour later, our landline rang, and I picked up.

'Is this the home of Masroor Ahmed Khan?'

'Yes,' I said.

'Your father has had an accident at GT Road,' said the voice on the other line.

The first thought that came to my mind was that he would die. *This is how it happens!* I thought. Trained by years of riots to face a crisis, I calmly noted the name of the hospital and the caller's number. My cousin Tariq called them back and the helpful stranger on the other end told him where to go. After I told Ammi, she began to weep loudly. I knew the first thought that had crossed her pessimistic mind.

Tariq Bhai left at once in his old Maruti 800, drove fast and reached the hospital within fifteen minutes. 'Chacha has suffered wounds on his head, but it's not serious,' he called and told us from the hospital. But until we saw Papa, his head bandaged but walking on his legs, nothing made sense. It had been a close call. A car had hit the back of his scooter when he was making a U-turn at a road divider, causing him to lose consciousness.

'You won't ride the scooter now, Saad will drive you around,' Ammi declared the next day. Envious of Saad putting his dirty claws on Papa's scooter, I offered my services as well. I didn't even know how to cycle, but that didn't stop me from telling Ammi I would learn to ride a scooter and drive Papa around. She trusted me even less than Papa and declined, making full use of the power she wielded in the home. Masroor may have been the boss at the office, but the home was Parveen's domain – he had to bow.

With new restrictions and old age catching up to him, Papa began to turn into an angry version of himself. With no subordinates to shout at, he began yelling at Ammi and Saad, but never at me. However, he had ceased to be a friend. Papa was now only a father like other fathers in Aligarh, who kept scolding me for not growing up fast. 'You don't even know how to operate a bank account or make reservations on a train! How will you survive in the world?' he'd say.

'It's because you didn't teach me or allow me to do things that other kids did,' I wanted to say but didn't. He kept going on and on about the big, bad world out there. 'It will slaughter you like a little puppy on the road if you don't learn.' I just nodded and it made him sadder.

Sadness is like an invisible, dark cloud hanging above your head. Its darkness is dimmed on better days, but it comes back, blocking any ray of sunshine to your heart. While grief coexists with its sister emotions and quietly slips inside your mind, luring you into its warm embrace, sadness drives away other emotions. It cuts through the clutter of your mind like a sharp knife, purifying you from inside at the cost of joy. It, though, makes people more sensitive – the kind who'd be there around you when you fall, tell you ways to rejuvenate an injured heart or listen to your grievances.

Most Indian families, however, don't like a brooding person around. They prefer to be thrilled by the world and when problems come, be hysterical about them. Those who sit alone to ponder the pointlessness of it all are not fun to be around. This was likely why Hindu saints left their homes in their old age and escaped to the mountains: they wanted to be alone with their pensiveness, far from the prying eyes of their jovial families.

Papa was changed by his sadness. He was now the easily irritable patriarch of our family. The weakening of his body strengthened his anger. He had never scolded or raised his hands at us, so his yelling came as a surprise. 'You are not the son of a prince. Your mother has spoiled you,' he'd say.

Until now, I believed we were as well off as my classmates' families. Somehow, my parents had managed to give us a comfortable life through their sacrifices. 'We are not as rich as you think we are,' he'd say, as if to wake me up from my slumber. There was something else ailing his mind: during one of his anti-establishment stints in AMU, he was transferred from his position at Union Hall, but eventually called back as nobody else could deal with student leaders. For reasons best known to the university, his pension was counted from the day he joined back, reducing it to half of what it would have otherwise been. It was too low to bear the expenses of our family of four.

To keep earning after retirement, a friend told Papa to supply belt buckles to clients outside Aligarh. For a few days, big sacks were placed in our lobby, something Papa saw with disdain and Ammi saw as a necessity. Like a hastily made paper plane, the business wasn't able to take off. Soon, the sacks of belt buckles disappeared like lizards in winters, sold at less price to some acquaintance, never to return.

Money is a strange thing; it dictates how much people respect you, how far you can ride your scooter, how many times you can go out with friends, whether or not you can help your sick relative, where you can study, career risks you can take, the person you'll marry, and often, the number of people who will turn up at your funeral. The richer a person is, the more society ignores their faults, the more their normal qualities are exaggerated into sagas of nobility. 'Money hides people's faults, poverty makes them abject,' Papa often said. 'If somebody respects me because of the clothes I wear, do I even want them in my life?' he'd ask. But outside Papa's ideals, money meant everything.

I was the biggest disappointment of Papa's life. With great expectations, he had made me take subjects that could qualify me for both engineering and medical entrance exams. The teenage Zeyad was, however, more interested in girls and hanging around at dhabas. My self-confidence was gone, replaced by endless doubts. 'I am just a lazy, arrogant boy who is not even that bright,' I told myself. 'You have coasted so far without working hard. Now is the time of your endless decline,' my insecurity said. This made me hate myself. Though Saad also wasn't doing that great in his studies, the weight of expectations crushing him was probably not as great.

With some leftover money from his retirement package intact, Papa brought home something that he thought would propel us to work hard: a desktop computer. 'This is the age of computers, and it will help in their studies,' he said when Ammi protested the expense.

Though he liked computers, he had a strong derision for the other gadget making its mark in the world: the mobile phone. Even after repeated requests from Ammi and others, he wouldn't carry one. 'It's a prison. Do I really want the world to reach out to me *all the time*? If they want to talk to me, let them call me on our landline or better, come home to meet me,' he'd say. Iqbal Bhai, a friend of Papa's, echoed this sentiment. 'Boys and girls nowadays are constantly on their mobiles. Nothing good will come out of this obsession.' As I dared not ask Papa for money for a mobile phone, I secretly saved some money to buy a cheap Reliance phone.

After the arrival of computers and mobile phones, my life changed, but not necessarily for the better. I was now obsessed with my PC. I would soon learn its basics and advanced functions. Then I began using it to binge-watch Hollywood movies and listen to music copied from MP3 CDs. I eventually moved to an obsession that would take away years of my life: computer gaming.

This hobby would go on to dictate what career I would follow, what course I got into and what friends I found. I first began playing *Need for Speed* and defeated nerdy engineering students on their home turfs and won competitions at AMU.

Then I turned my attention towards *Grand Theft Auto: Vice City*. While Papa thought I was using the PC to study, I was mowing down imaginary people with my imaginary car, butchering them with chainsaws and becoming the mafia lord of Mississippi. Every day I would put on '*Beete Lamhein*' by singer KK and drive, kill and plunder on the pink roads of Vice City. I could escape the real world here, which was all about failing Papa's expectations, his deteriorating health, yelling and financial uncertainties. Here, I could do anything and become whatever I wanted.

Even though I was addicted to gaming, I was confident I would crack my entrance exams. 'Haven't I been acing exams at the last minute all my life?' I told Papa. But that didn't happen this time. No matter how much I tried, I couldn't understand organic chemistry and differentiation and integration, topics that formed a considerable chunk of the questions in the entrance exams. The facade of my intelligence was breaking down. I couldn't qualify for any of the entrance exams at AMU, but I was the first among my friends to finish *Grand Theft Auto: Vice City*.

Papa was heartbroken. It was the only time he cried about something to do with me. It was a sad day at home. 'Why don't you take up English?' he suggested. In Aligarh, a bachelor's in arts was what the boys who were the weakest in studies did. 'My friend is taking economics, it has better potential,' I said. 'Go for English literature. It is what you'd be better suited to,' he said. It made sense.

Along with English, I also took linguistics (Sayema suggested it) and Islamic Studies. I went for the latter because I wanted to know the history of Islam, the faith that the world media was obsessed with. Putting my father's engineering dreams to rest, I reignited my childhood dream of being a journalist. My graduation class was a shock. Most of the boys in English literature didn't know English. 'I opted for this course because I want to learn English,' said more than twenty students on the first day of orientation, to the chagrin of our class teacher.

For me, the course was too easy. I would rarely buy books or attend morning lectures. I sat on the back bench and read a novel as teachers taught the front-row kids. After class, like all AMU boys, I spent my days at dhabas and canteens, talking about politics, religion, films, music and girls.

At this time, there was nowhere in Aligarh where boys and girls pursuing their graduation could meet – except the Literary Club. I went there to meet girls but ended up rekindling my passion for quizzing. Within a year, I became the quizzing head at the club. I began devoting all my time and attention to it and became an extra-curricular king once again. I was back to winning prizes, but this time for the university. This was probably when Papa got cancer of the lymphocytes. Only I didn't get to know about it until he died.

I was in the first year of my graduation. I had begun escaping the situation at home by being outside all the time. There is still a big lapse in my memory about what happened at home in those days. However, the one thing I clearly remember feeling was an overpowering powerlessness and helplessness.

Cancer is a clever enemy. It slowly takes away your resilience and charm and destroys your family from within. To see a loved one reduced to bare bones is something the world doesn't prepare you for. Their strength is gone, gradually leaching out of their bodies in vomit and blood. With each passing day, the very energetic Masroor Ahmed Khan got weaker.

It is said that there are five stages of grief that terminally ill patients go through: denial, anger, depression, bargaining and acceptance. At first, Papa kept saying he would get better. 'Parveen worries as if I am going to die,' he would tell Iqbal Bhai, who sat with him in the drawing room every day for three hours. Then came the anger, and the victims were mostly Ammi and Saad. He would get angry over everything: tasteless food, unclean toilets, us not being able to understand him. I didn't have any idea why he was angry, but his attitude made me angry with him. I stopped talking to him.

He grew tired of shouting and then began the depression. He began talking of his impending death constantly. 'I am worried about what will happen to them after me. They aren't smart enough to deal with the world,' he would often tell Iqbal Bhai, making sure I was listening. He also talked about how he didn't have enough savings left. Day after day, he saw his pension and provident fund accounts reducing and his medical bills mounting.

Then came the bargaining and frequent swinging between extreme levels of hope and despair. Like a debutante storyteller, he would tell his life story to whoever listened and call people he hadn't talked to for a long time. He'd tell Iqbal Bhai that he was dying. 'This is how others have gone,' he'd say. He developed a sweet tooth, something he never had. He'd cry at little things. He would tell us weird things, like to take care of Ammi after he passed away.

*Why does he say things like that? He'll get better!* I'd think. I didn't know that cancer was building inside him. His lymphocytes, white blood cells that give our body immunity, were multiplying at an exponential rate, his organs failing, his body losing its vitality.

When somebody from a middle-class family gets cancer, they face tragic choices. What matters more – extending a few months of your father's life or saving that money to fulfil the needs of the family if, God forbid, he passed away? I was angry at the world for the unfairness of what was happening, for not being rich, for not being able to do anything. The only thing on my mind was to earn money, something Papa hadn't been too interested in. It was the only way I could get out of Aligarh, now a hellhole I wanted to leave behind. It kept going on for a year.

In the second year of my college, I saw a notice on the Arts Faculty noticeboard: somebody in Aligarh wanted content writers. It would turn out to be my first writing job. As my father dealt with cancer without my knowledge, I was busy writing dozens of articles every day.

I would just sit at my computer all day, put on my earphones to drown out the noise of the world and write dozens of articles every day on the topics assigned. The most common theme was 'How to get your ex back'. As Ammi kept crying and Saad drove Papa to hospitals and doctors, I was busy giving dating advice to strangers on the internet. 'Cut all contact,' I wrote. 'Don't be needy, work out, become confident, make your ex realize what they are missing, make them jealous by talking to hot people, dress up and go to parties,' I told strangers on the internet.

Other topics were how to unlock your Nintendo Wii, how to jailbreak an iPhone, how to find exotic food for your German Shepherd, how to impress women in Los Angeles, how to hire a limousine, how to find guitar lessons in New York. On each topic, I had to write more than ten articles, basically saying one thing in a dozen different ways. I realized this was something I was good at.

I would pour my anger out on blank Word documents. I would keep writing as Ammi and Saad cared for my ailing father. 'I must earn – that's the only way to rise out of this mess, not by being emotional,' I kept telling myself when Ammi talked to me about my apathy. 'I am earning my own money and taking care of our future,' I'd say if I had to be sent to get medicines. I'd only go if there was no way to avoid it. When I was not writing, I would be on the phone with my girlfriend, who was the only person who understood me. She motivated me to keep working hard.

As I was facing the highs and lows of dating, Papa got mysteriously weaker. He'd sometimes call for water, and I'd give him what he asked but didn't stay there for more than a few minutes. I was *sure* he wasn't going to die. It was the first time he had gotten ill like that, and I thought he was taking it too seriously, taking his cues from Ammi who always made a big fuss of any illness.

One of the few times he was not extremely sad was when in the final year of my graduation, I was felicitated by the vice-chancellor on Republic Day for the laurels I had won for the university. After the ceremony, we were invited to a supper at the VC house. Papa was very happy when I told him about it. 'I had told you, he would make you proud,' Iqbal Bhai said, and Papa seemed hopeful. Probably, the future wasn't that dark at all.

However, he died a few days later – without much hope and a list of worries about the future of his family.

A few hours before he passed away in a private hospital on a December afternoon, he called Saad. 'Both of you are very young, but you are older, and Zeyad will take time to understand. You must fulfil all the responsibilities of this family,' he said. He also apologized to Ammi for all the hurt he had caused her in his life. 'I have pushed you to the edge and been angry at you – please forgive me. I will answer for the rest of my actions in Allah's court.'

Ammi wept and said, 'No, you have only been good to me,' she said.

Unaware that the most tragic event in my family's history was taking place a few miles away, I was sitting in front of my computer, trying to break Ankur's record at *Need for Speed*, missing it by a fraction of a second each time. Nida Bhabhi, Tariq Bhai's wife, rushed into the drawing room and told me in a low voice, 'Chachha has gone.'

The first emotion in my heart was disbelief. I didn't know how I was supposed to react. Nobody very close to me had ever died. I couldn't process it at first. I only wanted him to come back. There was a part of me that knew this was going to happen, but when it actually happened, it was like someone squeezed the life out of me. Papa was not coming home, ever. He was right all along and I was just delusional.

It was a slow afternoon. I slipped into his room and saw his things, his slippers, his pyjamas lying on his bed. They were now orphaned. What would happen to his stuff? Those glorious tweed coats and those slightly loose shirts? Those dozens of white kurta-pyjamas that he'd wear at home while disparaging Western clothing? It was silent. I was alone at home. There was a hollowness in my chest that just kept expanding and taking me to an eerie numbness.

In the stillness of the moment that I can never forget, I kept looking at his things: his long, beautiful shoes without laces, the small briefcase that he would take so proudly in his journeys in the Lucknow Shatabdi Express, the old, brown shaving brush, the watch I had always seen him wearing. What would happen to them? And the small silver box in which he kept his nail cutter and forgotten buttons? There was still a half-eaten box of the protein biscuits the doctor had advised him to eat to put on weight. Should I have sat down with him before he went away to the hospital and made him eat the biscuits, a rare task that Ammi had assigned me?

It is in death you want to reverse so many things: everything that went wrong in the long arduous journey of being with the loved one who had gone away. More often than not, you keep thinking about what you didn't do. Like a bottle of sulphuric acid inside your body, these things that you didn't do keep burning inside you, taking away a part of your soul.

The silent afternoon turned into a noisy evening. Neighbours began arriving in our home, and I was the only person in the immediate family there. Ammi and Saad were still at the hospital. I thought of what would happen to Ammi now that all her fears, which I thought excessive, were coming true. 'I didn't do enough. I didn't do enough. I didn't do enough,' I kept saying to myself. That's when somebody told me that he had cancer. The elders had, for an unknown reason, decided I didn't need to know that Papa would never recover from his mystery illness. It was as if I didn't have the right to know about his impending death.

Then came the questions. Why us, of all people? Hadn't Papa been a nice and helpful person? Hadn't he helped kids from Upar Kot get into the university? Hadn't he refused all the bribes that came his way? Why him? Why cancer? Hadn't Bhura Pahlawan spent his life inhaling yellow fumes from sulphuric acid without getting cancer? Didn't workers inhale black dust all the time? Had this happened because I didn't offer namaz anymore? Was it because Allah was angry at me, for leaving his way after I got into college? Or was it the smoke from mosquito coils Papa used, the cigarettes that he smoked, or the countless milk teas he drank at work?

Didn't death happen to other people? Not to people like us. I mean, all my friends' parents, except one, were alive. Then I kept thinking about Ammi: how she would take it? I knew Saad was strong, but Ammi? People kept pouring in, comforting me, but could I be comforted?

It wasn't until I saw Papa's body being bathed the next morning that the feeling of him having passed away really set in, and my tears finally began to flow.

All our relatives from far off and near had assembled at home.
Papa's body was wrapped in a white sheet and placed on a stand
on the porch of the mosque where everyone, including Saad and
I, stood for the funeral namaz. *Am I actually standing in prayer
for my father's funeral? Is this just a bad dream?* I wondered. But it
wasn't. Slowly, his bier was lifted and carried on shoulders to the
Shah Jamal graveyard, one kilometre from our home. Everybody
wanted to lend their shoulder, and I didn't have the energy to
struggle for my chance. It was only after everyone was tired that
I got a chance.

The grave had already been dug just alongside his mother's,
waiting for him. Papa was lowered inside it and the gravedigger
began to fill it up, followed by all of us picking up handfuls of
soil and putting it in the grave. The maulvi kept reading some
prayers and everyone said '*Ameen*' loudly with tears in their eyes.
Lost in my thoughts, I came alive only when they asked for some
branches to hold the soil together. I rushed before anyone else. At
least, I could do that.

After we got home, being there felt strange. There were
thousands of fears and thoughts raiding my mind: What would
happen now? Would we get poor and live on the roads? How would
we finish our education on Papa's meagre pension? Why hadn't I
qualified for those engineering tests? Why did Papa die hopeless
and disappointed in his sons? Couldn't Allah have allowed him to
live to see some good times before he left us? Why did Allah make
cancer? To rob us of our dignity as we waited for death?

What remained with us in the months to come was a fast-
decaying old home. It had a lot of space in which we could be
together and alone in our grief. Saad began to sleep in Papa's
room. Ammi slept in the main hall. I spent most of my time in
the drawing room where, if Papa had been alive, he'd sit with Iqbal
Bhai and talk about the decay in the world and its ethics. Badi

Ammi was inconsolable. She'd just keep talking about Masroor, her youngest brother, closest to her, who went away too soon. Steadfast in her faith, she'd keep praying for Papa. The months kept passing away in a haze. We pretended to be healed and carried on with our lives.

Rainfall came early that year to make us remember that life is better if it flows. When it comes, everything stops. The flurry of water droplets arrives from the sky in such numbers that you forget what you were doing and look at the heavens in amazement and sorrow. The monsoon takes you to a state of mind where you are thinking about your life not in anger (like in the summer) and not in sadness (like in the winter), but you are living in that particular moment, looking at the water gushing down from sewers and cracks in the walls and making hundreds of concentric circles on the concrete floor.

In the ghetto, however, rain is not as romantic as in the posh areas. It's a time of anxiety. The roof of our main hall had begun to leak. It needed to be remade, but we didn't have enough money. Ammi would get it cemented every year on top, but it would crumble in a few months again. When it rained, Ammi would cover the terrace with polythene sheets, but nothing worked. Drop by drop, the rain would fall from the roof on to our beds, dining table and carpets. Ammi would place a tub under the leakages, but it'd just begin leaking somewhere else. Soon, we'd run out of buckets and tubs. Ammi would stop trying and just cried and prayed to Allah to stop the rain. It was as if, along with her, Farsh Manzil was crying too, mourning the passing of the youngest son.

After his passing, Papa's friends who sat in our drawing room and played cards every day, never came to see us. The relatives who had promised that they were there for us began to take advantage of us. 'Can we have the scooter if your children are not using it?' they'd ask. They'd come up with helpful suggestions which would only antagonize Ammi. 'I have a relative who wants someone to take care of his karkhana. It would not be a bad decision to send your sons to work there,' a relative would advise her.

'We can take care of ourselves,' she lied and kept praying to Allah.

When bad things happen, they often happen in multiples. When somebody passes away in a family or community, others tend to follow in quick succession. Entire generations come and go within a couple of years. Papa's passing had opened the floodgates. In the next few years, Naani would die of heart disease. Our cousin and Mehro Phuppho's son Rashid Bhai would die of lung cancer. Yasmeen Bhabhi, wife of my cousin Shakeel Bhai and the mother of infant twins, would die of breast cancer. It was as if somebody had cursed Farsh Manzil and sent cancer to destroy whatever resilience remained in us.

Badi Ammi would spend most of her time with her daughter, but she'd keep coming to her portion of Farsh Manzil. Often, she'd sit in a corner and cry alone. Sometimes, Ammi would join her, making Saad and me very uneasy. 'Both of you cry so easily – things will be fine,' we'd say – and cry when nobody was looking.

In a few years, Badi Ammi would also die of old age. In her last days, she'd beg her daughter to bring her to Farsh Manzil, but she'd die, at peace, in her daughter's home in Civil Lines. We'd go to bury Badi Ammi in the university graveyard, far from the graveyard where her father and my father were buried.

The season of death is mean. It brings emptiness, numbness and disbelief. You are left surprised by how cruel the world can be. Once it seemed impossible that bad things can happen to you. But when they do, they break your spirit. Anxiety becomes a habit. There is mostly nobody to console you.

After Papa's death, I never had the heart to go the way of his office, the Union Hall which had been such an integral part of my childhood. One day, I went there in the evening and stared at the always-defunct fountain outside his office. I had always wanted to see water coming out of it. And that day, my wish was granted. As I saw water oozing out of its nozzle and falling inside the tank in a seemingly endless cycle, I remembered the times he'd pick me up from school and bring me to his office.

I remembered the times I was the king of the office, where I would be a telephone operator or try to take the typist's job, where everyone tried to feed me and I was part of meetings on university politics. But why did he bring me here, tolerate my tantrums before he eventually got tired and sent me home with a peon? It dawned on me that it was a way to spend more time with his youngest child, who he'd once expected wonders from but who eventually disappointed him.

A few days later, I began remembering him by going through his almirah and seeing his things, something I'd have never dared when he was alive. On the top shelf, I found his collection of English books, kept hidden under the Urdu books. Most were by the American suspense writer James Hadley Chase. I picked *Tell It to the Birds,* and it was the most engrossing book I had ever read. One by one, I read all of Papa's books. To escape my sorrow and my reality, I just kept reading. Papa's books held my heart and gave me solace.

It was as if even after his death, my father was guiding me. Books became my next obsession in life.

# 16

# UNIVERSITY

LIKE SOME WINDOWS of our homes that are mostly closed, we never open some windows of our hearts. But on some days, we need that extra bit of light and that extra bit of love in our lives. Like ants carrying a burden too heavy for their little bodies, we live a life carrying the burden of thinking that we don't need that much love. Like disgruntled fools, we continue to live without this extra love for years – sometimes entire lives – but we need to open these windows of our hearts now and again. Take comfort from anyone willing to give it, ignore all the writings on the wall and make ourselves vulnerable again. This extra love makes us last another difficult day, another weak hour, another dark night.

The mind has its ways to recover from its losses. I coped with my father's death by escaping from the world. Those days are as hazy as December school mornings. To protect myself from the ancient misery of life, I began shutting off my emotions. Like side effects of a medicine otherwise good for you, being emotionally numb also means you shut out the good emotions too. So, I stopped feeling happy over anything. 'Everything is temporary, fleeting. Most people are fools who don't realize that nothing matters,' my thoughts told me. In time, I began considering this numbness a superpower. When I stopped feeling, the pain went away. It was a cruel remedy for all the ills of the world: just stop looking and you won't get hurt. The wounds kept festering inside, unnoticed.

But memories, after all, are a magical thing. When you are swimming in an ocean of memories, you'd never know which wave will next hit you. It has the power to bring you heaven and hell, sometimes together. When you peel a memory back layer by layer, it takes you down labyrinthine passages leading to forgotten places in your mind. Deeply associated with memories are feelings. Even if you think you have buried all your feelings in an irretrievable grave, they'd come back with your memories in waves, tsunamis and storms.

When I was busy escaping my feelings like a convict on the run, Saad was fulfilling the role of a big brother and became almost unbelievably sensible – keeping the promise he made to Papa on his deathbed. He did the bank formalities, filled out the pension forms and the death certificate formalities, and got the insurance sorted. While I remained the pampered, risk-taking but easily disillusioned younger sibling, Saad became the risk-averse, overly cautious, thoughtful, responsible big brother. Like all mothers, Ammi knew whom to trust. 'I can't rely upon Zeyad for any work. He'll just spoil it,' she'd say.

In those hazy days, the other way I responded to my grief was by immersing myself in the life of a graduate student at AMU.

A prestigious central university, AMU was founded in 1875 as a madrasa by a progressive and visionary Muslim reformer named Sir Syed Ahmed Khan. Condemned as a heretic and a traitor in his time, Khan founded the university to provide Western education to India's Muslims. He responded to the needs of his times and engaged with the British state to create an institution that played an instrumental role in educating young men and women from the towns and villages of Uttar Pradesh, Bihar and other Indian states. Most of these students came from families that have traditionally not gone to college.

During Sir Syed's lifetime, AMU remained at the forefront of the Aligarh Movement, a nineteenth-century Muslim renaissance and furthered the debate on the rights of Indian Muslims under the British. After his death, it became a symbol of a distinct *tehzeeb*, a citadel of Islamic culture in India, and continued to influence mainstream Indian political discourse, cinema, art, theatre and of course, always remained embroiled in controversies.

It still keeps educating over 35,000 students every year and remains one of the largest and the most economical residential universities in India. Its alumni include two vice-presidents of India, cabinet ministers, ten state chief ministers, dozens of top Muslim politicians, supreme court judges, journalists, writers, poets, actors, and historians. It is the only Indian university whose alumni became heads of state to four countries: India, Pakistan, Bangladesh and the Maldives.[1]

The first time I went inside the university, like a pauper being put into a palace, I was mesmerized by its architecture, the wide roads, the eucalyptus trees lining them, the nonchalance of the students on their rusty bicycles, motorbikes or cycle rickshaws.

With arched gates leading inside, the campus is home to havelis made from sandstone bricks turned into men's hostels (all donated by the nawabs and kings to Sir Syed's mission), architectural beauties turned into departments, an auditorium and amphitheatre named after John F. Kennedy, the most regal swimming pool building in the universe, a sprawling cricket pavilion and sporting arena, the biggest university library in Asia, and countless heritage structures. The most famous structure is perhaps the three-domed university mosque which lies a few meters away from the red-stoned Victoria Gate, a close second.

What connected this sprawling campus to the ghettos of Upar Kot was that both lived in past glories. 'The fate of Indian Muslims is closely related to what happens in AMU. What Aligarh says today, Indian Muslims will say tomorrow,' Papa would say. In my now distant-as-a-dream childhood, university for me meant Papa and the Union Hall – a historic building and institution whose lifetimes members included leaders like Mahatma Gandhi, Muhammad Iqbal, Jawaharlal Nehru, Morarji Desai and later Mother Teresa and Dalai Lama.

Like a tower of hope standing amid the ruins of despair, for most locals, AMU is a beacon of the city's prestige and most importantly, a source of income for a significant part of its population. This was particularly true for my family, acquaintances and family friends – everybody we knew was somehow associated with the university. 'Without AMU, many generations of India's Muslims wouldn't have received an education,' Papa used to say.

Historically, AMU long had a focus on educating women, forming one of the campuses where girls from Muslim families of north India had a place to study. In a time when sending women to colleges was still a dream, the stalwarts of women's education of their times, Sheikh Abdullah and Waheed Jahan Begum, created a safe space in Abdullah Hall. Even though they faced their share of resistance here, it became the alma mater of progressive Muslim writers like Ismat Chughtai, Salma Siddiqui and Zahida Zaidi.[2]

Unlike these women writers, most lads around me were more concerned with student politics, macho one-upmanship and mischief. Their saving grace was their terrific sense of humour and superb social skills, which they used when they skipped lectures and sat at dhabas. 'We learnt so much from the hostellers, developed friendships that have lasted decades, ones that your generation can't make,' Papa recalled.

AMU hostellers were well-known for concocting and carrying out bizarre dares. Among the many stories he narrated to me every night, Papa had told me about one of these shenanigans. Sometime in the 1960s, the hostellers of Sir Syed Hall, the biggest and oldest hostel, are said to have had an argument with the warden over the quality of the food. Making an excuse for not fulfilling his responsibility, the warden said: 'It is as difficult to improve the quality of the food as it is to get a camel up on the terrace of Sir Syed Hall.' The students took his statement to heart.

A few days later, the warden saw something nearly unbelievable: a camel roaming on the roof of the hostel.

After he had dared them, like clay-court wrestlers challenged by a rival, students had assembled to think of ways to fulfil this challenge. 'It was impossible to take the camel to the terrace through the narrow hostel staircase. So, a student reached out to a brick trader and borrowed a row of bricks. At midnight, boys assembled to make a giant staircase from these bricks near the outside wall and pushed the camel on it and to the hostel terrace. Nobody remembers if the warden kept his word but the story became a legend of the mischief that AMU students got up to,' said Papa, his eyes beaming with pride.

For most of its students. AMU is not just a university. It's a second home where they learn life skills and the ways of the world. It is a cultural centre where traditions thrive and memories are made. After leaving, most alumni tend to long for their Aligarh days so deeply that it is said to be common for them to cry at the mention of AMU.

However, it'd be fair to mention the disparity here again: it's mostly men who think of their days in AMU as carefree. Many women recount adventures of thwarting nosy wardens keeping a tab on their movements and who'd pass remarks on their characters, and of not being allowed to go outside except on Sundays. Even after all these restrictions, many of them loved AMU as much as the men, savouring their memories of being a student here.

I was also making memories of my own at AMU. After Papa's death, I remembered him by raiding his almirah for books. His favourite English author James Hadley Chase's stories introduced me to leading men whose destiny took them to the most unfortunate situations. It was almost like meeting friends and seeing them turning to crime because of extenuating circumstances. They all ended up in tragedy, Papa's favourite genre.

∽

Days passing as slowly as seasons, I would continue to escape home and instead consolidate my friend circle. I often debated with people who considered AMU a conservative space mainly because of its Islamic identity. In my view, it was like any other university, with students trying to spend their lives on less money, flattering teachers to get marks and attendance, and above all, finding a boyfriend or girlfriend. Ironically, I didn't care that much for my Muslim identity any more. Religion had now faded from my priorities to be replaced by books, movies, love and music.

My graduation class had over twenty boys from countries in the Middle East and the South-East Asia. I was close to them, helping them navigate life in India, giving them notes and suggesting ways to deal with the everyday racism they faced. As talkative as an insurance salesman, I made new friends and rekindled bonds with some old ones. Every day, Shamlan, Zeeshan, Kaleem, Anas and I would skip classes and sit at a tea stall in Suleiman Hall. Here, we would chat for hours about things I can't even remember now.

The biggest favour you can do for someone is to listen. From children blabbering cutely to old people recounting memories on their deathbeds, everyone likes to talk. Everyone wonders if they are weird, unlovable or foolish. But when a friend listens to you unburdening yourself, all these fears melt away. Like the only window in a prison cell, companionship gives you hope. You feel accepted.

When a word leaves your mouth, it moves out of your brain into the real world, where another person has a chance to understand you. Words sometimes lead to tears, sometimes laughter and sometimes anger. But eventually, they help us find who we are and what we want to be. It is between these little agreements and arguments that relationships blossom.

Friendships in Aligarh are forged through conversations over countless cups of tea, sitting at rusted dhaba chairs. As much as the boys on dhaba learnt from each other, as much they spread misinformation. Grandiose statements like 'If Shah Rukh Khan doesn't win an Oscar for *Devdas*, it means that the Oscars are rigged,' were often bandied about at these dhabas.

Even while criticizing these boys, like a true Aligarian, I was doing exactly the same thing, locally called *bakchodi*. At these dhabas, my friends and I talked about anything under the Sun: politics, books, philosophy, cinema (particularly Quentin Tarantino's films), the effervescent beauty of Monica Bellucci about which Kaleem wouldn't shut up, the architectural beauty of deserted Yugoslavian apartments, America's war on Iraq but above all, religion. My friends were equally divided between the believers and disbelievers.

'Do you know there is a perfect moment for a Muslim to die?' I would say to the disapproval of Kaleem, a sorted boy from Bahraich who wanted to go into the army.

'Will you shut up if I say I don't want to know?'

'Of course, I won't! It's right after you perform the Hajj. You have washed all your sins and are as pure as a child. That's when you should kill yourself and go to heaven,' I said.

'Then, you'd certainly end up in hell because suicide is the greatest sin in Islam,' said Zeeshan, a friend from school, correcting me. 'Remember to kill me as soon as I arrive from my Hajj flight,' I said, not intending to give up the debate.

I often borrowed novels on my friends' library cards as I kept losing mine. In class, I usually sat on the back bench behind some tall boy, lost in my novels as the teacher taught frontbenchers. I rarely read syllabus books and passed exams by reading summaries borrowed from friends, answer guides or just writing impromptu answers on the spot. Often perceived as 'the mad one', I would sometimes reach the exam halls after half the exam time was over, yet remained among class toppers.

My favourite author was now Graham Greene, a British author who wrote comedies and dramas about the modern world, its failings and its complexities. Greene's nuanced understanding of human beings and their flaws made me respect him. I also read books by Arundhati Roy, Jane Austen, Fyodor Dostoevsky, E.M. Forster, John Grisham, Robert Ludlum, Ken Follet, Orhan Pamuk and some other novels suggested by Ayesha Ma'am and Samina Ma'am, my favourite teachers in the English department.

As it was in school, I didn't get along with most other teachers at university (of the ones who knew I existed as many didn't). I lived like a shadow, entered class from the backdoor like a spy, got out sneakily after attendance. Then I'd go to the Literary Club in the Kennedy Complex to take care of my duties as the head of the quizzing forum. I had initially joined the club because it was the only place in AMU where I could meet girls, but eventually, I ended up learning a lot.

For a welcome change, life was being kind to me. I was now winning a lot of quiz competitions, in AMU and later at national inter-university fests. Apart from the quiz forum, I would organize a lot of events for the university. My relationship with my girlfriend was beautiful. I was also liked by the teachers of the English department. People knew me in the university and for some weird reason, even respected me, something I never got at home. 'I think you should take the entrance for the journalism programme at Jamia,' a club senior told me. I took the suggestion seriously and began preparing for it.

All the while, I was busy earning money by writing content articles. A boy concerned with the basics of life, I didn't spend too much on clothes or food. I only spent on my friends – the centre of my existence after the grief that awaited me at home.

One of the best times in Aligarh came in winter every year when the Aligarh fair or the *Numaish* was organized. A 150-year-old event, it was a festival of lights, food, merry-go-rounds and a chance for men to make their wives and children happy. 'The Meerut people consider their Nauchandi fair the best, but it's Aligarh's crowd that makes the Numaish what it is,' Papa would say.

Everyone flocked to the Numaish: the families of Upar Kot's lock workers, the baniyas of Mahaveer Ganj, the Sikhs of Nai Basti or the notorious AMU professors. They browsed hundreds of shops selling colourful toys, clothes, antacid pills, shoes, sunglasses, utensils, tractors – anything an Aligarhi might want.

The Numaish had an especially deep connection with the university and its culture – its Urdu *mushaira* was among the best in the world. 'Sir Syed Ahmed Khan participated in a play at the Numaish to raise funds for the university. Now, it's a place where boys come wearing traditional black sherwanis to woo girls from

Abdullah Hall,' Kaleem told me as we walked through the crowds, referring to the love stories that blossomed at the fair.

My favourite place in Numaish was Hullad Bazaar, where the 'hullad' or ruckus was. The loudspeakers were too loud here, and decent people chose not to venture in. It had the circus, swings and rides, the boy with two heads, the half-snake girl, and the stalls where men and women hunted coloured balloons with air rifles. Apart from the circus, the most crowded areas were what were known as variety show – a dance performance show with women in skimpy clothes. 'Why would any decent person come here?' Papa would say when I dragged us there because I wanted a ride on Columbus, a ship-themed ride named after the man purported to have discovered America.

The one place in Hullad Bazaar that Papa never took me to, no matter how much I pleaded, was *Maut Ka Kua*, the Well of Death. In it, a man rode a motorbike on the inside of a round wooden circle, going faster and faster to defy gravity. If he slowed down, he would fall to his death. The daredevil biker reminded the audience that if they kept going through the motions of life without thinking, they'd stay afloat. If they stopped and lost patience, they'd fall hard. When people got bored of watching motorbikes, they replaced them with a small car in this well of death, and it brought back the audience.

Like the Kumbh Mela, kids are known to get lost at the Numaish, some of them permanently. Every hour, there would inevitably be an announcement on the loudspeaker, 'A girl/boy named Shaista/Seema/Asif/Manoj has been found. His parents can collect him/her from near the *phawwara*.' The phawwara, the central fountain of the Numaish, worked as a sort of lost-and-found counter for lost children. But the fountain was exactly where my parents decided to lose me.

I was four years old when the Aligarh district administration took a too-ahead-of-its-time decision to install TV screens across the fair. Any child who had got lost was shown on these screens. That's when one of Ammi's friends came up with this evil stunt. 'Let's "lose" Zeyad. His face will look so cute as it is telecast all over the Numaish.'

For reasons best known to her, Ammi agreed at once. 'Go to the policemen standing at the Gandhi statue and tell them you are lost,' she said, giving me instructions for 'getting lost', my heart sinking to my bones. 'Don't look at us when you talk to the cops. We will be watching you from here.' In that horrifying moment, I thought she wanted me to be lost for real.

I looked at Papa, but he disappointed me with his cowardice. After the final betrayal, I walked to where Ammi told me to. When I looked behind, they weren't there. Like an abandoned shoe in a vast ocean, I was now *actually* lost. With no other option now, I walked up to the cops and gave them the speech I'd been told: 'My name is Zeyad. I am the son of Masroor Ahmed and Parveen Jahan. I am lost, please help me.' I don't remember what happened then and when I was put on the video screens, but I distinctly remember staring at the Mahatma Gandhi statue, believing it would come alive to rescue me if my family had deserted me. But my parents came and these thoughts were forgotten like the rumours of Upar Kot.

After Papa's death, our family simply stopped going to the exhibition altogether. The place that had once mesmerized me as a child brought only sorrow now.

In those days, I went to the university with my cousin Niki Baji, pursuing a Ph.D. in zoology at AMU, in their old Maruti 800. In conservative families of Upar Kot, it was seen as a good thing for a brother to accompany his sister or cousin, as there were many to say all kinds of things in my mohalla. Whenever Sayema or Niki Baji had to go outside, I couldn't say no to escorting them. It was a taxing and time-consuming duty. Ironically, when Sayema went to the university or to meet her friends in Civil Lines, she'd go alone. She later even went to Delhi for an internship alone. In a strange twist of destiny, she could go far away alone but never nearby.

As I began to read books that expanded my views and made women friends at university, I noticed how Upar Kot treated its own women differently. In the Hindu mohallas, you could see women shopkeepers! Little girls sat at paan shops to help their fathers, and women sold vegetables from carts. The only Muslim women in shops in those times were the ones whose husbands had died. 'I would never let my mother work like Hindu women. I will earn for her,' I'd think, steeped in the patriarchal mindset that prevailed around me.

Being a student, I also began noticing how Upar Kot was treated inferior to Hindu areas in terms of facilities – they had better roads, streetlights, hospitals and schools, while Upar Kot had only a few public schools affiliated with the university but no public hospital. Many boys had died in various riots because of this. In the case of an emergency, the best option was to go to a *jarrah*, locals who become surgeons because it is the family business. Whenever any political leader came there, locals would point towards the lack of any public (or even private) hospital in an area where thousands lived. One of them agreed to see one built in the mid-1990s, and thus began the long construction of a mythical hospital in Upar Kot.

A three-floor huge structure was raised in front of the Jama Masjid with much fanfare. It would become the area's biggest joke. For the next thirty years, riots came and riots went, generations perished, children became parents and fathers became grandfathers, but Upar Kot's hospital remained under construction. Thirty years later, a small clinic was opened and that was it! The U.K. is still waiting for a full-fledged hospital.

But it wasn't just hospitals. We didn't have banks, ATMs or good schools. Even though many Hindus were as poor as the Muslims, the facilities in their areas were unarguably better than in Muslim ones.

The only Muslim places that were comparable to Hindu ones were the university campus and professors' quarters. My friends from the university would come to Upar Kot, but only for shopping or to eat nihari or kachori, food that was far, far better in my area than in theirs. The level of attention that shopkeepers in Upar Kot paid to their merchandise was majestic. A nihari-wala would pour their curry like they were pouring liquid gold. Hindu shopkeepers would look at their jalebis and kachori more lovingly than they did their families.

Kachoris were like nihari for Aligarh's Hindus. 'The *puri-kachoris* in Aligarh are the best in the whole world – their oil runs in the veins of our people,' Sayema would say. In fact, the kachori-walas are among the richest people in their mohallas. Once, when police raided a kachori-wala's home, they recovered crores of unaccounted cash.

While waiting for our food at these eateries, I and my friends often talked about the ongoing controversies at the university. You see, AMU was a hive of controversy: once a year, *something* reached national headlines. This year's issue was Professor Siras, a teacher who was temporarily suspended by AMU for engaging in same-sex relations with a local.[3] 'He was suspended for the right reasons. Homosexuality is against the ethos of the university and Islam,' most of my classmates said. I was too engrossed in my own grief to care about someone else.

My view changed when I saw one of my seniors, Adil Hossain, debating this issue alone against dozens of boys. 'It is not the reporters' prerogative to investigate what is happening in Siras' quarters. He shouldn't be penalized for who he is,' he said with conviction dripping from his words. As it seemed right, I began to take Adil's stand whenever the debate came up. 'It's a question of Siras' privacy,' I would tell my friends.

However, I knew that the concept of privacy wasn't popular in Aligarh, be it in Upar Kot or Civil Lines. Like other small towns, everyone knew each other and what went on in their lives. Gossip was the biggest pastime in the city, and envy was rampant. Civil Lines, for example, was notorious for being the starting point for rumours about which girl was dating which boy. Nothing was a secret.

In Upar Kot, the situation was worse. Everyone had known each other for generations, and most families married within their mohalla. Some were estranged due to personal rivalries, but that didn't mean they weren't concerned about each other's lives. The relatives would gossip about your private lives; they would then tell their friends, who would tell their friends and friends of friends.

Because of my mother's protective nature, I was shielded from this culture and knew less about Upar Kot than about Civil Lines. 'You study hard and get out of here,' she'd tell me. And I did. I prepared hard for the journalism entrance test at Jamia Millia Islamia, one of the most prestigious mass communication institutes in India.

'I know you'd qualify,' Kaleem told me. His confidence gave me a boost.

I gave the test and knew I would be called for the interviews. I answered most of the objective questions using my quizzing experience and wrote comprehensive long essays. A senior told me, 'If you want to clear the interview, make a documentary.' I immediately put a team made up of Amir Pashtun, a friend from Upar Kot and Aligarh's newest computer genius, and Anubha, a school friend. Pashtun helped me shoot and edit the film, while Anubha arranged a camera for me and anchored it. My documentary was on the criminalization of begging in India.

During the filming, there was one story about Aligarh's beggars that moved Pashtun and me to our core. An old couple were living on the railway tracks after they were thrown out by their sons. One day, his wife went to defecate on the tracks and was hit by a moving train. 'I don't know whether she didn't notice the train in time or if she stayed there to die,' said the old man, who has been begging alone since then. Then there are the kids left at the railway station by their parents, who grew up on the generosity of strangers. We were moved by these stories, and it made us realize, despite everything we had faced in our lives, we were more privileged than many others.

It wasn't a great documentary, but it worked for the interview panel. For the first time in my life, I wore a formal shirt. When the results came in, I had topped the entrance exam for Jamia's journalism course. I was going to study where Shah Rukh Khan once had!

But there was one thing that stood between me and my dream – money. The Jamia course was too expensive and the only income we had was Papa's pension. It wasn't enough to take care of the course fee and hostel expenses in an expensive city like Delhi. Ammi was initially unsure but somehow managed to arrange it. 'You take care of the rent and food. I will do some content writing to take care of my other expenses,' I told her. After much convincing, she gave the go-ahead, and soon, it was time to go.

It was the summer of 2010 when I had to leave Aligarh. I had anticipated that Ammi would cry, but she was more restrained than I had imagined. After meeting family members and neighbours, I went down the Farsh and took a rickshaw. I passed through the street where I once used to buy comic books as a four-year-old.

I was fulfilling my dream. I was leaving Aligarh for Delhi.

Aligarh. A rich shopkeeper intending to fill his coffers for the future of his children. A small shopkeeper maintaining his ledgers and writing something in his secret notepad. A puri-sabzi seller cutting back on the quality of his goods to account for the rising costs of raw material. A labourer eating these puris after toiling in his workshop, happy with less quality but not willing to pay a rupee more. A daily wage earner dreaming of living to fight another day. Clerks and middlemen grabbing whatever they could get their hands on.

Aligarh. A ten-year-old boy sitting in fuzzy light in his gully cigarette shop trying to repair a defective Chinese lighter. A brother and sister sharing secrets and dangling their legs from their father's wooden stall, looking out when he goes to offer prayers. A group of bored men sitting at a tea shop in an alley and sharing conspiracy theories. A girl showing off her shiny *churidaar* to her friends and swirling like a carousel. An old woman bargaining with the vegetable seller until he agrees to her price. A gang sitting on a dirty slab and hatching an evil plan. A mosque-going kid talking to a rickshaw-wala with all the respect he can muster.

Aligarh. The city where like a tiger in a safari, I was neither caged, nor free. The city where my father had lived, spent his life and was buried. A city I loved but hoped to leave forever behind.

# PART 3

# Manhood

# 17

## DILLI

WE OFTEN PERCEIVE hope to be a fragile thing. But it is more resilient than we think it is, growing inside broken hearts like peepal vines from cracks in old walls. Their roots reach deep inside the centre of our existence, uplifting our spirit from being submerged under the stormy floods of despair. Like embers that burn inside our hearts, hope keeps us believing our souls can be healed. With hope comes realizations – the bitter, sweet lessons that want us to leave old scars and grow into a life where our hopes become a tangible thing. In the absence of realization, hope is nothing but a fleeting dream.

Ten years had passed by since I had left Aligarh. Though I had come to Delhi full of hope, subsequent years would bring on realizations – some hurtful, some delightful, but all of them necessary.

As I was packing my belongings in cartons on 25 February 2020, I realized that life keeps moving in circles. And as Delhi burnt I was completing another circle of my life. Like a refugee across time, I was running away from yet another home in yet another city. As I checked my Twitter feed for news of anti-Muslim violence in India's national capital, I was packing a decade of my life into three large cartons in an apartment in Delhi's Sarita Vihar. My ears were listening for Hindu slogans, the first sign a mob was assembling outside.

∽

Around 60,000 years ago in Africa, Homo sapiens migrated for the first time. Since then, employment, wars, disasters and natural resources have forced millions to migrate across villages, cities, countries and continents. As nation-states grew from the debris of civilization, migration became political – more people meant more competition. It resulted in them facing hostilities from locals, being disenfranchised of their rights, electrocuted or even shot down at borders for the simple act of trying to settle in a land they weren't born into.

It is not as bad for people like me, who had merely changed cities. We might not be shot at or put in detention camps on borders, but migration for us brings a series of changes. Everything undergoes a transformation – friends, clothing, food, and even the topics of casual conversation. Flatmates become our new family, and visiting our hometown loses its charm. If, by chance, we encounter people from our hometown in Delhi, we flee as if we've seen a zombie on a midnight hunt. Neither do we want to see them, nor do they want to see us, in our new lives. With time, people from our hometown fade away from our priorities, and we from theirs. The flock we once flew with becomes too distant, their songs faintly heard on the wind.

Though Delhi and Aligarh are just 130 kilometres apart, they are like two different planets. Delhi is people flaunting fancy clothes, couples strolling on Connaught Place, stealing kisses beneath the trees of Lodhi Garden. Women confidently driving cars and bikes, smoking in markets like newborn dragons, moving freely around without brothers escorting them, and dancing the night away in neon-lit bars. It's the land of materialism, where people mostly don't care what you eat, what you drink, if you pray or whether you live or die.

The city of incessant exhibition of power, it has been the seat of authority since the Delhi Sultanate and Mughal era. It witnessed the British constructing majestic structures to govern India, and now sees modern developers erecting towering skyscrapers for the city's population. Amid broad roads, iconic heritage sites such as Qutub Minar and Red Fort stand proudly, while luxury cars wait at traffic signals like impatient grooms, their immaculately dressed passengers blurting: 'This is why I hate Delhi!' When caught breaking rules, they will respond like territorial Rottweilers: 'Before you give me a ticket, do you know who my father is?' they'd say, or go on to talk about an influential relative in a ministry.

For migrants from small towns and villages though, Delhi is a land of financial opportunity and freedom denied to them. Religion matters, but it is not worn on the sleeve and kept guarded in deep corners of the heart – you can meet Muslims who love vodka, Hindus who eat beef and Sikhs who light up *chillums*. However, as a migrant myself, I often found Delhi to be a place where people are inexplicably rude. 'They are creeped out by niceness because it means that you are putting up an act. To pretend that you are not pretending, pretend to be rude,' a friend advised me when I moved to Delhi. It worked – whenever you behaved like an asshole, people trusted you more.

Delhi is the city of living in the moment. The chameleon that takes on different colours at different times of the day. The city of monuments standing as a silent spectator as people stare at them. The city of umpteen cafes and pubs, where customers sit for hours and talk as if the words were colours and their feelings the paint. The city of beehive-like markets, shoppers in their shorts and slippers, moving like a river through the shops of Lajpat Nagar, Sarojini Nagar and the many, many malls. The city of broken promises, of get-together plans being cancelled at the last moment because someone flaked out at the last moment. The city of sex, drugs and alcohol and the home of Akbar, Shah Rukh Khan, and Mirza Ghalib.

Delhi is the Punjabi boy flaunting bike stunts to impress a girl with colourful hair. The old couple that lives alone in their 4 BHK bungalow, far from their son chasing his dreams in Silicon Valley. The Purvanchali family struggling to make ends meet in a slum. The ghetto boy beefing up in a gym to impress others. The worker toiling in summer heat, living in cramped quarters, yet sending money home. The Haryanvi girl commuting to work, facing lecherous men in public buses, determined to prove her worth is not dependent on whom she marries.

Delhi is chaos. You live in small, dark apartments with no courtyards and small balconies. You manoeuvre capillary-like streets, zigzagging through a maze of hawkers, dancing an intricate ballet of avoiding rashly driven autos, stray animals or joggers with shiny sports shoes. You order *daal* from the place least likely to serve it with cockroaches. If Ammi would have served me the same food, I'd have vomited and created a scene!

Delhi is tragedy. For some reason, everyone is pretending to be happier than they are. While riding the metro, I would observe people and wonder why nobody ever smiled. All the time, their regrets and broken dreams kept jostling each other in the compartment. The only ones laughing were the college students. Older people looked at them with contempt and envy. 'The world will eventually get to you,' their eyes seemed to be saying.

When I arrived in Delhi to study journalism at Jamia Millia Islamia, I rented an apartment in Sarita Vihar with three friends: Amir, Ankur, and Zaidi. Amir and Ankur were friends from Aligarh, and Zaidi was Amir's classmate. Our apartment had three bedrooms and was located in the narrow alleys of Madanpur Khadar village, just a five-minute walk from a posh DDA colony. Before finding this apartment, my friends had faced numerous rejections due to their Muslim identity. Many Hindu landlords had explicitly stated, 'We don't want to rent to Muslims because they eat meat.'

Our area was as Hindu as it could possibly be. Nestled near a Shiva temple and a village meeting area where elderly men sat for hours every evening, it was a Jat-dominated mohalla. Amir and Zaidi were able to convince Usha Aunty, our landlady, only by baiting her with Ankur's Hinduness, the shining beacon in their arsenal. 'We are harmless college students and will pay our rent on time,' they said, like seasoned politicians, making promises we wouldn't keep.

The landlord couple were nice people and had influence in the area. It was mostly Usha Aunty, the woman of the house, who dealt with us. 'Just don't bring beef and girls into our house, the rest is up to you,' she'd say. Of course, we didn't listen. In addition to paying her late, I'd always have at least a dozen friends at home. 'You won't find such a big flat for 10,000 rupees anywhere,' everyone would say. Over the next decade, our rent remained unchanged. Whenever Usha Aunty hinted at increasing it, I would point out the frequent change of tenants in her other apartment, which meant the loss of considerable money for them.

Our home was the *adda* of our friends from Aligarh. They would stay for weeks, bringing their friends, girlfriends, and classmates to join the revelry. House parties happened almost every day, with loud music rattling the night and lasting until dawn, halting only at the landlord's indignant arrival at our door. 'Our children have exams tomorrow – you should care about that at least,' they'd shout. We'd lower the volume a bit, but someone would raise it again – until the landlords showed up again. This happened at least twice every week. Being vain like that also made us appear less threatening.

It was a time of fresh starts and pure happiness. In this world of youthful bliss, we resided in our new home, sharing secret jokes and believing that someday, the Sun would shine on us like a crazy diamond.

At first, my flatmates would drop me off at college. But soon, they lost steam like old engines and began waking up late. So, I took a bus, where I merged with the crowd, flowing like a pebble in a stream, breathing the sweat of strangers, fighting to stay inside. My destination was the not-nearly-as-majestic-as-AMU campus of Jamia Millia Islamia.

Jamia Millia Islamia rests in the bosom of Delhi, caught in a tug of war between its Islamic heritage and contemporary character derived from its students. A busy road cleaves through the sprawling campus like a scissor slicing through silk. Even then, the campus holds an aura of tranquillity, like an oasis in the midst of the cacophonous city with its verdant greenery, majestic trees and ornate domes. Standing proud and imposing, AJK MCRC, my department, seemed like a castle on the sidelines, reserved only for those deemed worthy, a haven for journalism aspirants.

The prodigal thankless boy, I was late to college almost every day. Beneath the kind demeanour, I knew most teachers hated me. Most of them just marked me absent when I came late. In return, I gave them a stare that said: 'Hell, do I care!' Then there was Ramesh Menon, my print journalism teacher, who marked me present with a smile. 'Come on time next week,' he'd say. I would never do it and carried the guilt inside.

I didn't look at anyone as I slyly snuck to the last bench. A textbook introvert then, I would go on to avoid my twenty classmates for months. 'I don't want fake pleasantries and ad-hoc friendships with nothing lasting,' I'd tell my flatmates, who were sure we were the coolest people around. But in time, I made friends. Himani, Nishtha, and Vaibhav were the first outsiders to the main group. Himani would become a lifelong friend and my mirror to the lessons that Delhi offered.

Then I got to know Esha Paul, an extrovert nefariously embedded in the social circles of our college. 'Can I drop you at Sarita Vihar? It's on my way to Faridabad,' Esha asked me one day as we got out of college. I couldn't refuse; it meant saving money and time. Soon, this became a routine. On our auto rides every day, we talked of things like serial killers, military coups, assassinated presidents, flying antelopes, why death is the ultimate purpose of life, and why she thought I would become a prophet and start my own religion.

Esha invited me to explore Bihari House, a dwelling shared by three of my benevolent classmates, a sanctuary for the popular people of my class – Nasir, Sushovan, Hugo, Surbhi, Taha, among many others. Anshuman, the master of ceremonies, would beckon us to indulge in his homemade chicken curry. 'I have made this especially for you,' he'd tell everyone. Shiv and Ramzauva, his comrades, were as welcoming as him. As time passed, I began to immerse myself in Delhi's culture, socializing as much as my arduous course allowed. A lazy caterpillar emerging from its cocoon, I unfurled my wings to embrace the vibrant city.

For a reporting assignment, I went to the Nizamuddin Basti, a Muslim ghetto that had sprung up around the 700-year-old shrine of the Sufi teacher, Hazrat Nizamuddin Auliya. It was a place where people lived amid hundreds of tombstones and graves – some even had graves inside their homes! I immediately found myself at home among the narrow lanes and the garbage. Nizamuddin Dargah became my favourite place.

To see Upar Kot-like poverty at a place in the middle of India's national capital often made me ponder the unfair nature of life. The children of Nizamuddin's slums gazed up at the stars of Delhi's unclear skies, their hopeful eyes dreaming of a life beyond what they had, until reality caught up to them, dampened their hopes and made survival their priority. Tazeen, a boy selling caps outside the towering mosque, asked me once, 'What option do we have other than sitting at shops?' My own privilege apparent to me like the mosque's tall minarets, I had no answer. There were many like him, born in the slums or coming from villages and small towns, their dreams shattered swiftly.

There is one thing about being a migrant. People think you belong to two places, but the truth is you belong nowhere.

In Delhi, I missed Aligarh, my old friends and my family. No matter how hard I tried to merge into the culture of the city, I'd be known by where I was from. In Aligarh, I'd miss Delhi's freedom and diversity of thought. I had now begun to speak like the Delhi boys I once despised. I saw faults in Aligarh's old traditions and ethos, and unfortunately, shared these reservations with local friends. 'Delhi's polluted air has morphed your brain,' they'd say. Other times, they'd be guarded, portraying themselves as more modern than they were.

Beginnings are usually perceived as good – moving to a new city, falling in love for the first time, the birth of a child, buying a new toy, buying new textbooks for school or finding a new job. While endings are seen as something to be afraid of – the death of a parent, a break-up, the end of a friendship, losing a phone with years of photographs, a car totalled in an accident on the highway. Amid beginnings and endings in two cities, you forget who you were, like an uprooted tree flowing endlessly in uncertain floodwaters. Many identities envelop your true self, simultaneously screaming to be released, surrounded by the fragments of who you used to be and what you stood for.

Amid this battle, a rebellious small-town boy dies to be replaced by a compliant man of the city.

∽

By the time my journalism course came to a close, Amir, Zaidi and Ankur had left the apartment and gone back to their hometowns.

I had, however, found other people to share the apartment with, facing no trouble finding prospective tenants. Here, I will live with my Aligarh friends, quizzing buddies, batchmates from Jamia, classmates from my old school, their cousins and friends of friends. In this very eventful decade of my life, I'd coexist with a whopping thirty-seven different paying flatmates and hundreds of 'guests'.

The fact that Madanpur Khadar was a Hindu-dominated area mostly didn't bother me. 'Delhi is beyond riots and communal tension,' I'd say if a flatmate brought it up. 'If a riot breaks out here, you won't be able to get out alive,' they'd say. Then the conversations between us would invariably turn towards escape routes from our apartment 'in case a riot occurred'. Everyone had their plans.

The plan of Chottu, a junior from Aligarh, was simple. As soon as a Hindu attack came, he'd run to our terrace with the speed of an ostrich, jump on to the adjacent terrace and sprint down its stairs to safety in a secret lane behind our house. His brother Saahil doubted Chottu's plan. 'The Muslim area is very far from here. Some neighbour will inform the mob that you are trying to run. As you get down the stairs, you will be killed.' His idea was, instead, to fight the Hindu mob till the police arrived. 'I'd call my influential friends and police connections and meanwhile, keep the mob afraid by throwing things at them. If they don't stop even then, I will throw the gas cylinder on them,' he'd say. I thought of Noorjahan Apa and how she saved our house – sort of playing a waiting game until help arrived.

My plan was utterly naive. 'While waiting for the police, I'd ask Usha Aunty to save us by appealing to her neighbours not to kill us. I'd then go to the balcony and give them an emotional speech that we are Indians like them and try to rouse their conscience,' I'd say to howls of sarcastic laughter. All of us knew deep in our hearts, if a riot *did* happen, there was no way for us to escape.

However, these fears seemed far too remote to contemplate abandoning this abode in the big city. Its walls had now become imbued with a sense of belonging and thousands of beautiful memories – and I was forever the man who lived in the past. Over a decade, the longest I'd been away from the flat was when I moved to Turkey for a year for a journalism fellowship with my classmate Nasir Lone.

Turkey stood as a land of magnificent mosques, each sight a captivating tableau, the beautiful conundrum that was Istanbul, the Bosphorus Bridge, the blue waters of Antalya and the graceful lanes of Izmir. The Turks, exemplars of hospitality and benevolence, indulged in forty cups of tea and a hundred cigarettes each day, their friendships often kindled by asking for a lighter. 'We dwell in Europe and go to office in Asia,' I and Nasir boasted to our friends in Jamia when we called them.

Turkey also showed us a different side of Muslim culture. 'Even hijab-clad girls smoke and drink here,' desi friends would say. I was more shocked when I saw a suit-clad, clean-shaven maulvi, looking more like a suave gangster, smoking a cigarette outside a mosque in Konya, the city of Rumi where I learnt the Turkish language. After spending a few months there, I and Nasir went to

Istanbul to report on the 2013 Taksim Square protests, the largest Turkish citizens' movement in decades.

All this time, my family was insisting I come back to India and start earning. 'Ammi, this year will help me in the long run. I will get a great job as soon as I land in India,' I'd tell her. But it took almost six months after my return to get my first journalism job as a sub-editor in the Delhi edition of the *Deccan Herald*. A very busy job, it left little to my personal life.

Realizations shape our lives more than we give them credit for. They can dawn on us like uninvited guests, desperate to talk to someone. Or jolt us to reality like electric shocks from a defective switchboard you knew needed to be replaced. Sometimes, they cut through our illusions like knives in butter, wading through lies assembled in the veins of our hearts to find the remaining bits of purity. They can come to us through strangers or in dreams on nights we struggle to sleep. Fragments of truth we need to survive in the chaotic world of ours, realizations find their way, always.

On a terrible Sunday night, returning home in my office cab after a long day, I reconciled with 'the fact' in our family that Papa somehow didn't 'do enough for us'. *What even was 'enough', if not a relative measure of our greed?* I thought.

'If you can't find time for us, what's the point of being together?' my girlfriend told me on the phone in a fight, something becoming more of a pattern than a rarity. Now an emotionless robot just programmed to survive, I was living like millions of men and women around the world – spending their lives without feeling, without enjoying what they do, with no time for themselves and their loved ones, always chasing something, but somehow telling themselves a lie that they are better off than their parents.

As I gazed upon the ethereal dance of headlights upon green signposts, guiding the path to Badarpur, Noida, Faridabad, racing by in a blur akin to the fleeting brilliance of the moon and stars, their radiance interwoven amid Delhi's tainted horizon, I had a realization: I was tired as hell. *While we blamed him for not doing enough, Papa did this soul-crushing work for over thirty years,* I thought and cried. In those tears, all my anger towards my father and the unmet expectations were wiped from my heart.

In the busy life of a Delhi journalist, I rarely called Ammi or Saad. Ammi will call me occasionally to enquire about whether I was eating right or whenever she heard rumours of a riot in Delhi. The first riots in my time in Delhi took place in October 2014, the Diwali after Narendra Modi became prime minister. It happened in Trilokpuri in northeast Delhi, where more than 2,700 Sikhs were once butchered during the anti-Sikh riots in 1984. 'But those days are gone. It will be handled,' my editor told me.

As I was editing stories on the riots, it reminded me of the 2006 riots of Aligarh which took away Shadab from her mother in a forgotten lane in Aligarh. The script remained the same – a festival, a temporary Hindu shrine being set up adjacent to the local mosque, giant speakers disturbing the mosque prayers.[1] It first led to an argument and then a brawl. Here, the rumours were not circulated by panicky neighbours but through WhatsApp. People kept sharing rumours on text to inform their community, leading them to assemble at the site. Stone pelting took place, over thirty-five people were injured, and shops were vandalized.

It was the time for another realization – that I had been telling myself a comfortable lie for years. 'A riot couldn't happen in Delhi now,' I had often told my friends. In reality, Madanpur Khadar, where Hindus and Muslim localities lay in close vicinity, was one of the most likely places for a Hindu-Muslim riot to break out. I stayed alert for a week, but when nothing happened, I settled into my old life.

The only time I would call Ammi or Saad was when there was communal tension or earthquakes. If a riot broke out in Aligarh,

I would tell Saad to move to Sayema's flat in Civil Lines, but, of course, he wouldn't. Distance had erased familiarity, magnifying fear's stature beyond those close to the scene of action. 'The soft people of Civil Lines are more afraid of riots in Aligarh than those who live in Sheher,' went the saying in Upar Kot. Now I was like them, panicking at every news of violence from the old town. In my dreams, I'd see Hindus entering my home and setting it ablaze with my stubborn Ammi and Saad still inside.

The imaginations of earthquakes were much more vivid. I didn't expect the century-old Farsh Manzil to withstand a strong earthquake. 'If there is one home in Aligarh that will crumble because of a minor tremor, it's mine,' I'd tell my colleagues. Dreading that my family would be buried under the rubble of our home, I'd call them in every earthquake.

This was what happened during the 2015 Nepal earthquake. I was now working at the Reuters office, which was on the tenth floor of a building in Connaught Place. As I was rinsing my hands in the washroom, I saw the whole room moving sideways. 'This earthquake will bring down Farsh Manzil!' The washroom still vibrating like a train compartment, I called Saad. 'There's been a huge earthquake in Delhi. Are you out of the house?' I asked. It was only after he agreed to run out immediately that I ran down the stairs like everyone else. We came back to the office after having ice cream and skipping an hour of work.

In 2017, I left Reuters to join Vice, who were setting up a bureau in India. In this role, I'd write weird uncanny stories and meet a lot of different characters – satanist cults, alleged witches, village porn sellers, prisoners, gun smugglers, drug peddlers and kidnapping kingpins. Astonishingly, meeting the people society is generally afraid of didn't frighten me at all. But soon fear would find me around my own home in Delhi, where things were changing faster than we had anticipated.

Amir had now returned to our flat to find a job in Delhi. Within months, he had a confrontation with a Hindu neighbour who threatened to set his dog after him. Before the fight escalated, Usha Aunty intervened. 'Don't think you can say whatever you want to my tenants!' she told him, saving Amir from a potential mauling by a dog. We were grateful to her for stepping in for us.

A few months later, as I was rushing to the office, a neighbour Usha Aunty had warned me to stay away from, stopped me. 'You live here?' he asked. It would have been rude to not have a chat. 'I have seen you leaving every day at the same time. What do you do?' he asked, and I told him.

'Wow! We are proud to have a journalist for an international press living in our humble mohalla,' he said.

Even though I was getting late, we smiled and shared greetings. Before I went my way, he asked, 'Oh, you didn't tell me your name!' he said.

I never did until anyone specifically asked me. I didn't want to give a neighbour a fake name. So, I told him. 'I am Zeyad Masroor Khan from Aligarh.'

Suddenly, his smile disappeared, replaced by a frown, disgust reigning on his face. 'Khan? Are you a Mohammedan?'

'Yes.'

'You have now lost all my respect. Everything else about you is fine except your name'.

'Bhaiya, we are also Indians like you. What is bad about being a Muslim?'

'You people create trouble wherever you go.'

'I have been living here for seven years now. Have I ever created any trouble?'

'That doesn't mean you won't in the future. We don't want Muslims living here. How did Usha Aunty give her house to a Mohammedan? She shouldn't be allowed to.'

I was taken aback. 'I am getting late for work. Let's talk another time,' I said politely. There was no point arguing. 'Please don't feel bad about what I said. You should be happy I told you the truth,' he said, smiling.

'Yes, of course, Bhaiya. I don't mind,' I said, smiling. But I did mind. Very much. I had a terrible day at the office.

In the following years, I encountered my faux-friendly neighbour multiple times. We exchanged inquiries about each other's well-being, but beneath the niceties, there were underlying hints of aggression. At worst, I imagined him to be the instigator of violence against me. At best, I imagined him saving me in a riot because I was always nice to him. *That counted, didn't it?* I was behaving exactly like Rasool who lived among the Hindus at the Farsh.

Other friends had told me how their neighbours talked about 'how Pakistanis have arrived in their neighbourhood' whenever they walked past them. *Is this real or in our minds? Was this happening because of the anti-Muslim violence and lynchings that had come to dominate the news space or was it really happening?* I thought, and overthought, with no way to be sure.

Then something strange happened at one of my workplaces. Rahat Bhai, the son of my father's eldest brother who had migrated to Pakistan, found me on Facebook and called me on the messenger app. I stepped out to have a long conversation with him about our home and family. As soon as I came back, my colleagues asked me, 'Which girl were you talking to for so long?'

Without thinking, I replied, 'No, no, it was just my cousin from Pakistan.'

The expression on their faces changed dramatically. 'Pakistan?' they said cautiously. It was as if I had committed a crime.

'Oh, they were in Pakistan but have now settled in Canada,' I told the truth, trying to diffuse the tense atmosphere I could see building up in the room.

A year later, fear began to haunt one of my flatmates, when he had a fight with a neighbour for parking space. 'He was angry that I parked in a spot he thought was his, asking me where I was from,' he told me one night. I told him he might be overthinking it. 'All victims of lynching are overthinking? This is *exactly* the kind of place a lynching might take place,' he'd say, inconsolable. Thereafter, he stopped parking in the space. Few days later, a friend from Aligarh parked at the same place. 'Is this your car? The next time someone parks here, his number will come,' the neighbour told my flatmate. After this, he had constant nightmares of being lynched. He moved out within a month.

Meanwhile, I had changed a lot. My circle of friends had evolved to include both women and men. I found myself attending social gatherings with ease. 'You don't look like a typical Muslim,' people would remark. Most Hindus, even the progressive ones, had a binary perception of Muslims. One is a fundamentalist, patriarchal figure, donning a skullcap, eager to blow themselves up for Islam, the other is an exotic, modern individual, relishing in biryanis, indulging in Urdu poetry. In Aligarh, I was the former; while in Delhi, I personified the latter. Subconsciously, I had also begun presenting myself as the latter, striving to earn acceptance from my liberal friends.

But I wasn't alone. Many Indian Muslims, especially the privileged, have to unconsciously or consciously dilute their Muslim identity. In this silent negotiation, they become 'the agreeable Muslim' who can hold official positions and move around in elite circles. This don of agreeability shapes everything – their language, demeanour and expressions. In this symphony of cultures, the agreeable Muslim becomes a paradoxical figure who adorns the facade of acceptability while eroding their self.

'Idealism is bad for business,' my colleagues in the newsrooms would say. And as time went by, my own idealism with journalism was going through a transformation. I had come to realize that journalism does offer you only a limited scope to change things, often it becomes a tool for the powerful. And, in addition, there is a very specific type of glass ceiling for Muslims in Indian newsrooms. They were there, apart from their capabilities, because companies had to look 'diverse' and 'cosmopolitan'. For that, they needed Muslims in the newsroom. It was as if they were shouting (but not actually saying), '*You are a nuisance we have to deal with, so we will.*' We were fit to be tolerated, but never to be personally engaged with to hear their side of the story. 'Why do Muslims keep crying all the time?' was something you heard often. When it was not said, it was conveyed through silences, gestures and shrugs.

To survive in these newsrooms, Muslims were expected to keep their 'radical' political beliefs to themselves, be nice and polite, and show not even minute signs of anger for things happening to their community. They were there to churn out stories about the 'Muslim condition' that the editors wanted because there was a market for it – not because they were important to hear. It was probably worse for Kashmiri journalists, who likely had the added pressure of being 'a friendly guy' (and not a terrorist) compared to a 'mainlander' like me.

In elite English newsrooms, Muslims are expected to be 'minority reporters' even if they are adept at writing about other things. I often thought, *if this glass ceiling is present in journalism, where else does it exist? Does it exist in politics, administration, law enforcement? Does it exist in the arts, poetry, marketing and academics? Or God forbid, does it exist everywhere?*

‿ි

In 2019, when I was working for Brut, a French video platform, something historic unfolded in Delhi. On 15 December, police violence erupted against students from Jamia Millia Islamia, my alma mater, and the videos of the incident went viral. These students were protesting the Citizenship Amendment Act (CAA), a law that had ignited a nationwide discourse on citizenship, religion, and identity. The police brutality transformed the protest into a powerful Muslim-led mass movement, with Shaheen Bagh, a Muslim neighbourhood in south Delhi, emerging as its focal point.[2]

Once a casual spot for me to meet friends and eat out, Shaheen Bagh had suddenly transformed into a national symbol of resistance. While reporting from there, I couldn't help but draw parallels to the Taksim Square protests I had seen in Istanbul. While young, college-going students had led the movement in Turkey, this was led by women who peacefully sat blocking the main road, asking the government to scrap the controversial act.

Shaheen Bagh became a magical centre of solidarity as people from diverse backgrounds united against legislation restricting Indian citizenship for Muslim immigrants. Regardless of class, ideology, profession, gender, caste, or region, they stood together. The place resonated with the chants for religious equality, adorned with portraits of Ambedkar, Gandhi, and Azad. Unfortunately, most mainstream media outlets toed the government line, branding the protest as 'anti-national', 'paid', and 'jihadist'. Only a few journalists, including myself, highlighted how the protesters, many of them grandmothers, found innovative ways to convey their demands to the Indian government. Regrettably, these reports were overshadowed by pervasive hateful propaganda.

This experience left me disillusioned with journalism, feeling detached and disheartened. I hated the weighing of deaths; not all deaths were equal for journalists. I had seen media prioritizing an accident in an affluent area of Delhi over the rape of a two-year-old girl in a poorer neighbourhood. Murders of affluent people got much more news space than those of the poor. The tragedies of those in the big cities also got more attention than those in smaller towns. *Isn't it inhuman to weigh one tragedy over another?* I often thought.

Nationality further distorted this skewed perspective. An old workplace joke emphasized the glaring disparity: 'Two American lives are as newsworthy as forty deaths in India for the international audience. Deaths in Africa hardly make the front page, unless they reach the thousands, and sometimes not even then,' a colleague would say.

*How valuable would my life be if I died while reporting?* I thought and knew the answer. Only stories of celebrities and rich people got traction. Every day, I felt my spirit being crushed by media houses that were too bureaucratic, elitist, unimaginative or pro-government.

In early 2020, a chance meeting with Razi – a shady driver in Nizamuddin I often met for information – pushed me to finally take a break from journalism. Razi was the source for stories on crime, drugs and sub-culture. As we stood outside the Humayun's Tomb, I told him that I needed to rush back home. 'What's new in that? I have met you a dozen times. You always seem to be in a hurry. Tell me, Bhai, why do you keep running like this?' he asked me, taking a drag of a cigarette.

'Why do you keep running like this?' I kept repeating Razi's question many times. They hurt deep inside because they were true. Razi's words, like barbed arrows, found their mark within the recesses of my consciousness. Their sharpness pushed me towards a slew of realizations I wasn't prepared to face. The questions of identity flooded my mind like overflowing sewers that had been clogged with time.

Next week, I gave in my notice and told my family and friends. 'I want a sabbatical to concentrate on myself and my writing,' I told them. Only a few of them approved, but like a moth drawn to the flames of uncertainty, I was adamant. But before my last working day, something else arrived in Delhi – the season of violence I thought I had left behind in Aligarh.

# 18

# LEAVING THINGS BEHIND

WITH TIME, LIKE footprints in a distant seashore, lessons that I had learnt in my childhood at Upar Kot, had faded from my mind. 'Riots can't happen in Delhi in these times. There would be too much media scrutiny,' I'd tell my friends. And thus, like the Greek tragic figure Icarus, I continued to fly as high as I could, trying to build a life in the big city, forgetting that my wings were made of wax and the Sun was getting closer.

As the protests kept growing stronger, my friends had apprehensions that the tension could snowball into a riot. Like a gathering storm, the air crackled with the possibility of violence, lightning bolts of anger waiting to shatter the fragile peace. Shaheen Bagh, the biggest protest site, was merely two kilometres from my home. Zaidi, who had returned to live at the apartment in Madanpur Khadar after years, was the most concerned. 'I am the sole breadwinner of my family right now. I can't afford to die on the street in a riot,' he'd say. His cousin's entire family had moved into the apartment above us, and he had more reasons to be afraid.

As the roads were barricaded in Shaheen Bagh, a slender bridge connecting Madanpur Khadar to Kalindi Kunj was burdened with the task of being the only nearby path to reach Noida. Incessant traffic jams became the uninvited guest in the lives of people in Madanpur Khadar, and along with it, came rising anger against the Muslims. Zaidi, who came home from that route daily, could sense the incoming storm. 'I heard people saying Muslims need to be taught a lesson,' he told me. I didn't listen as I was busy flying closer to the Sun.

Amir and I, both now too comfortable in the decade-old flat, would mostly sidestep the question of security. 'At the first incident of violence in Delhi, we'll leave this apartment with you. If we are *that* unlucky that the first incident happens to us, then we better seek the help of a maulvi,' I'd say. But deep down in my heart, I knew Zaidi's fears weren't unwarranted.

All along, Zaidi would keep his ear to the ground for any sign of trouble. 'There is a meeting of village leaders that will march to Shaheen Bagh. It has the potential to turn into a riot,' he said. 'Has anything happened here ever?' I'd ask. 'It doesn't mean that it will never happen. Does it?' he'd say. His growing anxiety eventually resulted in a heated argument with Usha Aunty, the first time something like that had happened in years. 'If you guys go to Shaheen Bagh where those useless people are blocking the roads, you need to tell me,' Usha Aunty asked Zaidi one morning as he left for another long day at work.

'Those people are fighting for their rights. They aren't useless, the government is,' he replied.

It made Aunty furious. 'I think you people support Kejriwal in the elections. This protest drama is his strategy to win elections. We can't allow this in our home!' she said.

Zaidi ignored her, went down the marble stairs, opened the yellow apartment door with the BJP flag hanging on it and began walking towards the route he was afraid of.

Aunty then came to raise his 'insolence' with me.

'I will make him understand. And don't worry about us going to Shaheen Bagh. We are hard-working people with no time for all this,' I had, of course, lied. I went there regularly to report on the protests, meet friends, eat and hang around. I had to write a chapter for a book on the protests and I needed to observe what went on there.

I found Shaheen Bagh to be very different from how Usha Aunty had perceived it – a place where people were not 'useless', but concerned of their rights in a democracy and of the Indian constitution. It was a Muslim neighbourhood on the Delhi-Noida border, not much unlike any other Muslim ghetto in India, with high-tension wires passing through the narrow dusty lanes between residential and commercial buildings. The garbage accumulated on the street corners and tried to overpower the scent of tandoori kebabs arising from the many eateries. In a realm where shadows took their throne, sunlight was blocked by buildings and inhabitants sought light in the depths of their spirits.

Amid the battle between decay and life, this locality lay ignored in the elite consciousness until it became the centre of the nationwide protests and the biggest women-led movement India had seen. 'We won't leave until the government takes back the draconian laws and release those arrested from the campus,' said Shaheen Kausar, one of the protestors I interviewed.

'Modi shouldn't underestimate Muslim women. We will never leave the country where our ancestors are buried,' said another woman, in her eighties during an overnight vigil.

None of these overtures changed much. The mainstream media kept projecting the women protestors as 'paid' and driven by 'jihadist ideology'. News anchors called it 'the hub of anti-nationals' who were bent on dividing India. Many politicians made hate speeches against the protestors, often popularizing a hateful

slogan that had risen, '*Desh ke gaddaron ko, goli maaro saalon ko.*'
Hate kept accumulating against anyone who was against the
government, particularly if they were Muslims.

࿂

On the fateful night of 23 February 2020, the season of violence
returned to Delhi after years like a dormant beast awakened from
a slumber. At first, a mob of goons aided by policemen attacked
the protest site of Maujpur in northeast Delhi. Then like a wildfire
spreading through the jungle, the flames engulfed the Muslim
colonies of Karwal Nagar and Babarpur. The next morning
brought more destruction, as Muslim homes and protest sites
in Kardampuri, Gokulpuri, Seelampur, Jafrabad, Chand Bagh,
Gokulpuri and Shivpuri were attacked.[1]

The places, where slogans of peace and solidarity had been
reigning for months, became sites of death and destruction. Mobs
ransacked people's homes, set them on fire by bursting cylinders
and went on a killing spree. Passers-by with beards or wearing a
skullcap were beaten. Others were identified by taking off their
pants to see if they were circumcised. Then they were bludgeoned
to death by rods and lathis or just shot point blank after their
religion was confirmed. It was clear that the Muslims of Delhi
were facing a deadly pogrom.[2]

Hearing the news of the many tragedies unfolding in the
national capital, tensions reigned at our 'Muslim' apartment in
a Hindu ghetto. We were constantly on guard lest somebody,
especially *that* faux-friendly neighbour, decided to rid their locality
of Muslims. I thought of the 'escape plans' I had discussed with my
friends over the years, but was mostly depending on Usha Aunty
to safeguard us in case of an attack.

My friends weren't that naive. 'You had said that we would
leave the apartment if there was any violence in Delhi. What are

you waiting for?' Zaidi asked. Too attached to my home of over
a decade, I slyly made the condition more specific. 'The violence
is mostly confined to northeast Delhi. If something happens in
south Delhi, then we leave,' I said.

'You are just waiting for the bomb to go off!' Zaidi replied.

On the morning of 25 February, I was sitting at my apartment,
exhausted, traumatized. Unlike the violence in Upar Kot that we
had normalized, there was a sinister edge to what was happening
in Delhi. I didn't want to leave my flatmates alone at home in these
circumstances. I wasn't allowed to take leave during my notice
period, so I opted to work from home. 'I promise I'll concentrate
on my stories,' I told my boss. I couldn't. I was just glued to Twitter
and on my phone, my anxiety ebbing and rising like tides in an
ocean.

To anyone who cared, it was obvious that the violence was
a meticulously orchestrated ballet of death, demolishing one
protest site after another with the fluidity of a slithering serpent.
After destroying one site, the serpent moved on to another. For
the killers, the new dawn brought new possibilities. Today, they
would attack Muslim neighbourhoods in Brahmapuri, Shahdara,
Durgapuri, Gamri and Bhajanpura. A slogan reported by the
media, shouted by killers as they stabbed to death innocents was
'Hindustan me rahna hoga, to Jai Shree Ram kehna hoga.' The same
day, protest sites at Khureji and Khajuri were attacked by the police
and the accompanying mob.[3]

'Desh ke gaddaron ko, goli maaro saalon ko' was turned into reality
by killers now ruling the streets of Delhi, looking to kill anyone
Muslim: the community news media had firmly established as
traitors in their minds.[4] Before being killed, many of the victims
were forced to chant the slogan of 'Jai Shree Ram'.[5]

All of this was happening as US President Donald Trump
was in Delhi on his India visit. As the world's most powerful

man paid tribute to Gandhi, the global mascot of non-violence, at his memorial in Delhi, people were being slaughtered a few kilometres away.

My phone buzzed and rang endlessly. I was part of various online groups that helped people with relief aid and rescue. Whenever I could find verified information, I posted it on social media to caution people to stay away from those areas of violence. Then I coordinated with volunteers who could rescue people from these conflict zones. In between this, I saw the update that caused my stomach to churn: the protest site of Hauz Rani, just outside my office in Saket, was attacked by police and a mob. The violence wasn't just limited to northeast Delhi, it had reached south Delhi.

'It's only a matter of time before Shaheen Bagh is attacked and the violence spreads to adjoining areas like Khadar. We are now sitting ducks there,' Zaidi said when he called me from his office.

After a few minutes, my friend Ismat Ara, then a freelance journalist, called. Returning from a reporting assignment in northeast Delhi, her voice was trembling with sheer fear. 'Zeyad, I beg you don't go to any reporting assignment today. They are even attacking journalists. I was being chased by a mob, but I got out by telling them a Hindu name!' she said.[6]

'But I was planning to come to northeast Delhi,' I replied.

'Don't even think about it. If there wasn't a media van here that came at the right moment to rescue me, I might well have been dead!' she said. It wasn't the thought that she would have been killed despite being a journalist, but the anxiety, the utter hopelessness in her tone that caused my heartbeat to flutter. Vainly, I tried to console her, ending the call by promising to leave my home and go to stay in Jamia.

Home. A sanctuary of solace, built not from bricks and mortar, but of countless memories. The place where I had transformed from a boy to a man. A place where love had bloomed, tears were shed and laughter had reigned – now sadly a place that might become our crematorium if we didn't leave it soon.

I kept looking out of the window. Every sound felt like a mob was assembling outside. *Is the man who had once warned me not to live here assembling a mob to burn us to death right now?* I kept thinking. It wasn't an unrealistic thought. A few hours earlier, an eighty-five-year-old woman, Akbari Begum, eagerly waiting for a grandchild to be born, died when her house in Delhi's Bhajanpura was set on fire by a Hindu mob.[7]

I, on the other hand, was a young Muslim man – the perfect enemy.

I pushed these thoughts out of my head and went back to posting alerts on Twitter and sending my hastily written story to my editor. Before I could think of a plan to escape my 'home', I got a call from my friend, Rafiul Alom Rehman, an activist and academic I had once interviewed. He was crying. 'Zeyad, please save my friend. He will burn to death!' he said, his voice choking.

'Calm down, tell me what happened?'

His friend Mursalin lived in Ashok Nagar, a mixed-population locality in northeast Delhi. An armed mob of over 100 had surrounded his home, chanted religious slogans and set his house on fire with him inside. 'He has been texting me frantically. If help doesn't reach him, he will suffocate to death,' he said, now weeping profusely.

'I don't know what to do, Rafiul, but let me try my best.'

I reached out to a few local activists in the area, shared Mursalin's contact and one of them reached Ashok Nagar to help him.

'His phone is now unreachable,' the activist told me.

*This guy is dead,* I thought. I had failed to save him.

For the next hour, I doom-scrolled through my Twitter feed and kept glancing at our balcony at every little sound: a child crying, a mother screaming at her son and a man calling out for his friend. The sun was going to set soon. *The day is when the spontaneous attacks happen. The night is when planned, targeted killings happen,* I thought. I could easily visualize the panchayat leaders in my area assembling to meet for their evening hookah and planning to kill the Muslim tenants living in that area.

Just then, an SOS was passed on one of my journalist WhatsApp groups. 'A thief has been beaten up by a mob in the Madanpur Khadar area of New Delhi. The situation around the area is said to be tense.'

*Thief? Or a Muslim whom somebody wanted to find an excuse to beat, later proved to be a thief? Should I continue to take a chance?* I knew waiting wasn't wise, but going outside had its own risks. Delhi, my home for a decade, was now a dangerous city for my frightened mind, where everyone was a potential killer whose conscience had numbed. Where death had conquered the street corners, swords waited to slice our necks and guns waited to shoot us down as traitors. Where students and activists were seen as enemies, and mobs with weapons seen as the saviour. Where hopes died an uneventful death and words ended up in meaningless sentences, stripped of their ability to comfort loved ones.

My phone rang. It was Rafiul. 'Mursalin is alive! He escaped through the terrace. He just called from a safe place.'

This gave me some hope that we could still save ourselves. I called Zaidi. 'I am packing our things. Let's go to Neyaz's place in Jamia,' I told him. Neyaz Farooquee was a friend, journalist, writer and senior from Jamia.

As soon as Zaidi arrived home, we began making a plan. There were no autos outside and going on foot with bags on our shoulders from a Hindu locality kind of shouted that we were Muslims leaving, ready for the slaughter if a mob caught us. *Then we would be called suspect thieves,* I thought. No Muslim friend would come to pick us up from Khadar. There was only one solution. 'Let's call an Uber,' Zaidi said.

It was easier said than done. As soon as we put the destination as Jamia Nagar from our accounts with Muslim names, all the Hindu cab drivers would cancel. And no Muslim driver would come to pick us up in Madanpur Khadar.

One of the reasons I hadn't lived in the Muslim-majority Jamia Nagar was that most cab drivers simply refused to go there. Everyone who lives there knows that it would generally take at least thrice as many attempts to go there than to other places. We wanted to book a cab to Jamia when there was communal violence happening on the streets! For the next hour, we tried booking an Uber but to no avail.

'Zeyad, try Ola,' Zaidi said, as he tried to convince another Uber driver to come to help us escape our home. But our luck changed when I was able to book an Ola cab, that too with a Hindu driver! Preparing myself for another disappointment, I called him.

'I am just reaching in 5 minutes,' said the voice on the other end.

I couldn't believe it. 'You are coming?' I asked.

'Yes, I'll be at the location in five minutes.'

We were still unsure. 'Do you think this is a ploy by a Hindu driver to lure us outside and give us to the mob?' I asked Zaidi, speaking my thoughts aloud, cutting short our celebration.

'This is our only hope. Let's go with it,' Zaidi said.

We picked up our bags, locked the door and quietly went down the stairs without telling Aunty. There wasn't a mob waiting for us in the deserted lane. We walked nonchalantly, passing the village elders busy with their evening hookah discussions. As promised, the driver arrived soon, but the three minutes that it took to get out of our area were the longest of our lives. 'Please don't stop if somebody flags us down,' I told him as he started the ride. The highway was deserted, but we didn't encounter any difficulty reaching the Jamia campus.

'Isn't this where the protests are happening?' our driver asked us, looking at the street graffiti with slogans of protest.

'Yes, students have been protesting here but it's safe,' Zaidi told him.

'I know. I have been here before. They had been protesting for months, and there was no violence,' he said.

As we left the campus and entered the narrow lanes of Noor Nagar where Neyaz lived, we were grateful to this guy for driving us to safety. As we got down, we thanked him profusely.

'Bhaiya, I don't know how we would have reached safely without you,' Zaidi said.

'I was just doing my job,' he told us, reversed his car, turned into the slim lane and got lost in the streets of Delhi.

$$\backsim$$

As we rested in Neyaz's fourth-floor apartment in Jamia's Noor Nagar, we kept watching videos that captured the day's violence. Children had witnessed gruesome murders of their parents, their homes set on fire and dismembered bodies of their siblings floating in the drains.[8] Schools and hospitals in Muslim neighbourhoods had been torched. Over fourteen mosques in Delhi had been attacked by the mob.[9] The official death toll was fifty-three people, most of them Muslims.[10]

The police stood by like spectators, most victims said. Videos circulating on social media showed cops abetting the rioters or acting against already-injured victims. In one video, policemen were seen hitting three men lying on the road, screaming in pain, with batons. A cop demanded them to shout 'Azaadi'— the rallying protest cry. Another continued to strike them brutally, asking them to sing India's national anthem. Tragically, one of the men, Faizan, later died in police custody. His mother claimed that he was brutally assaulted by the police and then denied necessary medical treatment, leading to his death.[11]

At Neyaz's place, this was a strange, sad gathering of old friends. Absent were the usual jokes, laughter, intellectual banter, gossip, and nostalgic reminiscing. The conversations solely revolved around staying alive in days to come.

'I think you should move to Jamia, it's safer,' Neyaz suggested.

Zaidi said, 'We should do what right-wingers say and go to Pakistan. Nobody will mind.'

I wanted to become a hippie, grow long hair, change my name and move to Pondicherry where nobody would know that I was a Muslim.

'Let's just move to a posh colony. Only the rich are safe now,' Zaidi said.

Huddled in Neyaz's home, we deliberated our options throughout the night. Unlike fortunate ones like us, numerous Muslims were in relief camps, no homes to go back to, their lives irreversibly altered. *What was the fate of the wife and eight daughters of Mudassir Khan, shot dead when he went outside to buy medicines? Or the family of thirty-two-year-old Sanjeet Thakur stoned to death in Chandbagh? Or the mother of young Mehtab, burnt to death in Brijpuri?* I kept thinking.

These thoughts compelled me to face a dreaded decision – leaving my apartment in Madanpur Khadar. It was where I spent the prime of my youth. Between its walls, I had somehow coexisted with thirty-seven people, played card games on exam nights, blasted Deep Purple songs to my neighbours' annoyance, fell and lost in love – everything that a good Muslim boy isn't supposed to do. The memories of these ten years flashed before my eyes. *You can't live in the past forever,* I told myself.

We healed our broken souls at Neyaz's place for three days. As violence had subsided now, Zaidi and I decided to retrieve our belongings from Madanpur Khadar – and then bid farewell to our apartment forever. He called his cousin, who lived above us and had mostly stayed there in these tumultuous days. 'It's safe now. But a rumour of violence has spread, causing a minor stampede and shops to shut down,' he told us. We covered our faces with masks and sunglasses, took a cab and reached our apartment – now engulfed in a sinister vibe.

As I packed my belongings into boxes, a bittersweet revelation washed over me like a sudden rain – without a job or a place to stay, the only reasonable alternative I had was to go back to Aligarh. In a cosmic rewind, I decided to go back to the town I wanted to leave forever, where everything began for me. My life was being reset, returning to where it all began a decade ago – completing a loop that destiny had probably planned all along.

With this, the memories of violence in Aligarh I thought had been erased from my mind, came back not as mere ripples, but as relentless waves. The trauma, the smart fugitive I hoped I had caged, had just gone into hiding, only to return with new superpowers and push my dreams into the cliff of despair.

Every day in India, and in many other countries, Muslims are asked to leave their identities behind and merge into the mainstream. After a riot, pandits and mullahs ask those who have lost property and loved ones to 'leave everything behind' for the benefit of everyone. Many of us even train our minds to leave behind our old selves faster than we can create new ones – parting ways with friends we have outgrown, or lovers who are not sexy, ambitious, intelligent or kind enough as we wanted them to be. 'Know that nothing lasts forever. You should move ahead in life before life leaves you behind,' Badi Ammi would tell me when I was a child.

What we leave behind and what we keep may be one of the most important decisions we ever make. Like hammers on molten iron, this will forge us into the people we grow up to be. But do we really leave anything behind, or is all this 'moving on' a lie we tell ourselves to be able to swim in the treacherous waters of life? Do we forget people we love – the ones we left and the ones who left us – or do we simply bury them in a part of our minds, like hidden folders on a computer?

People, traumas and memories we try to forget, lie in wait like dormant volcanoes ready to erupt, simmering beneath the surface of time. They'd come back to us in strange ways, through old photos, people you knew, songs you heard with them, movie characters that remind you of them. The more we try not to remember them, the more they grow like seeds in the soil of our minds, their roots entwined with our very being.

At first, people believed that the Sun moves around Earth, but scientists found that it is, in fact, Earth that moves around the Sun. Could it be the same for us? That when we think that we are leaving things behind, it is the 'things' that are making these choices. So, when I thought that I had moved past my identity, my faith, the riots and the trauma of my childhood, it was they who had somehow left me behind, just to return at the time of their choosing. Did riots ever leave me? Did the wailing of Shadab's mother ever leave me? Did my father's death ever leave me? Or were they just hiding in some obscure dimension of time, to come back, catch me off-guard and smother my resilience into the ground?

As I carefully placed a decade of my existence in three heartless cartons, a truth was forever imprinted in my consciousness: the only thing we should leave behind was the illusion of a belief that we can leave things behind.

# 19

# HARIGARH

IT'S 2021, A year since I escaped the riots in Delhi and came back to Aligarh. A pandemic has become an invisible dictator of our lives, telling us not to touch anyone – or else death, through a new virus in its kitty, will creep up on us. Everybody is afraid of their loved ones dying, while their own mortality stands like an elephant in the room. A recession looms. The dreams of the Indian middle class are on hold, those of the poor are dying a slow death. The rich are seemingly comfortable but hurting inside, lost in a world of dystopia, depression and existentialism.

Aligarh is a changed city. In August 2021, as we tried to process the trauma of the deadly second wave of the pandemic, like a phoenix rising from the ashes, the sad debate of Aligarh-versus-Harigarh arose from the dead. The city's district council passed a unanimous resolution to do something that had once been a joke at Farsh Manzil – rename the city as Harigarh.[1] Even though it might take years for it to happen officially, the seeds of this slow metamorphosis had been sown, taking root in the collective imagination of the people.

In this imagination, Harigarh stood as a symbol, a bogey, whispering its belief, that everything in India belongs to the Hindus. A place where any notion of a Muslim history or nomenclature is deemed oppressive. A town where Muslims are scorned, their significance dwarfed to morsels of insignificance. In this new town devoid of historicity, Hindus can only be reduced to Hindus and Muslims to just Muslims – their humanity now as consequential as a mosquito in a jungle. The transformation of Aligarh to Harigarh might have started earlier, but it gained momentum with the arrival of a virus seemingly smarter than proponents of the new name.

When I arrived in Aligarh after the Delhi riots, the first pandemic wave had tightened its grip on the world like a snake wrapping around its prey. Like nearly half of the earth's population, we were in a lockdown, quarantined in our homes, afraid, confronting our mortality, distancing ourselves from friends, family and lovers. With days as slow as a slumbering cat, kites filled up Upar Kot's skies like poetry written in the language of the wind. As much a loner at heart as a hermit in the wilderness, I didn't mind being cut off from the world.

Aligarh was a ghost town. The roads were deserted, and the shops were shuttered. The bustling streets lay silent, like a carnival had packed up and left without a trace. The marketplaces resembled barren wastelands. No smell of human sweat lingered in the air. The group of children walking the narrow lanes of Upar Kot, singing Bollywood songs in chorus, stayed at home. Hawkers, who once sold bird-shaped-sweets, hustled to borrow money from relatives finding tricks to avoid them.

In Upar Kot, economic uncertainty reigned. 'If the lockdown is extended, I don't know where our next meal will come from. All the progress our family has made in these years will vanish,' Shakir said when he came home to share his philosophy of the world. He was the lock worker whose uncle was once killed by a police bullet.

Aligarh soon normalized the lockdown too. Despite a million public health advisories, many in the town, both Hindus and Muslims, did not wear masks, sat in communities, drank tea and propagated conspiracy theories. 'Corona is just a hoax spread by China,' they'd say to their friends, nodding their heads back and forth like a pendulum. When their neighbours began to die, they'd sink deeper into their denial, moving on to other theories.

I had naively hoped that this health crisis would unite Indians in addressing the flaws of our healthcare system. But it was a pipe dream. Instead of rallying together, like always, India opted to scapegoat the familiar 'other' – us, the Muslims.

Following the discovery that members of the Tablighi Jamaat organized a COVID-19 super-spreader event in Delhi's Nizamuddin area, Indian Muslims faced a surge of Islamophobia and hatred. The country's notorious TV media fuelled this bigotry by irresponsibly promoting terms like 'corona jihad' and 'Tablighi virus', suggesting that Muslims were intentionally spreading the virus to harm India, even at the expense of their own lives.[2] The government wasn't far behind – a minister in the ruling government called it a 'Talibani crime'.

As someone who had been a part of Tablighi Jamaat and seen them at their best and the worst, I felt a deep sense of injustice. The event had happened when India had a few hundred cases, and the government restrictions were not yet in effect. Jamaatis might have been out of touch with the rapidly changing times, but the subsequent demonization, arrests, and relentless persecution they endured were entirely undeserved – somewhat of a ploy to shift the blame from the state machinery's failure to contain COVID despite warnings. A few of my otherwise secular, liberal Hindu friends, joined this sad bandwagon. 'See the video. They are deliberately spitting at people!' one told me on the phone. Another expressed the desire to ban Muslims from entering her area.

In the consciousness of the nation, it was firmly and unquestionably established that Muslims had spread the virus in India. We were perhaps the only country in the world where the global pandemic was turned into a matter of religion.

Muslims in Upar Kot, and likely across India, were hurt and angered by the act of associating the pandemic with their faith. A Hindu neighbour just poured salt on their wounds. Every evening during Maghrib prayers, fuelled by rising religious nationalism in India, he blared a hateful song on loudspeakers: *'Ram ji ke kaam me taang jo adhayega, Ramji ki kasam, woh zinda nahi jayega.'* A week later, a Muslim boy went to an *aata chakki,* a flour mill, near the same house to get his wheat ground. Three men held him hostage and beat him for hours, for apparently no reason at all. The Farsh was tense again, bringing back bad memories. *Thank God, everyone is locked inside,* I remember thinking.

Meanwhile, in Kanwari Ganj, the milk seller from whom Bade Papa had been buying milk for decades, decided to put up a notice outside his shop. It said: 'No milk will be sold to Muslims.' Bade Papa moved to milk packets for some time. These days, it wasn't rare to see Hindu kids fleeing from burqa-clad women. 'The corona is coming!' they yelled as they fled like sacred rabbits. In Aligarh's Shivpuri Colony, a Muslim man was beaten up and rendered unconscious while attempting to purchase medicine.[3] 'You people are spreading the coronavirus,' the mob shouted as they thrashed him, sending him to hospital.

It wasn't as if Muslims were only held responsible for the spread of the disease; they were being punished for it. This was a sign that in the decade I was away from home, the riots had given way to something more sinister: targeted hate, alienation and mob lynchings against Muslims. Harigarh wasn't just limited to an obscure resolution; it was finding its feet in the physical realm around us.

I was depressed, unemployed, unloved and lonely. In my thoughts, fears lurked like restless beasts. I had left my job and financial security to be a writer, but now doubts had woven its web into my mind. *I am not good enough*, I kept telling myself. I knew that the city's healthcare system was crumbling like a pack of cards. Many died because they couldn't find hospital beds and medical attention in time. Shortage of medical oxygen snuffed out lives in hospitals.[4] Tragically, many of the dead couldn't get proper funerals as graveyards and crematoriums overflowed with dead bodies.

I was terrified of losing Ammi, now more precious to me than ever before. However, the only way to show your love to her was to do something for her. So, like many across the world, I made shakes, dalgona coffee and banana ice creams – a flicker of joy in those stressful times. I now also listened to her stories I had never cared to hear before.

Being nice to Ammi came with its complications. As children, she had cleverly used the threat of her death to manipulate us into doing her tasks. Now she was actually old, a deadly virus was killing the elderly, and my brother and I had no option but to please her. 'Both of you should marry soon. I can't keep taking care of you until I die,' she told us firmly. Saad and I now had no option except to listen to her. She was everything we had and knew it.

In the decade I had been away, Ammi had changed a lot. Every day, she'd read Hindi newspapers, then spent hours and hours on Facebook and WhatsApp. She believed most things she read on the internet. 'Why do Hindus want to remove us as citizens of India? When I was a kid, it was different,' she'd tell me.

For the first time in her life, Ammi was unsure of her life in Farsh Manzil. 'I want to die in your father's house,' Ammi had often told us, but now that resolution had dissolved in the shadows. The woman who had once single-handedly taken care of her family in numerous riots was now afraid of living in Upar Kot. 'Muslims are not safe here any more. You should move abroad,' she'd say.

Saad, the former bully, who beat up children and threw them off the school rickshaw, had transformed into an angel. His old schoolmates wouldn't recognize the soft-spoken, conflict-averse and helpful man he was now. Every morning, like a dutiful son I could never be, he bought essential food supplies for our pandemic survival. He cared more about Ammi's needs and anxieties than I ever did, explaining things to her like *he* was the mom. 'You think and worry too much. Don't read fake news on Facebook,' he'd tell her. If I ever asked him a favour, he wouldn't say no. Like ghosts of the past, there was still a bit of authoritarianism left in him, but nothing that would harm a living being.

Sayema, settled in Saudi Arabia with her family, was also confined to her home. Like me, she had inherited anxiety from our mother. Despite being away for years, she called daily and stayed connected with our family and friends. She was also busy helping her children transition to online classes. 'India is reported to be dealing with Covid for the next two years. You should move out while you still can,' she'd tell me when we spoke, when she wasn't sending job suggestions outside India.

To distract myself, I found solace in books and news reports. Despite all the reading, like a fridge magnet, my mind remained fixated on the anxious atmosphere at home, interrupted occasionally by joyful family moments.

To escape this, I began to take long walks in my neighbourhood and observe people. Somehow, it helped me write. With an N95 mask on my face, I would walk for kilometres into the lanes of

Upar Kot I hadn't been to – every single one of them. It felt like the whole universe was contained in a place that nobody cared about – families, their complications, love affairs, conflicts, memories, dreams that mostly didn't see the light of the day – a community of Muslims who were now more despised than ever. *Will they be wiped out as Ammi says or will they live here like this till the end of time?* I would think. Ignoring those thoughts, I continued walking through the desolate streets, passing by dilapidated houses, rows of shuttered shops, Sufi shrines in Hindu spaces and the graveyard where Papa was buried.

Sometimes I walked frantically, a furious madman seeking refuge from the world, desperate to shield himself from reality. Other times, I strolled leisurely, a devoted lover, attentively absorbing every detail of my beloved city as if I were seeing it for the first time. After exploring the lanes of Upar Kot for months, I ventured into the other Muslim ghettos near me that I had never been to: Bhujpura, Nuner Gate, Babri Mandi, Mian Ki Sarai, Thakurwali Gali, Haddi Godam, Sarai Sultani and Shah Jamal.

Bhujpura was somehow, impossibly, poorer than Upar Kot. 'For them, Upar Kot is like Civil Lines,' Saad had once told me. I could now see why he said that. A mere two kilometres away, it was a realm of intense deprivation, where lower-caste Hindus lived alongside lower-class Muslims. In this desolate landscape where it was common for many to go to bed hungry, roads turned into a dirty muddy path and deaths in riots evoked no ripples upon the ink-stained pages of newspapers. Before this, Bhujpura had merely existed on the outskirts of my awareness, known solely for its frequent brawls revolving around cows and pigs.

Near Bhujpura were the 'better areas' of Super Colony and Madina Colony. These colonies were planned to be the prosperous and organized alternatives to Upar Kot, but eventually turned out to be worse. Super Colony doesn't look super in any way. Madina Colony, a far cry from the holy Saudi city of Medina, is a place where people jostled on bicycles and looked enviously at those with mopeds. These places have had their share of violence, never chronicled. Overburdened residents 'moved on' quickly from their losses in the endeavour to survive. Who would remember the unnamed boy who died in police firing during some riot a few years ago?

*What would a better future look like for those who live here?* I often contemplated. If someday, by God's grace, city administrators decided to mend the broad open drain, where everyone turned into a long jump athlete so their slippers don't get drenched in the human excreta, would it make any difference? If, magically, all the garbage disappeared in Bhujpura or Upar Kot, would it lead to a 'better' future?

I knew that the secret desire of most who live in Muslim ghettos like Upar Kot, Bhujpura and Super Colony, is to move out someday. Hidden within the narrow alleys and crowded streets, like an unspoken truth, lies a silent yearning for escape. However, if everyone's dreams to escape came true, would these ghettos cease to exist and become a relic of the past? Would the cramped streets and bustling markets of Upar Kot become mere memories, lost to the passage of time? Or will they be replaced by other dreamy people, who pretend to have claws but have hearts of gold?

If the hate against Muslims kept growing, as Ammi feared, will they be dispatched into mass graves? Or deported into detention camps, a replica of which I had seen in Shaheen Bagh? Or sent to Pakistan, where many Hindus still believe, after decades of independence, Muslims should have gone to after India's Partition? Did Papa make a mistake when he chose not to listen to his brothers and stayed back in India? The answer, as Bob Dylan would have put it, was blowing in the wind.

As my diverse group of friends gathered for an evening tea after an afternoon of working for Covid relief, an unsettling question lingered among us like a stubborn shadow: when and how would a planned genocide against Muslims begin? Or worse, had it already commenced? These conversations were never on the possibility of a massacre, but about appropriate responses 'when it happens'.

'In Delhi riots, mostly Muslim colonies on the border of Hindu–Muslim ghettos were attacked. Even here, people living in mixed-population areas are in danger. Only those tucked deep inside the ghettos are safe,' said Pashtun, one of the few friends who stuck with me through the pandemic. 'I think the attack will be financial. Slowly, our community will be alienated from mainstream business and boycotted economically to drive us into the ground,' said Ansab, a student from AMU. Both were as unhopeful as rudderless ships lost at sea.

Reading comic books as a child bestowed upon me the precious gift of a vibrant imagination. However, this blessing had now transformed into a curse, for my mind could imagine dreadful scenarios as well! As my friends conjured these scenarios, I saw an army of saffron-clad Hindus armed with revolvers and AK-47s, swords and knives in their hands, gathering around 'border areas' like mine, killing dozens and burning down shops. In my head, I could hear the gunshots, the profanity, and the screams of women in unison. I didn't have to try that hard.

Journalists have reported that large armies of Hindu militants have been training in various towns of Uttar Pradesh.[5] Their aim is to counter 'internal enemies' and the Muslims who they believe indulge in crimes like love jihad.[6] As I listened to my friends' predictions, I pictured trained militia shooting at my friends and relatives in border areas like mine.

Then I began to visualize scenes in localities like Bhujpura, Nuner Gate, Babri Mandi, Mian Ki Sarai, Thakurwali Gali, Haddi Godam, Sarai Sultani and Shah Jamal. I saw people being dragged into lanes to be killed and their homes, which they had carefully built over decades, being burnt to ashes. An army assembled with petrol bombs, country-made guns and knives. Policemen shooting boys in the neck, the stomach or the head – like Shadab and the other boys whose blood remained on the tarmac outside my home for days.

It made me angry. I knew anger could make people do things they didn't know they were capable of. So, I tried to calm my mind – now an uncontrollable Frankenstein – but like wolves on a hunt, my imagination kept running wild. 'The violence here will be planned to make Uttar Pradesh another Gujarat. This state is the new laboratory of Hindutva,' said Ansab. Hearing that didn't help either. 'If the Muslims of Uttar Pradesh, and in particular Aligarh, are subdued, nobody would try raising their head against the Hindu Rashtra,' said Pashtun.

In these conversations among Muslims, as common as a housefly in Farsh Manzil, the best-case scenario is them surviving and the status quo being maintained. A few privileged Muslims are protected from this reality, but those who live in India's many Muslim ghettos live it every day. Those with wealth and influence aspire to break free from their designated role as the nation's villains by moving out. Yet, their silver thread of hope now dwindles with each fleeting day.

During the protests against the citizenship bill in Aligarh, the city got a peek at how large-scale violence might pan out. The police entered the AMU campus like a tidal wave and attacked unarmed students with tear gas, batons and rubber bullets. Their rage no more a caged beast, they entered the hostels and thrashed the students hiding in washrooms. When the storm calmed, a student had lost his hand, another his eyesight, dozens were injured.[7] A symbol of pride for Indian Muslims, AMU, would never be the same again. From a vibrant centre of student politics, it became as pliant as a willow tree – probably forever. 'How can the cops enter a university campus, attack students without provocation and get away with it?' friends abroad exclaimed in shock. Apparently, in Harigarh, they could. Later, Allahabad High Court held the cops responsible and demanded action against them.[8]

In other towns of Uttar Pradesh, the police unleashed their wrath upon protestors, their bullets piercing the air, claiming the lives of over twenty.[9] A callous wind tore innocent lives apart like scattered leaves. Fear, an unrelenting demon, gripped our hearts, haunting our thoughts and testing our resilience. In the state capital, Lucknow, women inspired by the Shaheen Bagh protests and engaged in sit-in protests, were removed forcibly. As a final act of betrayal of civility, cops allegedly stole the blankets the women had accumulated to warm themselves on cold winter nights.[10]

For young Muslims – those who go to universities and understand their rights as citizens – these times are enshrouded in a fog of bewilderment. 'I'd love to go back to those simpler times when my primary concern was college,' a young, fiery Muslim activist says. Some like her respond by asserting their identity and engaging in political activism, while others fall prey to depression, PTSD, anxiety or substance abuse. 'Several Muslim youngsters I know are traumatized due to fear of violence. Many find solace in drugs,' she says.

When old friends meet, conversations turn to politics even before a simple 'hello' can be uttered. Jokes float through the air like secret messages. 'Promise to smuggle drugs and medicines if I ever go to a detention camp,' somebody would say. Like chameleons in a desperate search for camouflage, many have adorned themselves with optional Hindu names, ready to slip into the shadows if the dire need arises. Almost everyone has picked a country where they would run to when *the inevitable* happens. Some have got in touch with uncles settled in Canada, the US, Turkey or the UK, if they ever need asylum. Even someone like me, who felt safe even in times of communal violence, now worries about my family's future in my homeland.

In Harigarh, still in the making, the alienation of Muslims from the idea of India was nearly complete.

It's strange how we slowly alienate the ones we think we are trying to help or 'set them right'. In domestic life, this alienation manifests itself as a father pushing his unfulfilled dreams on his eldest son or daughter, forgetting to love them in the process. Or a wife or a mother using sarcasm and taunting to see a man realize his faults and 'be better'. The overbearing boyfriend who pushes his girlfriend to adopt his taste in music, cinema and literature, not realizing that everyone has a path, and it is our differences that complete us.

In Indian politics, this has manifested as the idea of Hindus trying to 'correct' Muslims so that they become 'civilized' like them. It's not rare to meet someone who believes they are doing us a favour by trying to push Muslims 'on the right path' and outside the 'shackles of conservatism'.

In trying to improve a person (or community), we make them doubt themselves. We think we are doing them a 'favour', but are only making them feel unlovable, useless and inept. We make them feel as if there is something wrong with them. Or we begin to use them as emotional punching bags. But the brain has its own mechanism, beautiful in its utility. When there is no love, the mind has its own techniques to save the victim from this trauma and doubt. Their defences kick up and they stop loving us back. This is how we alienate the people we love.

If the victims can't save themselves, they might vent anger on someone else or bury it deep inside them, waiting to explode like walking bombs of human sadness. Ready to inflict pain on others. Sometimes with guns, sometimes with just words.

I often think that the warning switch in my drawing room was a similar defence mechanism for the Muslims in my neighbourhood. But even in those violent times, there was an inexplicable and paradoxical sense of safety and belongingness, not a sense of impending doom. 'Whatever may come, the Hindus and Muslims will always come back to sanity. Where else would they go?' Ammi would often ask. I wish I had answers.

In September 2021, when the Covid caseloads had eased a little in Aligarh, I met Shakuntala Bharti, a firebrand member of the Bharatiya Janata Party, for an interview for a documentary. She had been arrested in 2006 for leading the mob that had attacked my home, ultimately leading to Shadab's death.

Bharti came from a humble Dalit background but became a politician after fighting her family. 'There wasn't electricity in our home. I used to study under the streetlight. What I am, what I have achieved, is on my own,' she told me, narrating her struggle against class and caste boundaries. She wore saffron clothes and a long vermillion teeka, the kind of person I imagined burning down homes when the *inevitable* happens. At her luxurious home in a very narrow lane in Gudiya Bagh, it was hard not to see her love towards her husband, son and Kalicharan, her dog.

However, her love extended to everyone but Muslims: in her narrative, they were nothing but troublemakers. On multiple occasions, Bharti had hit local headlines for multiple cases of violence against Muslims. When I asked her views on Muslims, the softness in her voice vanished as swiftly as madrasa kids after their lessons.

'Their religion has many problems. We are taught to love and to care like Ram and Sita, Shiva and Parvati. They are taught to lie and be barbaric. Their only aim is to spread their religion at any cost,' she told me between narrating various accounts of her entering Muslim mohallas and fighting them for some reason or the other. These convictions had earned her a name in politics and propelled her to the powerful position of being Aligarh's mayor. Capitalizing on hate for Muslims, Bharti was a success story – unlike most of her neighbours.

After Bharti, I met the members of Hindu Jagran Manch, a radical Hindu outfit at their office in Delhi Gate. They were a group of a dozen men, very well connected to the police, tasked to stop inter-religious marriages and 'fight Muslim jihadis'. They lived not more than a kilometre away from my home. 'In madrasas, Muslims are trained to spread their religion and the idea of jihad. They receive foreign funds for this. Everyone knows that, don't they?' asked Sanju Bajaj, the leader of the group, as if he wanted to hear an answer. His subordinates, wearing chains on their wrists, their muscles bulging, their eyes angry but with an expression of utmost devotion for their leader, nodded like bobbleheads.

'This has been going on since the time of Babar. They use swords to usurp our temple lands and the land of Hindus. We need to fight such elements at any cost,' he added. Unironically, his Facebook profile quoted a verse from the Mahabharata: 'If non-violence is man's supreme duty, then doing violence to protect dharma is even more important.'

*If violence erupted in Aligarh at some point, would these be the people who would lead it?* I thought. *Will they attack school buses carrying Muslim children from Delhi Gate? Will someone identify the*

*Muslims among them?* I had a sinking feeling that in Harigarh, there wouldn't be a Bablu, taking out his locket to prove that he was a Hindu to save a bus full of Muslim kids.

Sanju Bajaj's Facebook profile revealed another interesting detail: he referred to Aligarh as Harigarh everywhere. Although the change hadn't happened officially yet, in his world, the city had already transformed into Harigarh.

# 20

# CITY ON FIRE

FIRE HAS BEEN our close friend and a sworn enemy. From the moment we stumbled upon its enigmatic power, the course of human history changed. Fire became our means of cooking, crafting tools, and providing warmth for our families during winters. At its best, it is the symbol of creation and transformation. Without the Sun's fire, Earth would be nothing but a lifeless planet. At its worst, fire can be a merciless nemesis, reducing to ashes whatever comes in its path, humans or their possessions. In fire, I found the essence of our potential and contradictions; like fire, humans possess the power to both create and destroy.

Fire reminded me of the violence I witnessed in Aligarh, the Delhi riots and many acts of violence against Muslims that adorned newspapers. It sparked my deepest fears. Will Farsh Manzil burn someday, erasing my father's memories and the essence of everything I am? What about Ammi? Could I be beaten to death by strangers on a nameless street, like many had been? Like Noah's flood, these fears deluged everything I thought, everything I did. And the only thing I could hope to salvage were my memories – a reminder that I once existed, with all my pains and joys, contained within a strange realm of time.

Was it time to turn to God again? Is this why people turned to God? Most religions, especially Islam, insist that life is a test. 'Everyone is going to taste death, and we shall make a trial of you with evil and with good, and to us, you will be returned,' says the Quran. And if it was a test, was I failing? I didn't know. I was too busy being afraid.

As the lockdown became a memory, I continued to escape my fears through long walks in Upar Kot. I took comfort in observing people lost in their lives and found hope in their perseverance. Aligarh was like a city suspended in time. Locksmiths still made music out of their instruments. Women still stared at passersby from behind majestic wooden doors. Kids still spent their evenings flying kites and their nights running on the moonlit streets. Married couples still walked together in the market like they didn't know each other. Men still sat with each other in tea shops as Kumar Sanu songs from the film *Saajan* played on tape recorders. Ghulam Ali's '*Hungama Hai Kyon Barpa*' still wafted out of restaurants.

Deep within my mind, my old fears were still alive too. Like my five-year-old self, I was still afraid of venturing into the lanes of Hindu ghettos. However, the N95 mask gave me a cloak of anonymity, making me feel safe. This time, my purpose for strolling through Hindu ghettos wasn't to rent comic books, but to find myself and some long-overdue answers to my lingering questions.

Who is a Hindu? Do all of them secretly hate Muslims? Is the kind shopkeeper, who sells framed pictures and displays an 'Allah-Muhammad' painting alongside a portrait of Radha Krishna, an imposter? Can the old grocery seller, who is rude to anyone asking for credit, pose a threat to my safety? What about the teenager coming to the Farsh to smoke the cigarette he can't in his mohalla? Or the woman who sits at the shop where her dead husband once sat? Or the ones who crack secret jokes as they bend in spiritual greetings? Do they laugh and cry like us? Do they get depressed? Do they care for their loved ones like us?

In their lanes, I noticed the architectural beauty of the old havelis struggling to survive the modern times, the people going around for work and children running around for no reason – just like us. Of course, they had better facilities, cemented roads, bigger shops, ATMs and less garbage than us. But the more I ventured into Hindu ghettos this time, the more the exoticism and the fear began to wear out, the more I realized they were just like us – men and women trying to make sense of the burning world they were born in.

In January 2022, I met Surendra Kumar Bajaj at his shop in Upar Kot, a stone's throw from Jama Masjid. At sixty, his face a roadmap of stories etched in wrinkles, white hair peeking out from beneath a weathered cap, he sat like a seasoned observer amid colourful saris, dupattas and salwar suits for newly married women. 'This shop was set up by my father. He was an enterprising, social and practical man. He had travelled to Mumbai, Surat, Ahmedabad to establish it. Everything I know, I learnt from him,' he told me, his mind fleeting to his youth.

His father, Srikishan Bajaj, didn't die peacefully in his bed: he was stabbed to death by rioters in this Muslim neighbourhood, at the same place outside Jama Masjid where my school bus stop used to park. 'The curfew had been lifted the previous day after communal tensions. He was returning after having a paan at Railway Road. Some people surrounded him and stabbed him with a knife,' Bajaj told me, his eyes as blank as a void.

After being stabbed, the seventy-year-old old man kept walking to save his own life, until he reached a police picket in Baniya

Pada. The cops rushed him to a hospital. 'By the time we reached the doctors, he had bled to death. I couldn't even talk to him one last time,' he said. The killers were never identified or arrested. Bajaj continues to sell clothes at the shop near the place where his father was killed, providing for his family. Now, his two sons sit along with him.

The elder one of them, Honey, was once a journalist. Before joining the family business, he had worked at several Hindi newspapers for eight years. 'When I grew up seeing administrative negligence, our case files being sidelined and my father running around for nothing, I lost faith in the system. I desperately wanted to change it,' said Honey, who was able to study till his intermediate. 'I wanted to help other victims of violence get justice. Whenever there was a crime or an incidence of violence, I was always the first one to reach the spot and investigate,' he said.

I listened to Honey, the signs of anger easily visible beneath his calm exterior. In him, I could see a mirror to myself. Like me, he'd come into journalism for a sense of justice. Though we were born into different faiths, we grew up in the same area. Both of us had chosen to tell other people's stories because of similar angst: he was driven by the death of his grandfather, I by the death of my friend.

Neither Bajaj nor Honey, unlike the Hindus who made political capital out of it, made their tragedy about hatred towards Muslims. 'All of our life has been spent running a shop in a Muslim-dominated region. They are our friends, who have been with us in tragedies and moments of joy. It's not about what religion you come from, but what kind of a person you are,' said Honey. There was a surety in his voice that told me he meant it. However hard I tried, I couldn't find in them a sense of hate for Muslims. This was a paradox: if people who had lost loved ones to violence didn't choose hate, how did hate thrive in Aligarh? Then, what exactly was this beast we call hate?

While poets, writers and philosophers have written extensively about love, very few have chosen to engage with hate. Even acknowledging hate inside our hearts make us feel like bad people. Unacknowledged and ignored, hate thrives deep inside our hearts like a secret puppeteer, affecting our actions subconsciously. Even if we don't notice it, it slowly changes how we see the world. Like an internal wound, hate keeps festering inside, deaf to reason, inflicting harm upon ourselves before driving us to unleash repugnant rage upon others. It shields us from seeing our failures, so we can blame everything wrong in our lives and in this unjust world, on the target of our resentment.

A deep relationship exists between hate and fear, two emotions that often go together.

People fear what they don't understand and often end up hating it. This fear of the other, perpetuated by centuries of family histories that remain in people's psyche, has time and again found its way to burn not only my town but probably hundreds of towns in modern India. The proponents of this fear vehemently believe that their fear is, after all, righteous, and therefore, hate is the necessity of our times, if not a duty. As a society, we have never accepted that we are fearful and hateful in our hearts, and that's why we can't get over it. After all, can we ever get over something we don't even see?

In this quest to understand hate, I reached out to old Hindu friends from my school, and from them, I only found love – a respite from the hate that I had recently witnessed. They only had good things to say about Muslims. 'Most of my closest friends are still Muslims. Riots are just ploys to keep us distracted from important issues,' said Ankur, who now ran his family's hardware business from a godown in Gudiya Bagh. Another busmate from my Route No. 4 days, told me that whenever riots happened, her Muslim neighbours protected them. 'They didn't even celebrate Eid when my grandfather died,' she told me.

I also learnt from them that in areas where Hindu and Muslim communities coexisted, it was always a handful of elderly men and women, with friends across religious lines, who resolved conflicts when they arose. They stepped in to calm down angry boys looking for blood, dousing the fire of youth with the wisdom of old age. 'My Muslim neighbours warned me whenever there was tension around here,' a man who ran a coffee shop in Baniya Para told me.

Despite numerous riots, temples and gurudwaras still exist within Upar Kot, and mosques find solace in the embrace of Kanwari Ganj. These are examples that decades of animosity have failed to break Aligarh's spirit. Even with their diverse narratives and individual stories, Hindus and Muslims could still be friends with affection for each other – extending umbrellas during sudden rains, rushing for medicines in an emergency, paying for a rickshaw when you struggle to find change or asking about your family's well-being with an uplifting smile. How could I forget Bablu, the Atlas who saved my life from a mob? And dozens of my Hindu friends who have always been there for me?

In Aligarh, despite its imperfections, Hindus and Muslims still gather at dhabas, openly discuss grievances, and share light-hearted jokes. Neighbours and colleagues break down religious and political barriers through their gestures. Disagreements often arise as they do, but in Aligarh conversations over a simple cup of tea are often enough to mend any rift. Why kill each other with guns, when we are totally capable of killing each other with our words? More often than not, it is these conversations that keep our worlds going, despite the many odds.

One of the distinct features of Upar Kot is the secret escape routes or '*chor galis*' built into its architecture. These are narrow staircases that connect Muslim settlements in Hindu areas to Upar Kot. The purpose of these staircases is what it seems like: they assist people escape communal riots. Historically, they were used for evacuating Muslims during the riots that erupted in Aligarh in the 1970s and 1990s. They were likely built by people who felt their lives were threatened but lacked funds or courage to leave their ancestral homes.

Three such staircases are in my area: one connects Tan Tan Para to Gudiya Bagh, another connects Gosht Wali Gali to Kanwari Ganj. Similar structures can be seen in Baniya Para and Usman Para – secret staircases known only to locals and practically invisible to outsiders. One such staircase was also in Farsh Manzil, likely built by my grandfather in case the Muslims of Farsh needed to flee the violence.

The importance of these escape routes cannot be overstated. When there is a riot, a dead end could spell definite death for victims. In the chaos that follows targeted violence, time is both a friend and foe. At such moments, finding a safe refuge requires a combination of planning, thinking, and the kindness of neighbours. Only those who had memorized the labyrinthine paths of these ghettos had a chance of survival. These escape routes, now mostly covered by garbage, were life-savers.

Like these physical escape routes, we also create escape routes in our mind, that helps us simplify the world, rather than face its complexities. Or we try to escape under the garb of 'moving on' or 'leaving things behind', an impossibility. But none of these escape routes have helped.

Since I was a kid, I have seen my city on fire, burning in hate, scorching all of us inside. How can we extinguish a city engulfed in flames that have burnt for generations? The fires that have ravaged lives, leaving behind trauma and heat of suspicion? Our old methods, just leaking buckets of water, are not enough to quell this inferno. The fire brigade would never be able to reach our narrow lanes. The sole salvation for a city ablaze lies, of course, in a rainfall – but not the ordinary kind, but the one that brings the tearful embrace of the heavens' weeping touch.

It is the rain of forgiveness, falling from the skies, washing away the stains of resentment and bitterness that have poisoned our souls for far too long. The rain of coexistence, in whose embrace we acknowledge that we all dwell within the same darkness, recognizing that there is no singular truth and that our fates are intertwined. The rain of compassion, melting away the walls of anger guarding our hearts, each drop eroding the barriers that separate us. The rain of empathy that enables us to feel the weight of others' sorrows as intensely as we feel our own, dissolving the indifference of being aloof from the misery of others. The rain of respect that reminds us that we are but fragments of a greater mosaic, each carrying a story that can never be fully understood by another.

Like a prayer that has been answered, this rain will adorn buildings and alleyways, dilapidated walls, the forgotten crevices and the trees that keep to themselves. It will fall on children dancing on streets and their terraces, mothers looking outside their windows, fathers sitting in their lock workers' workshop. It will nurture seeds of hope that the suffering will no longer suffer, their alienation will be a distant dream, their fears will flow away in the drains, carried away by the currents of joy and acceptance. As divine intervention has yet to bestow this rainfall upon us, it falls upon us to make it happen. Perhaps, this is the test that Allah wishes us to confront. Perhaps, this is the struggle that the Mahabharata urges us to triumph over.

In his final days, Papa, a *hafiz-e-quran*, yearned to complete the last episodes of the *Mahabharat*. As I battled internal fires that consumed me, he asked my friend Pashtun to procure the *Mahabharat* CDs. Before he departed to face God, he desired to witness what the Mahabharata, a story from the land of his birth, had to offer – a closure yet unattained. Seated at my desktop computer, he spent hours watching the concluding episodes of *Mahabharat*, those he may have missed, in his last days.

India, despite its flaws, is perhaps the only country where such a scenario could unfold. We are, after all, a nation of contradictions. Like dancers on a stage, these contradictions entwine, weaving a symphony to make us embrace the human longing for meaning and purpose and contain the chaos within ourselves.

How did Papa give meaning to his life? Until his dying breath, he nourished his bonds with Hindu friends, embracing those hailing from Kanwari Ganj or Civil Lines, regardless of their political affiliations, irrespective of their class or caste. Even when cancer threatened to ravage his body and soul, Papa's compassion never waned: he never ceased the small acts of kindness he loved doing.

We, as a society, are in dire need to go back to these small acts of kindness. The only way to counter this hate, however mad and impossible it seems, is to love those we perceive as our enemy with all our traumas and memories and heartbreaks and loss of faith. If we were ever to win this fight against these twin emotions of hate and fear, it would be with a bit of madness, courage and love.

As I walked home that day, I chose love over fear. I was, once again, madly in love with my city and all its flaws, its lies and its secrets. In those moments, I remembered the bitter fights between me and my father, the liberal and the radical. He wanted me to get over my fears and live a life which was whole, assimilating in a heartless world I had yet to bear, a father sharing his wisdom with a teenage son who was angry, fearful and hurt inside.

But we were not just father and son, we were two Muslims making sense of our alienation in our own ways. I thought I knew the truth of the world and what it stood for. But I was a fool. Nobody who has taken birth in the world knows what the truth is. Even though I thought I was a rebel, I was forged by the same fire that had shaped my city. And thus, I was only responding to the times and how society wanted me to be.

I could now see Papa's deliberations in a kinder way than I had ever before. My father, the realist, who saw the world in its true form, rather than ideals, was perhaps closer to the truth than I was. To see the world like him, in its naked abstractness and not confining it into the man-made packages of idealism, was a rebellion in itself.

Once after the riots ravaged Upar Kot, I asked Papa why didn't he leave Aligarh for Pakistan, like his brothers had. 'It's my home. How could I ever live if I left my home?' he said and kept on shaving.

As that memory struck me, I found that like him, I will never have the courage to completely abandon my home, Aligarh – a beautiful curse, the city that I loved and hated but made me what I am today, the city where my father had chosen to stay and where he was buried. I was sure, like a phoenix, Aligarh would rise up again from the ashes, until it found a way to heal itself and all of us inside it.

In that moment, the trauma that had accumulated in my heart began to wash away. Forgotten and hidden memories began coming back to me. It felt as if time had turned back its relentless hands, and I and Papa were friends again.

In that poignant instant, a realization washed over me like the last torrential rains of the monsoon: I was now turning into my father.

# ACKNOWLEDGEMENTS

I WOULD LIKE to thank every person who encouraged me to write this book and supported me in this tumultuous journey.

First of all, I am deeply grateful to my three mentors: Neyaz Farooquee, a friend and writer who ignited in me a belief in my story; Anushree Majumdar, my agent and kindest of souls, who strengthened this belief; and Isaac Chotiner from *The New Yorker*, who not only gave a direction to my writing but also valuable emotional support in a gloomy pandemic year.

Mere words won't express my gratitude to Sonia Faleiro and her team at South Asia Speaks for inspiring me, and Anish Chandy from Labyrinth for his valuable lessons. I am especially grateful to Bushra Ahmed of HarperCollins India, for her patience in handling my anxious phone calls asking her to hurry the book 'as the world might end anytime soon'.

I can't risk not thanking my wonderful friends for making me hate myself a little less during the writing process: Amir, Ansab, Asnaa, Himani, Hugo, Ismat, Manjiri, Maroosha, Meghna, Nasir, Ruchira, Pashtun, Pranav, Shahrukh, Shamlan, Zeeshan and Zumbish. This book wouldn't have seen the light of the day if it wasn't for their love and support. And everyone else whom I can't mention by name – my colleagues and bosses at *Deccan Herald*, Reuters, Vice and Brut, my friends in Turkey, Jamia and AMU, and all the strangers who have ever given me hope through their random acts of kindness.

Among people I have worked with, I want to acknowledge the life and work of Danish Siddiqui, a colleague from Reuters and a top-notch journalist, who sadly passed away in the line of duty in July 2021. He continues to inspire us to do our best to tell stories that actually matter, time and again.

Of course, this memoir wouldn't be possible without my immediate and extended family, who had to recount old, buried memories for this book. The same goes for my neighbours, acquaintances and all the people of my mohalla, Upar Kot, who shared their stories with me fearlessly and gave me enough content to last a lifetime. I am also grateful to the lock workers of Aligarh and workers everywhere in the world for giving me hope through their resilience and courage.

Last but not the least, I'd like to express my gratitude to all the writers, poets, artists, historians, journalists and scientists, especially those from marginalized communities, who battle their families, society and governments across the world, to burn themselves again and again in a pit of self-doubt and uncertainty, to bring comfort, knowledge, healing and joy to others.

# NOTES

Scan this QR code to access the detailed notes

# ABOUT THE AUTHOR

**Zeyad Masroor Khan** is a journalist, writer and documentary film-maker based in New Delhi. In his decade-long journalistic career, he has worked with national and international media companies like Reuters, Vice, Brut and *Deccan Herald*. A South Asia Speaks fellow, he primarily writes on politics, marginalized communities, crime and culture. Three of his documentaries have been screened at international film festivals. *City on Fire: A Boyhood in Aligarh* is his first book.

**HarperCollins** *Publishers* India

At HarperCollins India, we believe in telling the best stories and finding the widest readership for our books in every format possible. We started publishing in 1992; a great deal has changed since then, but what has remained constant is the passion with which our authors write their books, the love with which readers receive them, and the sheer joy and excitement that we as publishers feel in being a part of the publishing process.

Over the years, we've had the pleasure of publishing some of the finest writing from the subcontinent and around the world, including several award-winning titles and some of the biggest bestsellers in India's publishing history. But nothing has meant more to us than the fact that millions of people have read the books we published, and that somewhere, a book of ours might have made a difference.

As we look to the future, we go back to that one word— a word which has been a driving force for us all these years.

Read.